CW00450117

Careening thru Cambodia

Keith Lowry

Careening thru Cambodia
Text & Photo copyright © by Keith Lowry 2020

All rights reserved. © 2020 by Keith Lowry

No part of this book may be reproduced or transmitted in any form or by any means, electronic or mechanical, including photocopying, recording or by any information storage and retrieval system, without written permission of the publisher. Condensed segments of Part I previously appeared in the "Land Mines" chapter of Episodes from a 20 Year Vacation. This is a work of semi-fiction. Characters have fictitious names and identifying characteristics.

Paperback - ISBN 978-3- 9819790-2-2
e-book - ISBN 978-3- 9819790-3-9

For access to photos please contact
klowrybooks5@gmail.com

By the same author

Episodes from a Twenty Year Vacation

✽

Höttlland

✽

Höttlland, Part II A Life after Deaths

Contents

PART ONE

Day One: Friday Dec. 10th

I was seated in the dimly-lit lobby of a Phnom Penh hotel, a room where the lingering scent of spent incense had failed to mask the inherent mustiness, when I looked up from the newspaper I'd been perusing, to see a gruff, head-shaved, bear of a man in khaki shirt and pants, swagger in and approach reception.

"Has Conrad Garson checked in yet?" he asked bluntly, neglecting to acknowledge the receptionist's existence with a simple "Good evening," and confirming my suspicion that he was indeed the man of the hour.

"Where's the other cameraman?" Franz had demanded to know, once I'd introduced myself and explained that I was in fact the "shooter" for this film.

"Conrad should be down any minute."

With a face locked in thinly-disguised disdain, he begrudgingly extended his hand to deliver an exaggeratedly powerful handshake, an obvious effort to set some less-than-subtle ground rules. As we stood there in awkward silence waiting for Conrad to appear, it was impossible to ignore the small cartoon bubble making its way from my gut to my brain, carrying the message, *"what did I do to deserve this guy?"*

It was hard to believe that barely two weeks had passed

since Conrad had called to announce he'd received a long-sought-after green light to produce a documentary for a German network. Given the short time span until filming was scheduled to start, I suspected I hadn't been the first person asked if I was interested and available. Seeing I was both, I had sought more details, learning that the film's theme was to revolve around Franz Petry, a former Warsaw-pact soldier whose post-Cold War future had led to his joining an agency with the mandate to locate and disarm land mines in war zones around the world.

"We'll be filming Franz in his workplace, this time in Cambodia," Conrad had explained, "as well as documenting how his family deals with his having such a dangerous occupation."

Twelve days later, the last vestiges of Germany were disappearing beneath the clouds, as passengers fussed their way through the private rituals of settling in. Fortunately, a benevolent ticket agent had banished potential narrators to other venues, granting me the luxury of an empty row for the long flight. Eleven hours later, Singapore loomed into view just in time to see the connecting flight to Phnom Penh leave without us. Aware that we'd been sentenced to seven hours in what was then billed as the world's best airport, Conrad and I had sought ways to ease the boredom. But with beer priced at $14.00 a bottle, that quest was quickly abandoned. In the end we simply planted ourselves in one of the airport's open-area lounges to watch the world stroll past, hazarding guesses as to which of the hundreds of patrons milling about was likely to buy a Rolex at one of the shrines to Mammon.

Having expected third-world bureaucracy upon landing in Phnom Penh, it came as a pleasant surprise when we sailed through passport control and customs within minutes. Exposed to muzak and processed air for the last twenty-odd hours, neither of us were prepared for the staggering heat and humidity, not to mention the screeching birdsong that awaited us outside the hissing-pneumatic doors. Seconds after spotting a man holding a hand-written sign with our names, we found ourselves splayed out on the back seats of the air-conditioned hotel shuttle. No sooner had the driver edged his way out of airport security, we were sucked up into a giant swarm of motorbikes blanketing the main artery into the city. In a scene straight out of the "Dodgem Car" ride at a county fair, we watched as suited businessmen cloaked in surgical masks, families of four astride a motorbike meant for two, and an army of deliverymen, burdened with objects of unimaginable size and shape, all competed for space amidst the unbridled chaos.

"Do you realize there are no traffic controls anywhere?" I said to Conrad, as a group of younger drivers whizzed past at what was considerably less than arm's length. With no stop signs, warnings to yield, or policemen windmilling directions, we proceeded unimpeded for several kilometres until forced to halt by a lone traffic light. Presumably meant to regulate traffic flow, it had ironically created a lengthy jam. Although the light was outfitted with an ingenious, colour-coordinated timer that informed motorists how much longer they had to endure this disruption, those with no time to be impatient, simply switched to the opposite side of the road, indifferent to on-coming traffic as they continued on their pressing journey. But despite all the bedlam, there were no bleating horns, no angry gestures, nor any other signs of blatantly aggressive behaviour. Instead, there seemed to be an ingrained courtesy and adeptness at work, encouraging drivers to simply, "go with the flow."

In the midst of the tumult, I couldn't help noticing how exceptionally clean the city looked. Certainly there were places that qualified as rundown or in need of urgent repair, and the conglomeration of overhead power lines clustered at every intersection suggested the infrastructure could have used a few improvements. But instead of being dismaying, it all contributed to a riveting atmosphere of orderly confusion set amidst frayed gentility.

As we continued deeper into the city's core, scenes flickered past like slides on a child's old ViewMaster. An endless array of small shops held sway, all selling what appeared to be identical products. Foodstuffs, clothing, daily utensils, even the proverbial kitchen sink was available, stainless-steel versions of which lay stacked between teetering piles of mattresses and the other assorted household tools on display out on dusty sidewalks, helping to create a colourful, surreal world that gave new meaning to the word "kaleidoscope."

"I see you two have met," Conrad acknowledged, when he finally emerged from the elevator. Greeting each other with a handshake and a slap on the shoulder, the pair traded a few anecdotes about their previous work together, before Conrad suggested heading out for a drink.

"We're both too wired from the flight and layover in Singapore to hit the hay so why don't you join us."

"Normally I would," Franz conceded, but I've been on an alcohol vacation for a few months now, and besides, there are a few matters I need to take care of before we leave tomorrow."

Eager to soak up some of the evening's ambience, Conrad and I had no sooner left the protection of the hotel's palm-covered courtyard, when we were accosted by members of the revolving bands keeping hotels under constant surveillance.

"You need Tuk-Tuk, mister?"

What some might call a form of motorized rickshaw, a Tuk-Tuk is basically a two-wheeled, double-benched, open-sided cabin that's been welded to the back of an aging motor bike. Judging from the assortment parked in our street, they appeared to come in all colours and conditions. And if this particular batch was any example, so did the drivers. All that is, except for one. For reasons that were destined to remain a mystery, we would fail to encounter a single female specimen during our entire stay.

Much like their counterparts in other parts of the world, the Tuk-Tuk operators outside our hotel were simply involved in the daily struggle to earn a living. What made them so different however, was their approach. Anything but overbearing, a polite inquiry or friendly wave was followed by a quick and respectful withdrawal once they'd registered there was no interest. No badgering, no jousting, no glaring resentment; your decision was simply respected.

A few minutes later we were stepping into the bustling street life of Sihanouk Boulevard, one of the city's main thoroughfares. I was immediately struck by the number of young faces drifting past. Statistics from a guidebook I'd read on the plane, had painted Cambodia's population as young, setting the average age at twenty-five, with half the citizens well below that figure. Such numbers came to life out on the pavement, with olive-skinned men and women, the latter with delicate features and large almond eyes lodged atop a logic-defying lissomness last seen amongst Singapore Airlines stewardesses. Despite the yearning for lost youth a young pretty face can induce, Conrad and I were quite enjoying the passing parade when the first telltale signs of encroaching jet lag started to appear. Hoping to safeguard our dwindling reserves, we decided to retreat to a nearby bar, occupying one of the last free tables in the darkened tavern. As our eyes adjusted to the weak lighting, we could make out a sprinkling of older, bored-looking European men strewn about the room, many in the company of even more bored-looking younger Asian women.

"Are you thinking what I'm thinking?" I muttered to Conrad, as we clinked glasses to toast our arrival.

"It does seem a tad obvious, doesn't it?"

As can happen and so often does when on the road, one refreshment stretched to three and it was after midnight by the time we returned to our hotel. Up now for nearly twenty-four hours, I flopped down on the bed, too tired to undress, much less commit any of the day's impressions to paper. As thoughts of the day's events whirled through my head, I tumbled towards sleep with one recurring question, "*how I was ever going to relate all of this to those back home?*"

Day Two: Saturday, Dec. 11th

For someone with more than thirty southern Manitoba summers under his belt, excessive heat should have been nothing new. It might have been easier to cope with had it merely been the high temperature. It was the stifling humidity that threatened to do me in the next morning, and this in the middle of the so-called "cooler, dry season." As it was, further moaning was cut short by the blast of a horn, announcing the arrival of refuge in the form of an air-conditioned Land Rover. Introductions were exchanged with our Cambodian driver as we loaded equipment and luggage into the vehicle, but once underway conversation between the four of us was held to a minimum, partly because of the early hour, but also thanks to the loud clanking of the air conditioner, which would hopefully keep life bearable for the five hours it was expected to take us to get to Battambang.

Known as Bat Dambang by the locals, Cambodia's second largest city is the regional capital of a province bearing the same name. I didn't know anything about the place other than the opinion of one blogger back in Germany, who claimed it had acquired the reputation of being little more than "a shit hole," an image that somewhat dampened my anticipation as I gazed out at the interim scenery. Heading north on National Route #5, the densely-packed neighbourhoods of Phnom Penh quickly dissolved into what seemed like the world's longest village. The deeper into the countryside we advanced, the more dwellings were built atop wooden pilings, set back ten or twenty yards from the road.

"These huts," I began, leaning forward as far as the seatbelt would allow.

"It's to protect against the rising waters in the rainy season," Franz interrupted, having anticipated the question. "When times are dry, it doubles as a shaded storage area."

A short while later, as my interest in the seemingly endless row of weathered domiciles was starting to sag, a brightly-coloured brick villa popped up in their midst. It was quickly swallowed by the thick foliage lining the road, but moments later a second appeared, followed by a third; all three sticking out like random gaudy baubles. Set behind high-cement walls topped with strands of razor wire, none of the two-storey houses, briefly visible through the driveways, showed any signs of being inhabited, a stark contrast to the scenes unfolding amongst the more modest dwellings. There, farmers in loose-fitting shirts and pants, topped by the familiar cone-shaped peon's hat, could often be seen raking out small pyramids of chili peppers to dry in the merciless sun. In other vignettes, brown-skinned youngsters, many unencumbered by clothing, scurried amongst the lemongrass and palm trees without a care in the world. Further along we passed a trail of elder siblings attired in the uniform of white shirt and black pants or skirt, walking, cycling or balancing on the back end of motor bikes as they made their way towards the next closest school. One such exodus, several kilometres long, ended abruptly at a walled-in courtyard teeming with more white-and-black splotches moving amidst racks of idle bikes.

Interspersed throughout the panorama of huts, schools

and occasional villas, were the roadside vendors. Those that appeared to be transitory, had their wares displayed on stands crafted to the back of a motorbike. The more established merchants had spread their goods on rickety tables or the ground in front of their homes. Undoubtedly forced to endure prolonged gaps between customers, many looked as if posing for a still life as we roared past.

At some point the paraphernalia of civilization gave way to large tracts of land stretching back to the horizon. Rice paddies of spectacular hues of green, sectioned off from each other by raised earthen embankments, lay draped across the landscape like a giant quilt. Despite the fact it was neither harvest nor planting time, workers of various ages could be seen toiling in the knee-deep water, observed by solitary cows lazily grazing along the narrow pathways. Added to these snippets of rural life were young boys in hopes of escaping the ever-present heat, leaping from rocks or bridge abutments into the brownish waters of collected pools or creeks. Then without warning, the fields receded and we found ourselves back within another channel of houses and trees, where long-skirted mothers, many with child in arm, could be seen circling around a large steaming pot in their front yards, preparing the afternoon meal. It was nothing less than sensory saturation, a landslide of impressions far too plentiful to be fully absorbed.

*

As a result of Franz's arbitrary decision to sacrifice lunch for an earlier arrival, it was just after four when we entered the outskirts of Battambang. Circling past a twenty-foot statue of Buddha set in the centre of a roundabout, I couldn't help wondering why anyone would go to the effort of constructing such a large tribute, only to give it a cartoon-like facial expression last seen on an Austin Powers spaceship. In any event, I deemed it wise to keep my thoughts to myself.

Darkness was still more than an hour away after checking in at our hotel, enough time for a short, exploratory jaunt through the surrounding neighbourhood. Once out on the pavement however, it was quickly apparent there was not much to see; that is, unless you happened to be fascinated by a profusion of phone-card stores and food kiosks. Of infinitely more interest was a row of open-doored workshops, where soot-covered men squatted on dusty, cement floors, enveloped in a grey-blue haze of smoke as they cut and welded metal objects into recognizable shapes. Other than myself, nobody seemed overtly concerned about the cascade of sparks spewing out into the street as they worked. But as interesting as it was, it was not *that* interesting, and I was about to bring the mini-tour to an end when I caught sight of what appeared to be some sort of oasis across the street. Slipping through traffic considerably less daunting than that in Phnom Penh, I entered a small park smothered in lush-green cacti and hovering palms. It didn't take long to discover why I seemed to be the sole beneficiary of the park's limited features. Given the wide assortment of litter soiling the grounds, it was not the kind of place many would feel inclined to kick off their shoes and spread their toes in the grass or whatever else might be laying around. Another component of the park that had not escaped abuse was a round reflecting pool. Strolling past its stagnant, slime-coated water, where another Buddha-like figure sat pontificating on a pedestal, I wasn't thrilled to see several species of faeces slowly disintegrating in the rays of the sun. Now armed with ample evidence as to the accuracy of the mystery blogger's blunt assessment of Battambang, no further incentive was needed to call it a day and return to the hotel.

Fortunately, by the time we met in the lobby shortly after six, the image of decaying debris had faded from the radar. With the next day's departure for the mine fields set for seven-thirty, a nighttime tour of the city was abandoned in favour of dinner at a restaurant Franz assured us was not far. Underway on foot, one couldn't help noticing that streetlamps in that part of the city were at a premium. With the reflected glare from passing motorists the only source of light, some diligence was required to avoid errant parcels that hadn't ended up in the park's reflecting pool. After walking adjacent to a block-long facade of bas-reliefs meticulously carved into a wall enclosing one of the city's temples, we cautiously crossed a busy thoroughfare on to a smooth marble boardwalk that looked to extend for several blocks. At the lower end of the promenade, dozens of people had gathered to dine, seemingly unperturbed by the exhaust and noise emitted by the steady flow of traffic. Meals were being dished up by sweating proprietors, whose mobile kitchen carts had been squeezed in curb-side amidst a ridiculously long row of domino-parked motorbikes.

As we continued up the boardwalk in the dim light, we could make out other figures up ahead. Once alongside, the shadowy outlines turned out to be a group of fifty or sixty middle-aged women. All aligned in orderly rows, the ladies were frantically mimicking the antics of a male leader, who with the aid of a headset microphone, was barking out commands to the beat of what one might describe as Cambodian disco. For all the world, they looked like an assortment of aging Radio City Hall Rockettes engaged in rigorous aerobics, more or less in unison. A few metres on, a second band of "dancercisers" appeared. Clearly not willing to be outdone by their neighbouring competitors, these women were shedding pounds to an even louder beat. By the time we left the boardwalk to cross a bridge into the city centre, three additional packs had been encountered, each of them hopping, waving and dancing their way to svelteness. The competing soundtracks continued to hold sway long after the participants were out of sight, echoing off the shuttered buildings as we moved through a web of dark and empty streets.

"I suppose that explains why I've yet to see too many fat Cambodians," I pointed out to no one in particular as we settled in at a table on the restaurant's second floor balcony. While Franz and Conrad proceeded to talk business, I was content to merely stare out at the clear evening sky, occasionally peering down through a tangled maze of cables to a street scene straight out of New Orleans' French Quarter; a French Quarter mind you, that could have used a coat of paint, not to mention a few more street lights. Sitting there in short sleeves, with the German winter a distant memory, the needle of my gratitude attitude moved solidly into the red as I looked forward to what the waitress had billed as the "best damn hamburger" in South East Asia.

Day Three: Sunday, Dec. 12th

Very early the next morning, Cambodia was in the process of losing a significant chunk of its appeal. The cause was an indistinguishable ball of noise best described as a demonic orchestra tuning up at the level of a screaming jet engine. Normally one of the first to stomp down the hall in search of such a racket, exhaustion and the fact the concerto seemed to be coming from somewhere outside my hotel window persuaded me to stay put, glaring up at the ceiling in the hopes it would soon go away. But three hours of stupor later, it was still going strong, loud enough to almost blanket the feeble beeps of my alarm clock. As I slowly pulled myself to an upright position, it was abundantly clear just how large a chunk it really was.

Grumbling over breakfast at a neighbouring cafe where the rule of "peel it, cook it or lose it," was about to undergo its first serious test, I learned from our waitress that the musical interlude, which still showed no signs of abating, was the by-product of a wedding reception planned for that afternoon. Much to my dismay, she also informed me there are two things that Cambodians like to do during the dry season. One is to prepare for the rainy season, and the other is to get married.

"You lucky," she said with a wide, toothy grin, as she refilled our cups with Jasmine tea. "This weekend, three weddings...here on street," she added, pointing towards a red-and- yellow striped tent being erected just across the road. Irked as well as puzzled, after finishing my meal, I left Conrad to dawdle over the remains of his breakfast and phone messages, to stroll over for a louder look. Hovering inconspicuously at one end of the wall-less tent, I watched as a group of roadies unloaded chairs and tables in front of a makeshift stage. At the opposite end of the tent, a second group was busy assembling what looked to be a mobile kitchen. All of this activity was being carried out under a thundering roar not quite to my musical taste. Nobody seemed to be paying any attention, much less objecting to this aural barrage, convincing me it would be pointless to issue a complaint, especially to the two-hundred-pound Cambodian standing near the speakers.

Approximately, a half-hour later, Conrad and I straggled into the land-mine agency's courtyard. Franz wasted no time in pointing out we were fifteen minutes behind schedule. Not in the mood for a lecture after such a sleepless night, I concentrated on packing the equipment into the back of the Land Rover before retreating to the rear seat, leaving Conrad to take the brunt of the remaining sermon. Despite Franz's protestations about our tardiness, we were still early enough to avoid being prey to rush hour delays. Within minutes of passing through the control gate, we had left the last factories and warehouses behind for the welcome tranquility of the countryside.

Much of the trip that morning was a replay of yesterday's scenery, and it was just after eleven when we pulled into a base camp not far from a small village. Having rattled over washboard roads for several hours to get there, I was itching to get out to stretch my legs. My exit, however, was delayed while our driver grunted and groaned his way through a series of manoeuvres meant to bring our vehicle into perfect symmetry with three other trucks parked in the remote lot. Military precision may be all well and good in specific situations, but it escaped me why such accuracy was necessary when these were the only vehicles within sight. The answer came when I glanced over to catch Franz's nodding approval to our Cambodian driver.

Now that the eagle had landed, we climbed out into a searing heat. Led to the much-appreciated shade of an open-sided tent, we were introduced to the base camp leader, a former major in the English army, whose name I instantly forgot. We were then greeted by the Cambodian members of the camp staff, all of whom were dressed in dark-green jumpsuits despite the oppressive temperature. After handing out bottles of cold water to ease our parched throats, the leader asked us to raise a toast in acknowledgement of the tasks ahead.

"Hey," I said to Conrad, after wiping away a small dab of chilled drool from my chin. "Did you notice how many of the staff are women?"

"Yeah," he mumbled back.

"Interesting concept of emancipation."

"How so?"

"Well back in Phnom Penh I had the feeling that women were discouraged, if not banned from driving Tuk-Tuks, but out here they're '*permitted*' to work with land mines."

Once the round of small talk and niceties had been completed, the base leader, whose name was again revealed when one of the staff referred to him as "Mr. Calvin," guided us to a nearby bench for what was to be our first safety briefing. This was important stuff. My life could have depended on it. I should have been listening, but I wasn't. Instead my focus had fallen to a raucous game of soccer underway in an adjacent field. Able to risk occasional glimpses without potentially incurring Calvin's wrath, I struggled to grasp the rules of a game where there didn't appear to be any goals, marked sidelines, or even a referee. To add to the melee, the opposing teams each seemed to have between thirty-to-forty players, all of whom were dressed in the black-and-white uniforms of Cambodian school children. All the same, if whoops and yells were any measure, one had the impression that "herd ball" was a lot of fun despite the oppressive heat. As the game's momentum pulled players to the far side of the dusty field, my gaze drifted back to the base leader, just in time to see him turn away from a series of charts to face me. For a moment I was back in a grade-five literature class, dreading I was about to asked for a measured response to a question I hadn't heard. It turned out to be a false alarm, but just to be safe, I nodded and leaned forward in feigned concentration while taking another swig of much-needed water.

"Excuse me," I interrupted a short while later. "But why is a land-mine detection base camp located right next to a school?"

Somewhat non-plussed by the question, Calvin yielded the floor to Franz.

"Cambodia has between four and six million land mines scattered across its territory," Franz explained, picking up a pointer to direct my attention to a map. "Having a school next to a base camp is just a sign of their confidence in our work."

16 |

"But wasn't the school here first?"

"True," Franz replied, casting a "*who does this guy think he is?*" glance at Conrad. "Maybe I should say they feel more at ease since they know we have worked to clear the area. They need this land so they can eat. And it's our job to make it safe... And now it *is* safe."

The game was clearly over. The noise had subsided and players had disappeared into a sun- bleached building at the far end of the field. Back on our side of the fence, a Cambodian assistant had taken over the podium and was now holding up a number of cards that had my full and utter attention.

"The most critical sign is the red skull and crossbones," the man explained in accent-free English. "Its purpose is to warn visitors of danger. Whenever you see this sign, do not enter the area for any reason. Go back in the direction you came or to an area you know is safe."

Asked to scrutinize several more signs before being directed to a nearby table laden with protective equipment, we watched as a second assistant assumed command and began reciting the rules to be followed whenever venturing into an area known to be mined.

"You must be dressed in a flak jacket and helmet at all times," he told us, as other staff members fanned out to assist us in donning the safety gear.

"Another important thing to remember is that while in the field, your face visor must remain down at all times. You are not to raise it until the team leader says it is safe to do so. That will be when you have reached the active base camp and not before. Is that clear?"

Conrad and I nodded in unison, exchanging looks of

bemusement at the sight of each other in full regalia.

"While proceeding to the camp," the instructor continued, "You are to keep the position assigned you. Follow the person ahead of you at a distance of approximately two meters. Under no circumstances are you to leave the marked route, which as you will see, will be clearly marked by red wires stretched along each side of the path. Any questions?"

Following several last gulps of water, a private incantation or two, we were off. If I'd thought it had been hot during the lecture, it was nothing compared to being out on the trail in helmet and flak jacket. With the sole object in the sky having already nudged the temperature past thirty-three, there suddenly seemed a real possibility of passing out before reaching our destination. In an attempt to distract myself from the suffocating heat, one eye was kept glued to the heel of my predecessor, all the while wondering what good the two-meter rule would do when it came to limiting casualties. Meanwhile, the other eye was busy glimpsing at a somewhat tiresome panorama made up of flat, uncultivated fields, that were occasionally interrupted by a clump of bushes or small trees. The singular source of interest on the sun-scorched terrain was a distant, lone mountain, so out of place one could have easily thought it had been dropped there by a clumsy deity. Oddly enough, what was missing were any feelings of real danger. There we were, treading as close as anyone would ever willingly want to get to a live-mine field, and yet somehow it was difficult to register any sense of dread, which in some ways was a danger in itself.

Twenty minutes and several litres of sweat later, our party arrived at the active staging area. Just as the black walls of an imminent collapse had started to creep into my peripheral vision, permission was given to raise our visors. Top items on the agenda at that moment were to seek shelter in the shade of an equipment gazebo, secure a bottle of water and look for something other than my shirt sleeve to wipe away the fluid streaming down both sides of my head. Once freed of my salty veil, thanks to a towel handed to me by one of the field staff, I caught sight of a dark-green torso some distance away. He or she appeared to be operating a metal detector but was too far away to get a decent shot. I was about to move the camera to a better position when a hand clamped down on my shoulder.

"Sorry," Calvin said, shaking his head. "Nobody's allowed closer than fifty meters to an active operator. You can shoot from here as long as you keep your visor down."

Far from thrilled at the prospect of re-entering that heat chamber, I nevertheless obeyed. Setting up at the allowed limit to follow the action as best I could, I listened as Calvin began to detail the delicate procedures involved in locating and removing a mine.

"The worker only approaches as far as the red wire," he said, as the operator stepped forward to guide the detector in a slow sweeping arc several inches off the ground. The fact that its reach extended less than two metres from his feet, illustrated just how slow the detection process was.

"If something is detected," Calvin continued, "the worker will place a coloured chip on the spot where the signal is strongest. It doesn't happen that often, but an area of one or two meters can sometimes end up with several chips. That doesn't mean they're all land mines of course, but we have to act on the assumption they could be."

"And then?" Conrad asked, having moved up to join us.

"And then, another team will attempt to retrieve whatever is setting off the signal. But I can't let you film that," he added. "It would be too dangerous."

"Interesting stuff," I whispered aside to Conrad, my voice echoing off the inside of the visor. "Might even be worthwhile if we could get close enough to actually see what the guy is doing."

"Just get what you can," he said with a shrug.

His explanation completed, Calvin indicated it was time to head elsewhere. Trudging back up the path we'd just come down, we hadn't gone more than a hundred meters when he stopped to point out a pair of green-suited workers partially hidden in the underbrush. From our new vantage point we could make out a man and woman sweeping through long grass with what looked like high tech "weed-eaters." Faced once again with limited access to the action, I wanted to at least make sure the shot was in focus. Experience at the first location had shown that trying to focus with the visor down was at best a hit and miss proposition. Aware that no broadcaster would accept such grounds for fuzzy images, I'd resolved the problem by lifting the shield to quickly focus and frame, a procedure that had taken no more than a few seconds. What I hadn't known at the time was that nobody had witnessed that transgression.

"Visor down," Franz bellowed a few seconds later, employing a tone usually reserved for domestic animals. With my visor already in the descending mode, I didn't bother to acknowledge the comment and continued to film. Seconds later, there was another tap on my shoulder. Fortunately, it was only Conrad, directing my attention to yet another pair of workers on the opposite side of the path.

Unlike their counterparts, this time there were no natural obstructions blocking my view of their actions. After quickly re-positioning the camera, I instinctively moved to focus, but not before casting a furtive glance to confirm Franz's attention was momentarily elsewhere. But no sooner had my surreptitious move been completed, a voice boomed out above the whirring weed-cutters.

"Visor down on site... at *all* times. That is procedure."

Unless you include two years as a Navy League cadet at the impressionable age of 14, I'd never been much of a military man. Dealing with authority had generally been a case of erratic swings between outright rejection and varying degrees of respect. But even with that nurtured ambivalence, I could accept Franz had a point. Responsible for the safety of the entire troupe, he was not in the mood or position to tolerate violations, whatever their basis.

Despite my overt precautions at another site shortly thereafter, Franz caught a third and final infraction, only to lose it.

"That's it," he shouted, swaggering over to stand directly in front of the camera.   "What you do with your life does not really interest me. But today you are in an area under my jurisdiction. If something was to happen to you, it would reflect badly on me and the whole organization. I am not about to let that happen, so I want you to pack up and leave the area immediately."

It was a critical moment to say the least. With Franz the linchpin of the entire documentary, antagonizing him further would not have boded well for a smooth production. Confronted with potentially losing face, one way or the other, I stepped away from the camera, raising my hands in a mock surrender while curbing any rebuttal. Hoping to defuse matters, Conrad moved between us, his frown an indication that he was as dumbfounded as me by Franz's outburst

"It's okay," he said in a low voice, as the group prepared to trudge back to base camp. "I don't really need ten minutes of weed cutting anyway. But the lad has a temper. Definitely something to keep in mind."

*

"Just how safe is safe?" I asked, breaking the silence that had been lingering since we'd departed the base camp. Accepting the question as it was intended, part curiosity and part ceasefire, Franz met me halfway, answering over his shoulder without looking back.

"A hundred percent," he said.

"But how can you comb every square inch of an entire country and be sure you haven't missed something? That just doesn't seem feasible. What if someone was having a bad day, slacked off a bit and overlooked something. Who would know until...?"

"As I said before, once we've designated an area as cleared, it is safe."

Less than convinced, I decided not to press the point, blithely unaware of how soon my theory would be tested.

"God, look at all the dust," I said to Conrad, drawing his attention to the choking clouds being churned up with every passing vehicle. "How can people even see where they're going?"

Undoubtedly used to such conditions, the majority of

moped drivers and their passengers caught up in the throes of the massive dust storm, acted unconcerned, offering up desultory glances or even an occasional smile as we passed and left them in our own lengthy shroud. Although some had resorted to wrapping a scarf or surgical mask over their nose and mouth, it was difficult to imagine it was doing much good, given the sheer tonnage of airborne earth.

"We're heading for a disaster," Conrad announced a short while later, as another oncoming motorbike disappeared into the bulbous plume trailing us.

"What do mean heading?" I asked. "What would you call this dustbowl we're in?"

"No, I'm talking about the accident that took place a couple of weeks ago."

Events such as the one Conrad had referred to, were normally not reported beyond Cambodia's borders. The only reason this one had made international headlines was because thirteen lives had been lost in a single flash. As it had taken place within Franz's area of responsibility, he'd arranged for us to meet and speak with some of the relatives of those killed.

According to Franz, the incident had involved a group of local chili pickers returning home after a long day in the fields. Traveling in an open wagon pulled by a motorbike, that was being driven by a local man familiar with the area, the group had been on a safely marked route when they came to a point where the trail crossed over a small stream. Remnants of the recently ended rainy season had made passage at the crossing impossible, so the driver had stopped to scout around for an alternative route. Believing that cow hoof prints in the mud provided reasonable assurance that no mines lay in wait, he had eased the vehicle forward, straying no more than a meter or two from the original path. Regrettably what he failed to take into consideration was that while a cow may be heavy enough to set off an anti-personnel land mine, its weight is insufficient to detonate an anti-tank one. To their tragic misfortune, a metal wagon loaded with thirteen people aboard was.

After nearly two hours of bone-jarring travel, we entered a small village that at first glance resembled a deserted movie set. Complete with dust whirlpools and tumbleweeds chasing each other down a dirt street, all that was missing was someone being tossed out of the swinging doors of a non-existent saloon. When our Cambodian driver stopped to ask directions, I used the opportunity to stretch my legs and have a look around. Except for a familiar looking kiosk or two, there was not a lot to see. Stirred by the sight of a potential customer, one merchant began vying for my attention by fanning his arms. Not in the market for any brightly-labeled packages of dish detergents, cooking oils or American snacks, I merely nodded and refrained from wandering anywhere near his stand. I was about to saunter off in the direction of an abandoned fountain, long since incapable of offering relief from the heat, when a curt honk summoned me back to the truck, only to learn we'd somehow missed our turn-off. Fortunately, we only needed to retrace a "dustance" of 300 meters before stopping alongside a wooden lean-to, one hefty breeze from collapse. Despite our reduced speed, a trailing cloud managed to briefly engulf the group of wide-eyed children sitting out front. As we disembarked, Conrad mimed that he wanted footage of the dozen or so smiling faces. In other parts of the world, children spotting a camera would have immediately started a round of waving and clowning around. This group of youngsters however, simply sat in silence, watching intently as I set up beside the truck. While in the process of getting several cover shots, Conrad, who'd been off in discussion with Franz and a local man, returned to inform me the woman we'd come to interview was in fact there at the kiosk. Making use of the camera, I found her seated amongst a group of middle-aged women at the back of the lean-to. What set her apart from the other inquisitive faces was a hollow, blank stare that bore straight through the lens and into the back of my head. Rising up with a start, I caught Conrad's chin with my shoulder, as he leaned over to confirm the woman in the viewfinder was indeed the mother of one of the victims, and grandmother to the small boy squirming on her lap.

As it had been determined that the best place to conduct the interview would be at the woman's home, I was sent across the street to scout out a location. There didn't appear to be anyone in the yard as I approached the hut with a combination of respect and curiosity. Calling out but getting no response, I ascended a short, makeshift ladder and poked my head through the open doorway. A quick survey of the sole room, basically the size of a small single-car garage, made it apparent there was no need to venture any further. Divided in two by a pair of blankets draped over a rope, the room's grey, rough-hewn walls and floor, made it too dark to shoot in. While still atop the ladder, I was suddenly besieged by images from another world, seeing myself wandering through a familiar house, flicking a light switch, running a tap, turning up a thermostat, before grabbing a snack from the fridge and settling down in front of the television. I was yanked back to the present by the realization that the residents of this dwelling were unlikely to experience such creature comforts... ever.

Having set up in the dirt yard at the front of the hut, we were about to begin the interview when the grandmother beckoned a young girl on a nearby stoop to join her. Holding a framed photo of her deceased mother, the young girl stood motionless the entire time it took the older woman to solemnly relate her thoughts on the event, the restless three-year old still squirming in her arms. Unable to hear what the translator was saying to Conrad, and not understanding a word of Khmer, my thoughts were overshadowed by a deep sense of embarrassment at the immense opportunities afforded us by the mere accident of birth.

"There's one more place I think you should see before we head back to Battambang," Franz said, as we watched the woman and her grandchildren turn away to avoid the dust blown up by our departure. As it turned out, the accident site was not far and within twenty minutes we'd arrived at a plateau overlooking a broad plain. To no one's surprise, there in the distance was yet another solitary mountain. In an attempt to raise the somber mood present since leaving the village, Franz chose to explain the origin of these isolated peaks as we unloaded.

"Five thousand years ago," he began, "Cambodia had yet to be formed. The Mekong delta was much further north, somewhere up near the border with Thailand. Over time, the tons of silt washing downstream from the Himalayas forced the seawater to recede. What was left behind was a flat fertile plain that is now Cambodia. Peaks like the one out there were simply islands in the former sea."

The geography lesson was suddenly interrupted when Conrad called out, pointing to a small vehicle approaching in the distance.

"Out there, in the valley. Can you get it?"

Scrambling to set up as the wagon drew nearer, the already substantial pressure to capture the event was increased with Franz's announcement that the advancing vehicle was identical to the one involved in the deadly incident. Making the moment even more poignant was the fact the wagon was full of men, women and children, all smiling and waving as I managed to pan and let them slip past out of frame.

Following another brief safety lecture, the three of us set off down a narrow, rutted trail. Once again the scenery was less than breathtaking, comprised mostly of empty scrubland, hyphenated by the odd cultivated field. As we continued to walk, it didn't escape me that there were no red strings anywhere to be seen. It wasn't until we had looped around a rudimentary animal compound, home to several skeletal cows and a few ornery goats, that I caught a glimpse of the familiar red skull and crossbones. Such reassurance, however, was short lived, as seconds later Franz directed us to turn right, away from the signs. Having been saddled with both camera and tripod, keeping pace with the other two was proving to be an effort. Just as the gap between us was getting large enough to warrant a shout, Franz and Conrad paused at the crest of a small hill. Joining them on the summit, I glanced back to see our truck in the distance, a reminder of just how close the victims had been to safety that day.

"I want you both to stay here while I check out the area,"

Franz called back to us, as we watched him descend to a dry creek bed and walk a short distance to the edge of a small crater.

"I thought he said something about areas being safe once cleared."

"Don't bother mentioning that again," Conrad warned, as Franz waved the all clear to advance. Stumbling through a brief performance of "After you... no after you," which ultimately would have been of no consequence had a mine been present, we both proceeded with caution.

Setting up on the edge of a crater approximately three to four meters across and two meters deep, I listened as Franz explained how the initial retrieval team had secured the area.

"It's standard procedure to first confirm the site is safe. In this case, it was even more vital considering that they discovered a second unexploded anti-tank mine not far from the original blast."

"That's information I could have done without," I mumbled to Conrad as we both stared down into the shattered earth. An eerie silence followed Franz's explanation, broken only by the rustling of dried corn stalks in a nearby field. I felt a chill rattle down my spine, as Conrad directed my attention to a twisted mass of metal lodged on a ridge ten to fifteen meters away. Looking more like a piece of abstract art than any recognizable mode of transportation, it wasn't until I zoomed in on the blue-coloured object that it became recognizable as a gruesome symbol of the power that had ended thirteen lives.

"It's almost the same time of day as the accident took place," Franz said, glancing at his watch. Up until then, his choice of words hadn't really bothered me, but there at the site, it was irritating to hear him still refer to it as an accident. Staring at the residue in the pit, which included a few empty water bottles and an overturned flip-flop, thoughts drifted to the lengthy chain of people responsible for our being there; infantrymen, officers, military leaders, politicians, advisors, bureaucrats, lobbyists, arms dealers, defence contractors, sales reps, manufacturers, assembly line workers, parts suppliers... were all testimony to the fact this had been no accident, but rather a crime.

Once a short stand-up by Franz had been recorded, I was in the process of packing up for the trek back, when I happened to look up to see two heads disappearing over the crest of the hill. It couldn't have been more than seven or eight meters to the relative safety of the rutted path, but I was suddenly filled with a sense of uncertainty. With "what if they did miss something?" lurking in the shadows, I managed to calm myself with the premise that anyone as strict in following regulations as Franz, would not have abandoned a colleague if there had been any prospect of danger...then again. In the end, it was a single deep breath that broke the impasse. Slinging the tripod over my shoulder, I grabbed the camera bag and covered the distance between two points in the quickest time history has probably ever recorded.

Day Four: Monday, Dec. 13th

The next morning, we were treated to our first daylight view of Battambang's central core. The range of shops, food stands and general hubbub on the streets was similar to that witnessed in parts of Phnom Pehn, but here the scenes unfolding pushed "teeming" to a whole new dimension. In the midst of the plasmatic flow of life oozing past my window, my attention was nabbed by a large placard when heavy traffic brought us to a halt. Unlike the small, unassuming plaques common to Europe and North America, the proprietor of this particular business had selected to use what could have easily qualified as a mini-billboard to advertise his wares. As the traffic eased and we slowly edged onwards, I found myself asking why, of all enterprises, the services of a psychiatrist were touted in such a blatant manner.

With the city proper behind us, it was quickly apparent that a good portion of the day's vistas would be less than scenic. Given the limited appeal of factories and warehouses, few of which carried any identifying logos, thoughts turned to the road itself. The stretch of two-lane asphalt we found ourselves on was not only plagued with numerous potholes, but also had the added luxury of rudimentary shoulders, presumably meant to serve as a haven for pedestrians, cyclists and motorbikes hoping to dodge incoming ordinance in the form of SUV's. A surprising number of these obnoxious dominators were underway that morning, most of them passing at whim, and signalling their general disregard for anyone who strayed in their way with a loud and prolonged blast of the horn. Our own driver's performance was considerably less perilous, inspired perhaps by the steady stream of criticisms emitted by Franz. Nonetheless, it was a relief when we pulled off the busy main highway to enter a bustling market town where the sheer number of people and animals afoot soon slowed our pace to a crawl.

"What are all these people doing here?" I asked, peering out at the shifting masses, many of whom attempted to peer back through the darkened windows.

"Surviving, I suspect," Conrad answered drolly, without looking up from his laptop.

Upon exiting the town, patches of what one presumed was green countryside started to appear. I say presumed, as the ever-present dust had transformed roadside foliage into a corridor of grime-coated sentinels. Combined with the withered scrub bush and otherwise scorched landscape, it seemed obvious why few of Cambodia's fifteen million inhabitants had chosen to settle in this part of the country.

Despite improved road conditions, we were still half-an-hour behind schedule when the driver turned off on to a trail canopied by large palm trees. Two hundred yards along, we rolled to a stop in a clearing filled with a jumble of parked motorbikes. Entering a concrete bungalow through a side door, we were greeted to a round of applause by fifty to sixty locals who'd gathered to hear today's presentation on the dangers of land mines. Men, women and children of all ages were scattered around the room; the men seated on benches and stools, smoking and chatting amongst themselves, while the women squatted or knelt on the bare cement floor, quieting those too young to appreciate the theme of the meeting. Following a brief introduction, the moderator began to explain the meaning of symbols on the plastic cards that had been handed out earlier to participants. Watching and listening intently to the lecture, no one in the audience so much as batted an eye in my direction as I moved through the crowd capturing candid shots of more faces than we could ever possibly use. Twenty minutes later, as the lecture was coming to a close, I skirted out a side exit hoping to catch the surge of departing guests as they clambered aboard their motorbikes. Forced to retreat to escape a billowing cloud of bluish exhaust, I suddenly found myself amidst a group of twenty or more white-shirted students. Apparently on break from a nearby school, the group of fourteen-to-fifteen-year olds had come to buy ice cream at a nearby kiosk, when they had been distracted by the sight of the camera. Initially greeted with smiles and a few furrowed brows, I spent a few minutes fumbling through rudimentary attempts at communication, answering the standard inquiry of where I was from, whether it was my first time in Cambodia, and did I like the country. Once those subjects had been exhausted, the general demeanour seemed to shift. Comments uttered by some of the boys were followed by a burst of giggles from the girls, making me suspect I was no longer being cordially welcomed, but rather the butt of jokes in order to impress the female members of the crowd. With the re-emergence of Conrad and Franz a few minutes later, I took my leave from the group, curious as to what sort of stereotypes I may have lived up to during our brief cultural exchange.

    With no further appointments scheduled, the decision

was made to stop for lunch before starting the arduous journey back to Battambang. Taking advantage of a detour suggested by our driver, it was not long before we were cruising along the dusty main drag of a nearby village. More of a hump than a road, each side rose up almost two feet before meeting in the middle, presumably designed in such a way to facilitate run-off and prevent the area from turning into a giant quagmire during the rainy season. What also made this village unique was the relative lack of activity. Instead of the masses of shuffling shoppers, only a few clusters of bored-looking teenagers were visible, straddled over their bikes at various spots along the roadside. Slow motion glances and prolonged stares were cast in our direction as we edged our way down the street, with the last clique treating us to a round of requisite adolescent sneers as our driver swung into a space in front of an outdoor cafe, directly across from their turf. Seating ourselves at one of the plastic tables perched on an undulating section of the dirt courtyard, we were granted a direct view of the outdoor cooking area; basically a tiny grill and deep fat fryer set atop a rickety wooden cabinet. Adding to my growing sense of unease was the noticeable absence of anything remotely resembling a fridge. Oddly enough, it was almost three years to the day that caution had been thrown to the wind in the seaside resort of Dahab, Egypt. Famished after an hour spent snorkelling on a nearby coral reef, the tantalizing odours wafting from a sidewalk bistro in town had seduced me into ordering a slab of beef, whose prior place of residence I hadn't bothered to confirm. As a result, the next two days had been passed sprinting between bed and bathroom, interrupted only by several painful visits from a needle-wielding local doctor, promising to restore my rapidly vanishing electrolytes. In an attempt to shake off such memories, I was mindlessly tracing figures on the sticky tabletop when my gaze gravitated to fumes rising up from a skillet on the grill. I couldn't help but notice a thick blue cable running out of the back of the cooking unit, snaking its way across the ground before ending at a large propane gas tank less than two meters from our table. Luck however, had been with us that day and instead of getting blown sky high, we were treated to a very tasty meal.

That evening back at the hotel, with no rumbling reminders of lunch present, I decided to spring for an over-priced beer from the mini-bar before retiring. Casually flipping through the guidebook while sitting on the bed, I happened to land on a page with a rather puzzling statistic. It seemed the entire country of Cambodia was endowed with a total of twenty psychiatrists. Why such details rated mention in a travel guide was puzzling, and it wasn't until I had drained my glass and snapped off the light, that I realized that the information might just come in handy, should another wedding reception break out in the middle of the night.

Day Five: Tuesday, Dec. 14th

On what was to be our last full day in rural Cambodia, we again found ourselves in uncharted territory, this time headed for a recovery base located north of the city of Pailin. Unlike the flat, scrub-filled terrain we'd grown accustomed to on previous outings, batches of isolated hills started to sprout fifty kilometres northwest of Battambang; the odd one decorated with a golden-temple spire poking through the thick carpeting of trees. Save for the odd road construction site, where entire sections washed away in the rainy season, were being replaced by Chinese roadworks companies, the drive went relatively smoothly. As a result, we were approaching the outskirts of Pailin earlier than expected. First impressions suggested the region was far from poor and a quick look at the trusted guidebook explained why. In the past, precious gems, timber and rice had accounted for the area's wealth, a fact the Khmer Rouge had apparently not overlooked when looking for ways to keep their struggling revolution alive in the early 1970's. Although most of the mines had long since been exhausted and timber and rice production severely curtailed by the number of land mines in the area, something still keeping this town of 23,000 relatively affluent. But whatever residents were doing to earn their livelihoods, not many were out doing it that morning. Minus the thriving markets, bustling crowds, and chaotic traffic, so prevalent in other cities, our progress through Pailin proper proved swift and painless.

"We're entering an area known as K5," Franz announced shortly after we'd left the town limits and entered a landscape more agricultural than what we'd seen on other trips. "It's a strip of land thirty kilometres wide, that begins at the Gulf of Thailand and runs all the way to Laos, a distance of between three and four hundred kilometres. It's the former front line between warring factions, the world's longest minefield and one of the most dangerous places on the planet."

"If this place is so saturated," I began. "Where the heck do you start to de-mine, if there is such a word... it will take forever to clear the land."

"More like forever and a day," Franz answered. "Some people estimate it could take 10,000 years to make Cambodia completely safe again. But you need to start somewhere."

The mere concept of having to live with the threat of mines for ten thousand years sparked an idea.

"Hey... here's a thought," I whispered to Conrad, when Franz had resumed his conversation with the driver. "Why don't they re-plant some of the recovered mines in the backyards of executives from companies who make them?"

"Do me a favour and keep Plan B to yourself," was his answer.

Although the base camp turned out to be less than fifteen minutes from Pailin, our arrival was once again delayed while the driver parked the truck under Franz's discerning eye.

"Remember your bleedin' visor," was the sum total of Conrad's advice, as we climbed out to be greeted by yet another former British military officer. In his late fifties, short and squat, with a rigid manner that suggested he was also a stickler for order, the base leader introduced himself as Gerald before taking us to meet the rest of his team. Already old pros in the safety lesson department, it wasn't long before we were tramping down a dirt track bordered on both sides by ripening corn fields. Thanks to the dips and swells in the path, a full load of equipment, and thirty something heat, sweating and wheezing were once again part of the routine.

"You sound like the truck's air conditioner," Conrad said with a chuckle, as he stopped to let me pass.

Forced to endure this collective torture for almost twenty minutes, it was a relief to see Gerald veer off down a narrow path that offered the promise of some shade. Several minutes later we were descending into a charred ravine, at the far end of which a green, field tent had been erected.

"Another five minutes and I would have evaporated," I warned Conrad as permission was given to raise our visors. "I've got so much salt on me, I feel like I just came out of the Dead Sea," I added with a groan. Hoping to compensate for the massive loss of fluids, I grabbed a bottle of water from a portable ice box, and slumped down on a bench in the cooling shade, making sure that the only parts of me moving were my throbbing temples. Respite, however, was brief. After what must have been the shortest ten minutes on record, Gerald sprang to his feet to announce, "Well gentlemen... I guess we should get a move on."

Despite having done nothing in the interim, a gargantuan effort was required to get to my feet, and an even larger one to not sit back down again and order a Mojito. But somehow automatic pilot kicked in and I reluctantly followed the others back up the path. As the group continued to wind its way through what had now become thick underbrush, I could see Franz and Gerald conferring up ahead. Although I wasn't close enough to hear what they were saying, their gestures reaffirmed how certain people can exude a military presence without ever opening their mouths.

"Gentlemen," Gerald barked, raising his hand to halt us at a point where two paths intersected. "You are about to have the pleasure of filming the removal of a live mine. But first, you must stay here while Franz and I inspect the site."

"And just exactly where is this live mine?" I asked Conrad, having noticed there were no reassuring red wires anywhere in sight.

"I'm sure we'll find out soon enough, one way or the other," he answered, in what I thought was extremely poor taste. Meanwhile, Gerald and Franz moved ahead some twenty to thirty meters from us. When beckoned to approach a few minutes later, it was somewhat alarming to look down into a hole at their feet and see two brown cylinders lodged in the earthen wall.

"These mines are of Chinese origin," Gerald informed us, matter-of-factly. "When activated, they will spring out of the ground before exploding, thereby causing maximum collateral damage."

"What does he mean 'will'?" I asked Conrad, acutely aware that we were in the middle of the Cambodian jungle, miles from any medical assistance, in a location that seemed the last place one would ever expect to find a land mine, making it the perfect spot to plant one.

"They are capable of taking out everything within at least

a five-meter radius," Gerald added reassuringly.

Having seen quite enough of the ordinance up close, I was pleased to learn that Franz would obtain close-up footage of Gerald extracting the mines, while I filmed from a safer location some distance away. Once both cameras were set up and rolling, I couldn't help wondering how I might react if a muffled boom was to suddenly occur. But before I could speculate on the financial implications of owning world-exclusive footage, the entire procedure was over.

Back on the trail, I was able to catch Gerald's attention long enough to ask why mines weren't simply detonated where they were found rather than risking their removal. It must be said he made a concerted effort not to sound too patronizing, although his facial expressions could have done with a bit of practice in regards to appearing sincere.

"Sometimes we have no choice. We have to detonate on site," he explained. "But when ordinance is blown up on location, shrapnel will either contaminate areas already cleared, or add metal fragments to sectors yet to be scanned. That would increase our workload substantially."

In a scene reminiscent of the "Cone of Silence," in the 1960's TV series, "Get Smart," a good portion of Gerald's explanation was lost to the muffling effects of his lowered visor. What I did retain was that whenever possible, workers would place detected ordinance in another nearby hole already lined with sandbags, before covering the devices with more sandbags and detonating them from a safe distance.

"The sandbags limit the explosion, directing it downwards where it can do less harm," he informed, before bringing the lecture to a close and quickening his pace.

Back at base camp, re-energized by the realization that all

my extremities were still intact and functioning, I was busy loading the gear back into our dust-laden truck when an inexplicable urge to whistle suddenly came over me. It was a revealing moment to say the least as I never whistle... ever.

Sprawled out in the back of the truck, awaiting our departure, my heretofore elation was dimmed by the announcement that our next destination was to be a place Franz referred to as "the killing caves." But before there was a chance to dwell on the implications of that ominous description, Gerald stuck his head in the window to issue a last-minute invitation to join him and his senior supervisors for lunch. Leaving the Cambodian workers, a troupe of unsung heroes if there ever was one, to fend for themselves, fifteen minutes later our small group was seated around a large wooden table on the patio of a restaurant located in the middle of the jungle, surrounded by scents from an assortment of flowers and lush vegetation.

"Anybody up for a bit of crocodile?" Gerald asked probingly. "I'm serious" he insisted, when nobody responded. "It's really very good and it's local."

"What do you mean by local?" I wanted to know, recalling the previous images of young boys jumping into creeks and ponds en route to Battambang.

"They're in the rivers here in the region. Tigers as well... mind you, not in the rivers. The tigers are pretty rare, but a local farmer said he spotted one a couple of weeks ago in the fields not far from our base camp."

Concluding that Gerald at least *appeared* to be in control of all his faculties, the group reached a unanimous consensus to lessen the local reptilian population. As is often the case when colleagues gather, especially ex-military ones, conversation shifted to shop talk once food orders had been taken. Peppered with random bursts of hearty laughter, not to mention a whiff of bravado, the banter revealed that most of those present had neither families nor close ties to their homeland, having been drawn to their trade by a hunger for adventure and the urge to help others. Unable to add much to the focused discussion, I sat back, realizing that although I'd had come to dislike Franz's persona in a very short span of time, I still harboured a smidgen of respect for the line of work he had chosen. (*Months later, that respect would suffer a significant dent, upon learning Franz had been actively involved in planting mines during his tenure with the Warsaw Pact military.*)

In the end the crocodile looked and tasted like rumpled chicken; not bad but nothing outstanding. The best part, I suspect, was that you had earned the right to say you'd had it.

As lunch wound down over coffee and a dessert that looked capable of dissolving fillings, Gerald lowered his cell phone long enough to let us know he'd managed to arrange for a final surprise. Fifteen minutes later, we were back in the truck, headed for what we'd been told was a nearby munitions dump. Getting to the actual site involved hiking an additional three-hundred metres along a deeply-rutted channel slashed through a field of long grass. Our goal was another small hole, which according to Gerald, was to be the final resting place for three small Russian-made rocket mortars. Unlike the two cylinders removed that morning, which in many ways had resembled rusted soup cans, the sight of these mini rockets, complete with pointed nose cone and fins, was considerably more unsettling. To make matters worse, a language breakdown resulted in the Cambodian assistant placing the mortars in the hole before I could film his doing so.

"He's too quick," I complained to Gerald. "He needs to wait until I nod before starting the action."

Ordered to repeat his actions, the assistant cautiously removed the ordinance and proceeded to gently set it back down in the hole. Once footage of the re-positioned mortars was "in the can," Conrad and I left the trio to the business of attaching the detonation wires.

"Any idea why the fifty metre regulation for non-staff wasn't in effect just now," I inquired.

"Not a clue, but don't start asking questions like that again. Just be glad nothing happened and that we'll soon be out of here... See those things?" Conrad asked, as he slowed his pace and directed my attention to a row of white, gauze-like patches lodged along a ridge running the length of the field. "Know what they are?"

"No idea," I answered, puzzled by the fact each object had a distinctive inch-wide hole at its centre. "They look like candy floss that somebody sat on."

"Close... they're tarantula webs."

Although it didn't appear that any of the occupants were at home, my gait had already quickened by the time Conrad added, "If you see one, keep away from it. They're supposed to be aggressive and very fast."

Highly cognizant of where I placed my feet while setting up for the money shot, I made sure I'd framed and focused before Franz, Gerald and the assistant rejoined us in the parking lot. This time the latter heeded Gerald's advice, and waited for the signal to proceed before attaching the wires to the detonator box.

Beyond a sudden spurt of black smoke and a short tongue of orange flame, there wasn't much to see. A fraction of a second later, an echoing boom swept past, accompanied by a wave of compressed air strong enough to flutter my pant legs. Almost immediately particles of shattered earth could be heard dropping like rain within throwing distance of our position. As the smoke dissipated over the field, I was drawn back to images of the accident site. Feeling compelled to ask Franz how the blast we'd just witnessed compared to the one that had killed the chili pickers, I was taken aback to hear the sobering news that the controlled explosion represented only a quarter of the power that had been released that day.

Anyone remotely familiar with the events that took place in Cambodia between April 17th, 1975 and January 7th, 1979, knows how "the killing fields" got their name. Consequently, it didn't require a huge leap of the imagination to figure out what awaited us as we passed through an unmanned gate at the base of Phnom Sambeau mountain on our way to what Franz had called the "killing caves." Skirting past a collection of abandoned market stalls laid out beneath a canopy of shadowing trees, we ascended a steep, winding road until arriving at a cement courtyard so disheveled, it looked as though it had suffered through a recent earthquake. Presiding over a derelict temple on the far edge of the courtyard, a forlorn looking, paint-chipped Buddha sat in the haze of the sinking sun. Other than a pair of saffron-robed monks crossing the square, the only activity was several merchants hovering at stalls along its border. Having been to the site on several previous occasions, Franz quickly guided us to the path leading to the caves. Several minutes later, we began our descent down a long concrete staircase, into what looked more like a natural amphitheater than a cave.

"People were brought here," he explained, as we reached rock bottom and stepped out on to the black-and-white tiled floor of a large grotto. "Purported enemies of the State, which given the circumstances at the time could have been just about anyone, were tortured in the temple back at the courtyard before being marched up to that ledge," he continued, gesturing to a nearby rocky overhang. "Then one by one, they were thrown down the shaft to their death."

With those words still echoing in my ears, I moved over to the shaft where a collection of jagged boulders lay scattered along its lower contours. Although Franz was now a good thirty feet away, I was able to hear him explain that more than 14,000 victims had met their fate within feet of where I was standing. Earlier, he had advised us it was not forbidden to film in this sacred memorial, but now that we were there, it nevertheless felt intrusive to do so. Attempting to document aspects of the shrine as respectfully as possible, I was unable to escape the memories created by a visit to the Nazi concentration camp in Mauthausen, Austria. In *that* hell on earth, numerous prisoners had met a similar end, flung to their deaths at the camp's notorious stone quarry. Several minutes later, Franz's sonorous voice pulled me back to the present.

"They killed the adults here. Children, fourteen and younger, around a thousand or so, were thrown down another shaft not far from here."

Moving to the opposite end of the grotto, I caught sight of a lone monk sitting cross legged amidst an array of

Buddhas and burning candles. There to guard the vestiges of those who'd perished, he nodded knowingly as I stepped forward to pay my respects. Accepting his wordless offer to light a stick of incense, I was bending down to place the smouldering tribute at his feet when distracted by a brightly-coloured cabinet stacked with several dozen human skulls on its open shelves.

Evening shadows were beginning to creep across the checkered floor by the time we returned to the top of the stairs.

"Why here?" I asked Franz in a lowered voice, turning for a final look at the cavern below. "Why like this?"

"This was a holy shrine before it became a cemetery," he answered. "The Khmer Rouge knew that and used it as a final insult before sending people to their grave."

"And the method?" I repeated.

"As gross as it sounds… because it was practical. Simple as that. Practical buggers, the Khmer Rouge. Access here was easily controlled so there was no chance of witnesses. By throwing people down a shaft, they saved on ammunition and the need for burials. The same logic was used in the killing fields, except there people were murdered with shovels or had their throats cut with sugar-cane leaves to save on bullets."

The sense of detachment with which Franz had related this information was a stark reminder of how routinely such acts had been carried out in the name of the revolution. By the time it was over, some two million people, reputedly twenty-five percent of the population were thought to have perished.

"It's a real paradox to see these friendly, helpful people

today," Franz mused as we rejoined the highway for the drive back to Battambang. "Maybe that's why I don't trust a lot of Cambodians. They may smile all the time, but you never know what they're thinking."

Day Six: Wednesday, December 15th

Although the past four days had been nothing less than a feast of sensory overload, a part of me was glad to see it coming to an end. Standing in the compound the next morning, awaiting the truck that would take us back to Phnom Penh, my penchant for reflection was diverted by squeals and shouts drifting over a nearby cinder-block wall. Careful not to slice my fingers on the strands of razor wire on its top edge, I peered over to see dozens of tiny red-uniformed grade schoolers cavorting in a drab, gravel schoolyard.

"Franz was right," Conrad said, having crept up the small incline to join me at the wall. "All these people ever do is smile. But what is there to smile about when so many have so little?"

"Maybe the answer is in the question," I countered, as we continued to watch the miniature Cambodians at play. Just at that moment, Franz came bounding out of the main office building, dressed in a fresh set of khaki fatigues. He seemed to be in an exceptionally good mood, announcing that our trusted companion for the past five days would be remaining behind in Battambang. For reasons that weren't forthcoming, the return trip to Phnom Penh was to be made in the comfort of a brand-new Range Rover. Once underway, cocooned from reality more than ever, it was hard to ignore the element of decadence as we settled in for the five-hour journey. With Franz at the wheel of a vehicle capable of higher speeds, it was shortly after one when we arrived back in the capital. Having fully expected the next few hours would be spent location scouting, I was pleased when Conrad proclaimed the rest of the day "shoot free," suggesting a part of it be spent relaxing at the hotel's rooftop pool. Although lounging at poolside did prove calming for awhile, it came with a price; that being the indelible image of oneself as some latter-day colonial baron, leisurely basking in the sun while peons toiled in the fields below. With a boat trip on the Mekong scheduled for the coming weekend, it seemed a much better idea to head for the riverfront to scout out a potential craft. As a result, an hour was as much relaxing as I could take.

Thanks to the less than frightening power of my hotel shower, a detectable odour of chlorine was still clinging to me as I hopped out of the Tuk-Tuk on to the grand promenade. In the process of telling my driver not to wait as I planned to take my time exploring this part of the city and had no idea when or if I would be in need of his services again, I was met with a bewildered look. Despite repeating my declaration, he simply nodded vigorously and climbed into the back seat with obviously no intention of leaving. In no mood for an argument, I merely shrugged and turned away, assuming he would eventually get the hint in a day or two.

A short while later, standing atop a long concrete embankment, I was gazing out at what I presumed was the mighty Mekong, when my attention was snared by an erratic flotilla of foliage drifting along in the swift current. A quick glance in my trusty guidebook informed me that the greenery floating past was actually doing so in the Tonle Sap river, having been swept downstream from a lake of the same name located in the centre of the country. Hoping to fill in a few more gaps in my porous knowledge of the region, I retreated to a nearby bench to learn that the Tonle Sap river was a somewhat ambidextrous waterway. During the dry season when water levels were low, the river flowed southward, eventually hooking up with the Mekong not far from my current vantage point. In the rainy season however, it pulled off the remarkable feat of reversing direction. This switch had to do with the melting snows of the distant Himalayas, which when combined with monsoon rains, ballooned the size of the Mekong. Once that mass of water reached Phnom Penh, it caused the Tonle Sap to back up, creating a current that flowed all the way up to the lake itself, a distance of some 125 kms. With the surrounding countryside being so flat, huge sections simply disappeared under the water, forming what amounted to a seasonal inland sea. Here in Phnom Penh itself, the vertical drop from the upper edge of the sloping embankment to the rippled mud at the water's edge, looked to be somewhere in the neighbourhood of fifteen to twenty feet, an indication of how much the water level changed between seasons.

Now thoroughly informed about the features of the Tonle Sap, I abandoned my studies for a stroll further along the waterfront. That day, some twenty to thirty tourist boats could be seen parked along the shoreline. Slotted diagonally like tightly packed sardines, one could have theoretically walked from the deck of the first to the last without ever touching the water. Most of the vessels had been painted in an array of garish colours, presumably in hopes of their standing out in the crowd. The problem was that with so many employing the same promotional gimmick, there wasn't anything that really distinguished one from the other. Making my way along the muddy shoreline, careful not to step in any of the water-filled holes, I couldn't help noticing the scarcity of on-board activity. Half-way through my mini-inspection tour of this armada, I realized that all of the boats were too large for what we had in mind. What seemed more sensible was something the size of the fishing skiffs I could see out on the river. But with little chance of making contact with them, I relinquished my quest and shuffled back towards the promenade.

Had it been unknown beforehand, it wouldn't have taken long to determine I'd landed in the tourist section of the city. Aside from the heavily trafficked riverfront drive, the first clue to my whereabouts was the assortment of blinking neon signs. Hundreds of coloured tubes, hawking accommodation for as low as $8.00 a night, vied for attention with others pushing hour-long Thai, Khmer or Vietnamese massages for even less. Added to this mix was a jumble of bars and clubs, all elbowing each other for what they claimed was the happiest hour on the block. For the discriminating tourist there was even a shop for coffins, which oddly enough didn't seem to be doing a thriving business. Had this been a city in North America or Europe, I would have likely hailed the nearest taxi and headed for quieter climes. But for some reason, here all the activity and droves of humanity was enamouring; so much so that all I could do was plunk myself down on another bench, lean against the trunk of a towering palm, and try and take it all in.

In no rush to return to the hotel after I'd had my fill of the endless tumult, I drifted over to a nearby temple complex I'd spotted earlier, curious to see whether "non-monks" were allowed to venture inside its inner sanctum. Just how much I'd been bombarded while absorbing life outside the complex became apparent the moment I passed through the ornate-gated entrance into the grounds. Coveting the new-found silence as the sounds of the city quickly fell away, I by-passed the main temple, whose steps were littered with tourists, to saunter through an empty garden. Off to my right, I noticed a group of orange-robed monks gathered around a table, animatedly conversing over a pot of tea. After taking a photo from a respectful distance, I crossed the flagstoned courtyard to the side door of a smaller temple. Abandoning shoes and socks at the door, as a sign requested, I entered a cool, darkened room that at first seemed to contain little more numerous rows of round pillars. The sole visitor, I could hear my warm feet squeaking on the patches of the cold, marble floor not covered by red woven mats, as I moved towards the centre aisle. There at the front of the room, two large golden Buddha statues sat on a raised platform, bookending what appeared to be a smaller black replica of themselves. Overseeing these three deities was yet another Buddha, this one portrayed resting on a divan in a large mural directly above its counterparts. Amongst the paraphernalia assembled in front of the platform were ceremonial bowls, flags, donation boxes, flowers, incense, paintings and still more Buddhas. Numerous other figures were scattered along the sides of the room, including four life-size, golden statues that resembled Mahatma Gandhi in the lotus position. All in all, the decor made it feel as though I'd stumbled into a religious garage sale. Intrigued as much as puzzled by the sheer amount of tributes, I was about to take my leave when out of nowhere an elderly monk scurried past. Muttering something indecipherable, he gestured for me to wait, before disappearing through a side door flanking the stage. Upon his return a few seconds later, strands of white-and-yellow bulbs above the stage flickered to life, turning the entire arrangement into a mini Las Vegas. Startled by this unexpected display of enlightenment, I could feel a stiff smile attach itself to my face as I glanced back and forth between the clearly proud and expectant monk and his creative work. After feigning interest for what felt like a respectable amount of time, I clasped my hands in thanks, bowed my head and exited. Only once outside did I realize I'd been expected to leave a donation. Seeing as rectifying that faux pas meant repeating the process of unlacing my boots, I chose instead to make my way to the rear of the compound, where I came upon a number of intricately carved stone burial monuments amidst smaller auxiliary shrines. Painted in light greys, and pastel oranges and yellows, they brought to mind a series of multi-tiered cement wedding cakes. Moving further through the well-kept graveyard, I eventually caught sight of a pair of monks sitting quietly on the balcony of a two-story residence. Exchanging acknowledging nods as I passed, I found myself wondering just what it was monks did on their day off.

As I continued to stroll through the peaceful grounds, up ahead I could make out a large decorative archway, signalling the route back to a world abuzz. But before returning to the reality of central Phnom Penh, the temple had one last surprise in store. Much like the childhood pleasure of discovering and exploiting a squeaky floorboard until parental comments warned of the risks of continuing, I stumbled through an invisible curtain that separated my current and imminent worlds. Stepping halfway through the arch, instantly enveloped me in a wave of sounds coming from the busy open-air market across the street. Pausing to swing the same foot back one pace, I was returned to the sanctity of the temple grounds. Forward...clamour. Back... tranquility. Forward...din. Back...silence. Despite a small group of Cambodians staring, pointing and chuckling at me from across the street, I spent several moments piercing and re-piercing the veil for my own enjoyment.

Having finally left my sanctuary to enter the crowded market, my first impression was that it was genuine; free of the barking hucksters of a Petticoat Lane or a Moroccan souk, where the singular goal often seemed to be the blatant milking of tourists. Considering the market butted up alongside the tourist zone, such authenticity was no small achievement. Quickly caught up in the invigorating pace of market life as I moved through the crowded aisles, I soon lost track of time, barely noticing when the bazaar's overhead lights fluttered to life. When I did become aware of the late hour, the encroaching darkness failed to deter me from walking back to the hotel. Setting off on an unfamiliar route that followed one of the main venues paralleling the river, I was soon ambling past the block-long-wall bordering the Royal Palace, stopping at various locked gates to catch a final glimpse of the arched pagoda roofs before they dissolved in the rapidly fading light. Repeatedly accosted by bottled-water merchants hoping to close a final sale before heading home, I wove my way through the stream of tourists exiting the palace grounds, to arrive at the edge of a large plaza. Just at that moment a long row of streetlights clicked on to full power like a string of falling dominoes. Despite this supply of illumination, the yellow cones of light fell off quickly, making it difficult to see what was going on beyond their reach. It was only as I approached the far end of the plaza that a group of figures emerged, soundtracked by the heavy traffic and a familiar disco beat. More numerous than their counterparts in Battambang, I couldn't resist stopping to observe the hundred or more silhouetted gymnasts limbering up to dance their night away.

✻

What with it being our first evening back in the capital, I had been looking forward to dinner at one of the dozen or more restaurants within a two-block radius of the hotel. Given the close proximity of the eateries, Conrad and I knew we would be a big let-down for the troupe of Tuk-Tuk drivers stationed in the courtyard.

"How many times do you think we'll have to say 'no thanks,' before we get to the restaurant?" he challenged, as we exited the air-conditioned foyer, straight into a wall of humid air.

"I guess it depends on how far we want to walk."

"Come on, hazard a guess," he urged.

"Okay, I'll say three... maybe four, if there's a lot of them out there tonight."

Much too conservative in my estimation, the number of participants in the predicted onslaught had risen to five before we'd even covered a full block.

Partly because of its ambience, and partly due to pure

laziness, we ended up selecting a restaurant on the corner of the next block. Shown to a table on a comfortable treed-in patio, we ordered a round of mojitos before sitting back to peruse the menu. Nearby, a woman with a set of miniature xylophone mallets was coaxing oriental music from a stringed instrument I'd never seen before. Our drinks arrived just as I'd convinced myself to try something called Fish Amok, a concoction of baked fish, coconut, and lemon grass, served in a banana leaf. Despite an accompanying photo that made it resemble something packed in a bowl of mud, I hoped it would taste better than it looked. Shortly after placing our orders, a man in jeans and hooded sweatshirt approached our table.

"Evening Gents," he greeted with a cocked finger. "American?"

"Even better," I replied.

Judging from the look on his face, it was not the answer he'd been expecting.

"Sorry, I'm Canadian. He's German," I said to a fading scowl.

"Yeah, I'm sorry he's Canadian too," Conrad added. "Because his German is terrible."

Jerry, who introduced himself as the restaurant's manager, *was* American, as it turned out, a conclusion his accent, mannerisms and greying ponytail had already hinted at. Watching him respond to a question Conrad had about an item on the menu, I was reminded of the character Christopher Walken had played in the Vietnam movie, 'The Deer Hunter,' prompting me to ask how he had ended up in Phnom Penh.

"Back in the States I was married to a Cambodian," he

began. "After so many years, we decided to come visit her homeland. Came here for three weeks, eight years ago."

"And you never went back?" I asked.

"Oh sure we did. We stayed in California for another year. I didn't realize it at first, but I'd fallen in love with this place during those three weeks. Kept thinking about it all the time... Was making me crazy. I just knew I had to come back to get it out of my system."

Sensing he was devoting too much time to our table, Jerry slowly extracted himself from our discussion and wandered off to greet the next batch of customers, adding a final remark. "As you can see... It didn't work."

Day Seven: Thursday, December 16th

Abruptly at quarter past six the next morning, sleep ended rudely when a construction crew began noisily working on a nearby building. Cautiously swinging myself out of bed to avoid aggravating an already sore back muscle; likely the product of too much walking, my yet-to-focus vision fell to a small dark spot on the floor in front of the minibar. The first inclination was to think it a stray leftover from last night's snacking binge, but before reaching for my glasses to confirm, I knelt down for a closer look. As I couldn't recall the last time I'd seen a snack with legs, I gave it a gentle poke. With no response, it seemed reasonable to assume that the morsel was no longer of this world. Once my glasses were firmly lodged on the bridge of my nose, it was clear that a cockroach, the size of a small turtle, had somehow met an inglorious end during the night. Grateful it had chosen not to explore or expire in my bed, I retrieved it with a tissue, wishing it well before sending it off to its next possible incarnation via the toilet. Needless to say, the breakfast buffet received a little extra scrutiny that morning.

Over the years as a cameraman, I had come to recognize that one of the primary benefits of an early start, was the prospect of an early wrap. Today was another example. With all the planned interviews with mine-retrieval employees completed by two, I was once again cast loose to take advantage of being thousands of kilometres away from a "normal" winter, a privilege made even more pleasurable by the fact that someone else was paying for it. Topping my hastily arranged agenda was a return to the riverfront district. But before hailing a Tuk-Tuk, I decided to traipse to a nearby supermarket to secure some nutrition that would hopefully keep me going until dinner. Traipsing however, was perhaps not the right word, as that tends to imply waltzing along lost in thought, without a care in the world. Negotiating would have been more accurate, for if it wasn't the hundreds of haphazardly parked motorbikes, or aggressive SUV drivers emerging from underground park houses that hindered me, it was the steady flow of customers frequenting the series of smoke-billowing food stands along Sihanouk Blvd. Added to that were the mobile vendors and panhandlers, ebbing and flowing in rhythm to any perceived expression of interest. Once having made it past those obstacles, there was still the array of half-finished, unprotected construction sites on the sidewalk to contend with.

"*Why is 'Jingle Bells' playing in a land that's ninety-five percent Buddhist?*" I asked myself, as the familiar melody graced the in-house airwaves. Momentarily caught up in images of distant snow, I was jarred back to the present when the song suddenly switched swerved to a version I'd never heard.

"Bells on bob tails ring, making spirits bright... hmm, hmm hmm, hmm, hmmm... oh jingle bells, jingle bells."

"*Hmm, hmm, hmm, hmm, hmmm...What is that?*" I thought, glancing around the check-out line to see if any other customers were puzzled by the new lyrics. When it was obvious that neither the cashier nor other patrons were perturbed or had even paid it any attention, I simply stuffed the nourishments into my knapsack and left, unable to dislodge the lingering tune for several blocks.

After several hours spent haunting the nooks, crannies and back alleys of the riverfront area, I inadvertently ended up in a narrow street clogged with wall-to-wall souvenir stores. As escape meant retracing my steps back through the smoggy haze of heavy traffic, I concluded that now was as good a time as any to resolve the burdensome task of "*what to buy for the folks back home?*"

"*How difficult can that be in south east Asia?*" I thought, recalling an expressed wish that I return with a "nice Buddha," as I pushed open a stiff door to enter a shop that looked to house hundreds of them. Ignoring those beyond my budget, not to mention my baggage limit, I was browsing under the gaze of a grinning salesclerk, when my eyes drifted to a white-stone model wedged in between several bronze colleagues.

"How much?" I asked my attentive appendage, lifting the chosen model free of its assigned slot, to expose a dust-free outline.

"For you, make special deal," she assured me. "Twenty-Five dollar. Only one stone. Twenty-five dollar... Very good price."

"Hmm," I murmured, nodding and shaking my head at the same time. Following a script learned in Morocco twenty-five years earlier, I told her it was too much and moved to set it back in its row.

"How much you pay?" she demanded, stepping forward

to block my way.

Aware that the same piece, if even available, would be triple the price or more in Germany, I by-passed the obligatory poignant pauses and haggling to blurt out, "I'll give you twenty."

Grabbing the Buddha out of my hands, she was half-way to the cash register before turning back to say, "You got deal."

Out on the street, nursing the sting of a hasty bid, I consoled myself with the thought that she, and not some large consortium would make good use of the extra dollars I had just parted with. All that needed to be done now, was to figure out how the hell I was going to get the five-pound ikon home in one piece.

*

It was just after six that evening, when Conrad answered the door with a handful of papers, a telephone cradled between his ear and shoulder.

"You go ahead without me," he said, holding his free hand over the mouthpiece. "I still have a few calls to make and emails to send. I'll join you if I can."

Too famished to be disturbed by the fact I was eating alone, I finished my meal quickly, grateful that no replacement chat partner was making the rounds on what must have been Jerry's night off.

"*How many times am I going to find myself in Phnom Penh,*" I muttered, loudly enough to turn the heads of several expectant Tuk-Tuk drivers before the hotel courtyard. In no mood to go back to my room and watch the sole English channel till I passed out, I approached the one driver who hadn't propositioned me, to negotiate a price for an hour's worth of "night seeing." Once a deal had been agreed upon, the driver darted out onto Sihanouk Blvd. without so much as a passing glance at other traffic. Heading east towards the river, he eased into the roundabout carousel that encircled the enormous Independence Monument, and began mumbling something over his shoulder that was immediately lost to the buzz of a passing motorbike. Turning right where turning left would have taken us past the plaza now void of "dancercisers," he continued his muffled narration, diligently pointing out the new Australian Embassy coming up on our left. Letting that less than awesome information pass unanswered, I contented myself with other passing sights while enjoying the night's warm, if somewhat odorous breeze. Well on the way to no place in particular, traffic had thinned considerably by the time we turned off the main road; so much so, I was actually able to hear the driver announce that we were headed for "Diamond Island." By the time we'd crossed over one of several bridges leading to said island, and entered an area that looked as though it had been artfully landscaped by a fleet of rampant bull dozers, I'd managed to banish all images of Ricardo Montalbán and Tattoo. Gazing out across the treeless void, it was possible to make out the glowing lights of a large complex in the distance. Just as we managed to get close enough to identify the structure as a modern shopping mall, the first raindrops had begun to fall. Although the rainy season was officially still five months away, that didn't prevent the drizzle from rapidly turning into a downpour. Within seconds my entire left side was drenched, and the basin of the Tuk-Tuk had begun to fill with run off. Hoping to salvage his fare despite the elements, the driver leapt out to lower the side panels, taking his own dousing in stride. Temporarily wedged into a line of idling cars, I watched as dozens of nattily dressed Cambodians dashed between their luxury automobiles and numerous trendy clubs lining the complex. It didn't take long to determine that this was not a part of Phnom Penh I wished to see or remember, so I leaned forward and signalled the driver to head for home. Glancing back through the mist as we drove back to the mainland, I was grateful that the powers that be had at least had the decency to stick the monstrosity on an island.

By the time we arrived back at the hotel, the rain had let up. Standing in the courtyard, discussing a reduced fee for the shortened excursion, I couldn't resist asking the driver his thoughts on what we'd just seen. How representative of the populace his opinion may have been is open to question, but it was nevertheless dismaying to hear him boast that Diamond Island was very popular and viewed by many as a big step forward for the community.

In the midst of peeling off my wet clothes in the dry sanctuary of my room, I couldn't stop thinking how much of what I had just witnessed, contrasted with life in other areas of the country. What was disheartening was how Western influences seemed to have led a number of people to associate "a better life" with shopping malls and fancy cars. Although I suspected that if given the chance, many Cambodians would jump at the chance to trade places with a "Westerner," and all the material benefits that purportedly entailed, a part of me wanted to believe that some people would still choose the simplicity of rural life over so-called modernity. Seeking to bolster that theory, I dug out the guide book one last time before climbing into bed. According to the author, the form of Buddhism most widely practiced in Cambodia is called Therevada. Adapted from Hinduism in the 13th or 14th century, its ultimate goal is "nirvana" or "extinction of all desire and suffering in order to reach the final stage of reincarnation." Put another way, practitioners are encouraged to accept their lot in life no matter what hand they've been dealt, to focus on becoming a better person. Envy is frowned upon in the belief that those in better circumstances will make efforts to pass some of their good fortune down to those with less. By striving to live an honourable life, believers will be able to reduce the number of their rebirths before ultimately reaching nirvana.

"Sounds great in theory," I mused, as I closed the book and tossed it on the night table. With the delirium of half-sleep already gnawing at me, I flicked off the light and flopped down on the pillow. In an instant, thoughts reverted to the morning's "snack," and the burning question of whether it had progressed far enough along its path of enlightenment to have earned its last ticket out of here.

Day Eight: Friday, December 17th

An early breakfast, brought on by a restless night, meant there were several hours before our scheduled interviews were set to commence. I was hovering over a city map and my customary morning dosage of steamed noodles, vegetables, rice and tea, when Conrad joined me in the breakfast nook.

"Did you know that we're only a few blocks from Toul Sleng?" I asked.

"And who, pray tell, is Toul Sleng?" he asked, catching the roving waiter's attention for a cup of coffee.

"It's not a who, but a what. It's one, if not the most notorious of the former Khmer Rouge prisons. If you're interested, we could grab a Tuk-Tuk and take a look before our appointments."

At first glance, the former high school reminded me of an abandoned embassy complex somewhere in war-torn, south-east Asia. Located in a central suburb of Phnom Penh, three of its four triple-story concrete blocks formed an inverted U around a grassy field dotted with palm trees. Each and every floor on the unpainted blocks was fronted by a building-wide balcony, behind which were a row of open doorways and glass-less barred windows.

After purchasing our tickets at the main entrance, Conrad and I decided to part company, agreeing to meet up again in an hour or so. My first stop was Building A, where for no apparent reason I felt drawn to the second floor. Half way along its lengthy balcony, I entered an empty classroom where a small group of visitors was listening to their guide shed light on the horrors that had taken place within these walls.

"Then they would take a three-foot bamboo pole sharpened at one end and drive it down the prisoner's throat until it came out his lower abdomen."

Needing no further clarification, I quickly backed out of the doorway and moved to the next room that was fortunately devoid of informative guides. The sunlight streaming through a lone window in the rear wall, focused attention on a metal bed frame in the centre of the room. A rusted toolbox, roughly the size of a car battery was sitting open at one end of the bed. Inside lay a jumble of wooden and metal instruments, obscure enough to defy imagined uses. As I eased my way across the grimy-tiled floor to the window, thoughts of Nazi concentration camp memorials I'd visited in Germany came floating to the surface. Unlike most of those sites, whose buildings had either been razed or largely sanitized for public viewing after the war, this room left the visitor with the distinct impression of having only been recently abandoned.

The ground floor classrooms of Building B had been turned into a large photo gallery, with row upon row of glass-covered portraits. Much like their genocidal predecessors in Nazi Germany, the Khmer Rouge had kept meticulous files on each of their intended prey. As a result, hundreds of faces of all ages and genders, left behind after the regime was overthrown in 1979, now stared out at visitors, each bearing a number pinned to their clothing. Undoubtedly ordered to assume a neutral expression, some had nonetheless conveyed the knowledge of their imminent fate.

I departed the gallery through an opening that had been crudely smashed through a classroom wall, to enter what initially appeared to be a room full of unfinished chimneys. It was in fact a series of open-brick cubicles where prisoners had been chained to a post in the floor, and kept under observation by patrolling guards. Measuring no more than four feet by five, the cells were lined up side by side, with twenty per room in the four chambers I passed through before reaching the end of the building. Back outside in the courtyard, I happened to notice that Building C was the only structure whose balconies were enclosed by strands of barbed wire. I was in the midst of pondering the reasons behind such a measure, when a passing guide happened to deliver an explanation to his group.

"The wire prevented prisoners from jumping. Death was not something victims were allowed to take into their own hands."

Curious what had prevented prisoners from jumping from other balconies, the guide moved off before I could seek an answer.

With twenty minutes remaining until we were scheduled to meet, I headed for the last building in the compound. As the first room only had statistical construction charts and architectural photos on display, I passed through quickly. Halfway through the second room, much more crowded than its neighbour, I was snapped out of a growing aloofness when a trio of visitors moved aside to reveal one of the roughly-drawn paintings adorning the walls. Whatever vague barrier of incomprehension had been building in me, was shattered by the crude depiction the painter had made of the devices and instruments these grotesque torturers had used in their work. Directly below the painting were the actual utensils themselves. Moving from picture to picture, each more upsetting than the last, I was aware how quiet the packed room was, save for the shuffling of feet and occasional gasps. Many of the obscenities that had been carried out in the prison were there to see in that room, including fingernails being pulled out, people being water-boarded into unconsciousness or beaten with iron bars. Just as it seemed the horror could not possibly get any worse, I came to the most staggering picture of all. In it a guard was seen to be using garden pliers to cut off the nipple of a woman's breast, while a second accomplice held an open-doored cage up to the bleeding wound. Inside the cage was a curled scorpion waiting to strike. The image stunned me into a mental and physical paralysis, and for a moment I felt as though I might lose my breakfast. It wasn't until a group of noisy Chinese tourists followed their guide into the room, that I was able to regain enough equilibrium to squeeze past an elderly couple stalled in the doorway and out into the courtyard. Relieved to be away from the overwhelming sense of dread, I slumped down on a nearby bench as a light rain began to fall. It took awhile for some semblance of sanity to return, but once it had I retreated under a makeshift awning set up to protect the courtyard bookshop. Still caught up in the images I had just viewed, I was browsing through book titles when I came across a jacket blurb stating that of the fourteen thousand prisoners that had entered Toul Sleng, only seven had survived. Convinced it had to be a misprint, I felt compelled to ask the clerk behind the counter, only to have the number confirmed. In the midst of trying to fathom yet another unfathomable component of Toul Sleng, I glanced up to see Conrad emerging from Building D. For several minutes we had nothing to say to each other as we stood there staring out at the empty courtyard. Finally, it was Conrad who was able to muster thought into voice.

"What was the point? I mean, what was the bloody point?" he said. "They knew the people sent here would never leave alive. They knew they were fated to die with or without a confession. So why torture them? They couldn't have all been spies. What did it gain? What kind of monsters would do such things?"

"I read in one of the brochures that they used to play loud rock music during the day to try and drown out the sounds of the prisoners' screaming," I said. "But not so loud that residents in the area couldn't occasionally make out the cries of agony... a less than subtle reminder that they could be next."

On the ride back to the hotel, with my eyes mindlessly glued to the back of our driver's bobbing helmet, thoughts drifted back to Building D.

"How did this all happen? I wanted to know. *"Who were the perpetrators? What could have possibly driven them to such madness? And more importantly, how many came to justice after the regime was overthrown?"*

✷

It was shortly before one when we pulled up to yet another high-walled enclosure, this one guarding what was to be Franz's new home in Phnom Penh. Still busy with the morning visit to Toul Sleng, Conrad and I unloaded in silence, acutely aware that if we had any hope of concentrating on our work, a line in the sand needed to be drawn. Passing through the unlocked gate, a shared glance somehow helped to focus on functioning.

After viewing footage of the group funeral held for victims of the anti-tank mine explosion we'd investigated earlier in the week, we conducted brief interviews with Franz and a colleague in less than two hours. Thankfully, after we'd wrapped, Conrad declined the invitation to join the pair for a late lunch, and we returned to the hotel. As thoughts of Toul Sleng continued to swirl, I turned to the sole source at my disposal, hoping to gain more insight as to how the Khmer Rouge had emerged and operated. According to the limited information in the guidebook, the regime had often "recruited" boys from the countryside, some as young as fourteen, feeding them propaganda that city dwellers were largely to blame for the limited prospects of their lives. Subsequently given a weapon, a uniform and a doctrine, these young soldiers were then encouraged to extract revenge in the name of the revolution. What the guidebook didn't reveal was how many of these young recruits had ended up serving in places like Toul Sleng.

✴

It was half past three when Conrad knocked at my door.

"If you're up to it, I'd like to head off into town to get some more footage of daily life in Phnom Penh," he announced.

A welcome distraction from the events of the morning,

our first stop was the Central Market, an immense pale yellow, Art Deco building that wouldn't have looked out of place alongside the Fontainebleau hotel of 1950's Miami. Inside however, turned out to be far less appealing. In contrast to the hustle and bustle of other markets, there was only a meagre collection of bored-looking sales staff, too apathetic to even accost the few customers cruising the aisles. Judging it a lost cause after fifteen minutes, we moved across the street to an outdoor vegetable market, where, encouraged by the footage we were able to capture, I convinced Conrad to accompany me to the market I'd visited the previous day. Wandering through the maze of stalls once more, this time with camera in hand, I happened to spot a band of young children clambering on a wooden-slatted wagon similar to the two-wheeled carts North American settlers had used on the prairies more than a century ago. Unlike the reaction of the rural children to the camera, here it suddenly became a contest to see who could clown the most. Fortunately, the group quickly lost interest and didn't bother to follow me as I moved further up the aisle. As had previously been the case, I was again met with friendly reactions from a variety of merchants. A prime example of that cordiality came when I inserted myself between two vegetable stalls, hoping to grab a candid shot of the activity in the crowded aisle. Down on one knee, with my eye cupped to the viewfinder, I was in the process of framing when I felt a tiny hand on my shoulder. Turning to meet its owner, I was confronted with twin black pools of wide-eyed innocence. The four or five-year-old observer however, had not been the only member of my audience. Fanned out behind him like a small choir, a half dozen adults stood quietly, straining to catch a glimpse of what I was up to. Raising the viewfinder, I invited them to see for themselves and in an instant the entire group surged forward, crowding around the small monitor to view a scene they'd no doubt witnessed a thousand times. Smiles, chuckles and nods of approval made the rounds as several moved in front of the camera to be recorded. Shortly after completing the shot, my attention was diverted by a loud cheer coming from a cluster of men nearby. Huddled beneath a snowy television precariously perched above an array of fresh vegetables, most paid me no notice, too busy showing support for their favourite kick boxer to acknowledge my presence. Those who did, did so with a friendly wave or smile before reverting to the action.

Having captured enough "local colour," we were preparing to head back to the hotel when Conrad realized we still needed an establishing cover shot of the market. That was easier said than done given the low-level of the tarpaulin and metal rooftops covering the market stalls. Fortunately, after scouting around for several minutes, I spotted an apartment block less than a block away. After agreeing to meet Conrad back at the market's main entrance, I set off for the building, assuming that I would somehow be able to obtain the needed shot from a higher perspective. Getting there however, involved overcoming a number obstacles, including people who were determined to pass through the narrowest of crowded spaces on their motorbikes. Initially unable to locate an entrance when I reached the base of the apartment block, I asked an elderly merchant how I might gain access. Rising up from a rickety stool, he quietly pointed to a darkened alleyway that looked anything but inviting. Up to that point, there had never been any reason to think I was at risk carrying around equipment likely worth more than the annual wages of most marketeers. Bolstered by that track record, I entered the alley to discover a narrow stairway sandwiched between two mould-flecked walls. Forced to ascend diagonally on steps almost as steep as the rungs of a ladder, I eventually reached a rather treacherous looking third-floor balcony that ran the length of the building. Sensing that lingering might make me appear to be an intruder, I edged forward along the gangway, squeezing past two curtained doors I hoped didn't open outwards. Several knocks on the final door were answered almost immediately, making me suspect that my ascent had not gone unnoticed. But even before I could explain the purpose of my visit, the young Cambodian girl in front of me glanced at the camera and beckoned me in without a word. Following her through the small kitchen, where her back kept disappearing between rows of hanging laundry, I entered a living room where a young man on a mattress stirred long enough to nod hello. After directing me to the door of the front balcony, the pair simply left me to my own devices.

"*How did these people know what I was here for?*" I asked myself while gazing down at the shot I'd been seeking. "*And how do they know I'm not ransacking through their belongings right now?*"

Letting the camera roll for a couple of minutes, it wasn't lost on me that there weren't many places in the world where a complete stranger could expect to be ushered into someone's private quarters with no explanation or persistent pleading required.

With the shot of the multi-coloured rooftops "in the can," I delivered a sincere "Okun" to each of my impromptu hosts and made my exit. It was only after I'd already descended to the bottom of the stairway that I realized I'd neglected to offer them anything in the way of compensation for their troubles; a regret that lingers to this day.

*

In what had almost become a ritual by this point, that evening after dinner, Conrad begged off conducting a pub crawl with the excuse of more pressing work. Seeing as tomorrow's call time was set for noon, it seemed an opportune time to try completing the previous night's rained-out tour. With yesterday's driver nowhere to be found, I negotiated a price with a new recruit who for some strange reason, struck me as the first Cambodian I'd met with a potential for evil. It was not so much his manner, as the expression on his face when I explained I simply wanted to be shown "the night life of Phnom Penh, away from all the prominent tourist venues."

Much like his predecessor, the new chauffeur was also obsessed with delivering endless amounts of information, despite having advised him that most of what he was saying was being lost in the drone of traffic. Having taken me at my word to avoid "touristy sites," he headed for a section of the city completely unfamiliar to me. In fact, I was about to inquire as to our whereabouts and intended destination when we swerved off the road and came to a halt at the awninged entrance of a hotel that looked to be considerably less than five-stars. Turning to face me as the Tuk-Tuk's engine shuddered into silence, the driver asked, "You want good lady? Ten dollars, very cheap...You like Chinese or

Vietnamese?"

Momentarily distracted by the shabby decor of the hotel, it took a few seconds to catch the drift of his sales pitch.

"No... No thanks," I mumbled, suddenly conscious of how naive it had been to request a non-touristy tour without expecting it to contain some "special deals."

Presumably used to customers who needed prodding, but not in the mood for a lengthy debate, the driver simply shrugged before re-starting the Tuk-Tuk and heading back into traffic. It wasn't long however, before I realized my refusal should have been expressed more adamantly. Less than five minutes after leaving the hotel, we were making a second stop, this one directly outside a raucous night club. Despite the dim light spilling out of the doorway, it was possible to make out a number of women sitting inside at the bar. With no intention of expending any energy until a potential client crossed the threshold, only a few cast a lazy glance in our direction before ultimately branding me a snooper. After making it abundantly clear to the driver that I was still not interested, we slipped off into the darkness leaving the women to nurse their drinks.

If silence was any measure, the driver appeared to have finally heeded my rejection, freeing me to concentrate on other nightly sights and sounds. In addition to the number of young children still roaming the streets at this late hour, one scene to catch my attention involved a large family gathered around a makeshift table in their front yard. Caught in the harsh glare of one of those rarest of animals, a streetlight, they all sat patiently awaiting a late evening meal cooking over a nearby open fire. No sooner had that vignette been left behind, we were racing down a deserted street, skirting along a lengthy pock-marked wall until a familiar entrance loomed into view. Bathed in a chilling, yellowish light, Toul Sleng looked even more menacing than it had that morning. Not surprisingly, the nightmarish sight and recollection f what it represented brought any hopes of enjoying other venues to an abrupt end. Peering back at the prison as we veered off down a side street, I couldn't help but wonder why of all the locations condemned to darkness in the city, this one deserved to be illuminated.

Following a final half-hearted rejection at yet another 'fun club', it was clear the show was over. Back at the hotel a short while later, I felt it only fair to add a few dollars to the agreed upon fee, seeing we'd been gone longer than expected. Going by the disgruntled look on the driver's face however, it appeared my gesture had fallen short of his expectations.

"We gone more two hours," he blustered, pointing to his watch. A cursory glance at my own confirmed otherwise, but I was not eager for a lengthy discussion. Unintentionally speaking loud enough to attract the attention of several other Tuk-Tuk drivers huddled nearby, I calmly informed him that we'd been on the road for no more than seventy-five minutes. Waving the bills already in his possession, he spouted a few choice Khmer phrases that required no literal translation.

"Look pal," I said, peeling off another dollar and handing it to him. "We agreed on six dollars, and this makes nine. If you like trying to hose people so much, why don't you just become a fireman," I added in frustration.

Half expecting a cold-steel blade to penetrate my back before reaching the hotel door, it was only a chill I had to shake off as I entered the cool lobby and headed for the elevator. Watching the squeaking doors slowly close on another twenty-four hours of Cambodian reality, it struck me that the mild dust-up which had just taken place outside, was somehow a fitting end to a less than perfect day.

Day Nine: Saturday, December 18th

Right from the start, Conrad had known it was unlikely to make for exciting, edge-of-your-seat viewing. Nonetheless, with no other options available to portray the family, it was decided that a good portion of the morning would be spent following Franz, his wife and three kids through the streets of Phnom Penh; capturing the nuances of what it takes to set up house in a new place and culture. The task was trying to say the least, but despite an hour in the chilly offices of a phone company arranging for a telephone, and another squandered setting up an account at a local bank, frazzled nerves had yet to surface by the time both objectives were achieved. That left shopping, the primary goal of which was to collect as many tools and utensils of domestic life that could be strapped aboard a Tuk-Tuk. Two hours and numerous shops later, the family was headed home, loaded down with pillows, mops, buckets, a toaster, a ladder and an assortment of other perceived necessities. In spite of the spectacle of this virtual household on wheels, nobody else on the road bothered to give us a second glance.

With the subsequent delivery of goods to his new house, my formal dealings with Franz had come to an end. Judging from the shuffling feet and awkward glances as we stood at the gate, it was apparent neither of us were likely to shed any tears at the impending farewell. Although the episode with the visor had failed to return as a topic of conversation in the intervening days, it had not been forgotten by either party. Fortunately for all concerned, the awareness that our paths would likely never cross again, granted us a trace of magnanimity. Prepared for his handshake this time, I met him with reciprocal force before wishing him and the family the best of luck with the new segment of their life.

Knowing the next day's agenda called for a half-day on the river, I returned to the hotel to pass the remaining hours of daylight at the rooftop pool, wondering what still lay ahead and scribbling postcards to friends back in the "real" winter, that basically said *"I'm here and you're not."*

Day 10: Sunday, December 19th

"Can you imagine what it's going to be like out there today?" I asked Conrad, before poking my head out the side of the Tuk-Tuk to gain some breezy relief without losing it to a passing road sign. "We're gonna fry in this heat."

Despite an early morning shower and loads of cosmetic amenities, my deodorant was already failing me by the time we arrived at dockside. Most of the colourful boats seen earlier in the week were missing, their slots now occupied by a series of small skiffs from which fishermen and their families were unloading the morning's catch. In their midst, lay the mid-sized boat we'd arranged to charter with the help of one of our regular Tuk-Tuk drivers. As we schlepped our gear down the concrete steps of the embankment, I couldn't help noticing several tourist groups off to our left, struggling to align themselves behind the colour co-ordinated umbrellas of their respective guides. Why they were there was a bit of a mystery seeing as there wasn't a single tour boat in sight. In any event, once on board, the guides and their charges were left to swelter on the shore as our vessel eased out into the swift-moving current.

There was considerable activity on the river that morning. Up ahead numerous small fishing boats, silhouetted against a blazing sun, could be seen plying the waters of their staked-out territory. Without disturbing their activities, we approached just close enough to capture men casting and collecting nets, while women helped transfer the haul into blue plastic ice-boxes. Those children too young to help, often sought shelter beneath the distinctive metal arches that cleaved the skiffs in two. Passing within ten metres of one boat, offered a first-hand view of a young fisherman lazily gathering the last of his net in his hands. Pausing briefly to wipe his brow, he then proceeded to fling the net out over the water, watching it burst into a perfect flattened circle before descending to the surface in slow motion. Similar balletic scenes were taking place aboard other skiffs and the whole panorama would have bordered on idyllic, had it not been for a deep rhythmic chugging sound coming from a barge near the opposite shore. Linked to land by a long-snaking tube that terminated at what looked to be an oil derrick, the apparatus appeared to be part of a dredging operation, sucking up portions of the silt washed downstream from the north. Why they were dredging at a point where the river must have been at least half a kilometre wide, escaped me. They certainly weren't doing it for our benefit even though we were one of the largest vessels on the river that morning. Built to hold between forty and fifty tourists on a good day, Conrad and I had the pleasure of being the only passengers on our vessel. The captain was a man in his mid-to-late thirties, who spoke virtually no English, and remained closeted in his wheelhouse for most of the journey. Meanwhile, a woman of similar age, presumably his wife, was constantly scampering around the boat attending to various chores. One minute she was disappearing down a hole into the engine compartment, the next she was serving refreshments to Conrad and myself, all the while keeping an eye on the meal cooking for her two children. The elder of the siblings, a young girl of seven or eight, was entertaining herself, ardently teaching her doll the rules of life on the water. Her smaller brother, naked but for a bulky diaper, was seemingly content to silently swing in a nearby hammock, while watching the world glide by. Judging by the amount of personal belongings onboard, it was apparent we were travelling in their home; an assumption strengthened when the wife pulled aside a curtain behind the wheelhouse to remove a fresh diaper from a stack of neatly piled clothing.

Having spent twenty minutes filming from the tip of the bow, both legs dangling a foot above the water, I failed to notice when a small skiff docked alongside. Although I had heard faint, muffled conversation on the periphery, it wasn't until Conrad tapped me on the shoulder that I became aware that plans were about to change.

"Are you interested in seeing all of this real close?" he asked with a wide grin, pointing to the six-meter skiff now

attached to our port side. Five minutes later, I was as close as one can get to life *on* the Mekong, without being *in* the Mekong. Despite the treacherous wobbling that any movement entailed, I cautiously moved forward on the narrow boat to take refuge under its central arch. From there I was able to capture a shot of the owner proudly straddling the space between the stern gunnels. His hands gripped to a long wooden pole that was attached to a submerged propeller, powered by a loud, smoke-belching motor, he looked every inch like a Cambodian gondolier, as he guided his craft through the main current. Up at the opposite end of the boat, where the hull tapered off to form a small flattened platform several inches above the water, sat his wife, inadvertently caught in a pose that was a cross between the young mermaid of Copenhagen's harbour and the symbolic prow of a renegade pirate ship. Eyeing me warily from under the arch was their ten-year-old son, one of the few Cambodian youngsters I'd met who did not respond to attention with a smile. During a momentary lull in the action, I had the chance to glance around at the various belongings stowed aboard the small craft. Clothing, food, personal trinkets, and even a dented bamboo cage that was home to two exotic birds, suggested I was looking at the sum total of their reality.

By the time I turned my attention back to the bow, the young boy had moved forward to join his mother. Quite unexpectedly, the image of mother and son swept me back to my own reality as a ten-year-old. Excluding the time spent in school, many warm, summer days had been passed on baseball diamonds, beaches or biking trails along the river, with intervening gaps filled by the wondrous invention that had provided black-and-white treasures like "The Lone Ranger," and "Leave It To Beaver." Two realities that couldn't have been more different.

"The captain has offered to take us to a floating village on the opposite shore," Conrad informed me, as I waved goodbye to all three crew members as their boat drifted away from the mother ship. "I've told him to go ahead."

With enough time to prepare, I was already rolling by the time a fleet of weathered houseboats, yoked together in more ways than one, slowly emerged from the haze of the distant shoreline. Engulfed in silence as we grazed the outer edge of the village, the first sign of life came from an elderly woman in a black peasant's suit, buckled over a washboard on the heaving porch of her home. Busy rinsing the last items of a dwindling pile of laundry, she didn't bother to look up as she listlessly slid out of frame. A short distance later, that scene was replaced by a solitary arm stirring an invisible pot, as wisps of smoke rose up from behind the thatched wall of an outdoor kitchen. That image was in turn followed by two dark-skinned boys jumping from the bow of an arriving skiff, waving to us as they attempted to secure the moorings. A myriad of vistas of everyday life on the river continued to unfold over the next ten minutes, simple, mesmerizing, and yet unimaginable.

Day 11: Monday, December 20th

Traffic was at a complete standstill, not an uncommon occurrence for Phnom Penh. It had been relatively tolerable up to the point where we turned into a narrow street, made impassable by an armada of haphazardly parked Tuk-Tuks. Having rid themselves of their human cargos, drivers who weren't lounging in nearby cafes, lay drooped in the rear of their vehicles, browsing through newspapers and slugging back sodas while awaiting their clients' return. Aware that traffic conditions were unlikely to ease, our own driver suggested we abandon ship to cover the remaining distance on foot.

"What is it with these guys?" I asked Conrad, as we jostled our way through a conglomeration of people and vehicles. "Most of them just saw us get out of our Tuk-Tuk. Why do they keep on asking if we want another one? And where could they take us anyway? It's not like anything's moving."

The continuing barrage of requests was beginning to get on my nerves, yet I managed to remain in good spirits, in part by knowing that the market we were headed for, now less than a block away, would soon put us beyond driver's reach. We'd come to Psar Tuol Tom Pong, more commonly known as the "Russian market," to film life in what was reputed to be Phnom Penh's busiest and most well-known bazaar. According to the guidebook, the special moniker had been adopted in the early 1980's, when many of that country's citizens had frequented the market. Given that it catered to both locals as well as bargain-hungry tourists, we'd been duly warned that it could be crowded. But what we encountered was way beyond crowded. Initially, we were only able to penetrate the outer fringes of one of the multiple entrances. Further movement remained slow for some time, thanks to dawdling browsers deeper inside the narrow, weblike passages. With the slowed pace came the chance to glance at the many wares on display in the patchwork of stalls and booths. Shuffling past the merchandise, one had the impression it was possible to buy just about anything, including a substantial assortment of chintz and baubles. It was at one of the forced pauses that I made the mistake of scanning a tiny cove of suspended knapsacks a little too closely, making me fair game for the vendor whose enterprise we were stalled in front of.

"Normal thirty dollars. For you twenty-three. Only one left," a saleswoman proffered, already reaching for one she thought my eyes had brushed over.

"Not right now thanks," I answered, holding up the camera as a defence against her sale pitch. "Here to work. Maybe later," I lied, aware that the brand-name item she was holding up would be ten times the price in Germany.

"You buy later, you buy from me," she half-commanded, her voice trailing off as the line began to move again. Careful not to let my gaze linger too long on any one item as we continued towards the core of the market, I couldn't help noticing the extraordinary amount of repetition. Within a span of several metres, ten or more stands seemed to all be selling the identical products.

"Have you seen some of the prices on these things?" I

asked Conrad as we eased past yet another booth crammed with well-known brand-names. "How can they possibly sell this stuff for such prices?"

For anyone who'd picked up a newspaper or watched the news in the last two decades, the answer was pretty obvious. In the early 1990's, numerous giants in the international garment industry had flooded into Cambodia, hoping to take advantage of government incentives and cheap production costs. In their wake had come the local and China-based knock-off industries.

"It's weird," I said to Conrad during another gridlock. "You know these big firms are here, but I don't remember seeing a single sign for one of them anywhere on our travels. They must be playing it low key."

Growing tired of deflecting expectant stares, I took advantage of an opening in the throng to dart down a side aisle, signalling to Conrad I'd meet him back at the main entrance in half an hour. Away from the turmoil of the main corridor, scenes of more "normal" daily life began to appear. The first was that of a young boy no more than four or five, standing in a small plastic tray in the middle of the aisle as his mother gave him a shower from a watering can. A few meters beyond, a trio of adolescent girls sat with outstretched feet, giggling amongst themselves as they compared their talents at toenail painting. Still further was the vegetable section, where money and produce criss-crossed the airspace of a long shadowy aisle. Then without warning or planning, I suddenly found myself at the heart of the market, caught up in a wave of activity and pungent odours emanating from a dozen or more steaming woks. I'd landed in Phnom Penh's version of a North American food court, where peals of laughter and conversation echoed off the grease-coated skylights above a series of bustling makeshift kitchens. All that was missing were the ubiquitous, uniformed cleaners and grim-faced rent-a-cops that patrol Western malls for errant trash.

After observing and filming the action for fifteen minutes, I was attempting to ease myself back into one of the market aisles when my way blocked by a German couple furiously debating the best method of haggling over a wooden Mahjong set I would have accepted gratis. Sorely tempted to reveal that I knew what they were "jammering" about, in the end I decided to let them be. Nudging past them, I turned the corner and literally bumped into Conrad. We hadn't been separated for more than thirty minutes, yet during that time he'd managed to load himself down with a collection of soaps, scarves and other souvenirs.

"Oh, man, am I glad we ran into each other," he said with a sigh of relief. "I got a message from the network just now and need to get back to the hotel as soon as possible."

Despite having his own bag of surplus to schlep, Conrad agreed to take the camera back to the hotel, freeing me to follow through on my wish to return on foot, a journey I estimated would take about ninety minutes. Relying on a crumpled inner-city map I'd snatched from the hotel lobby, I set off in what my instincts suggested was north. Hoping to catch a glimpse of how people lived, I purposely tried avoiding major thoroughfares, following a route that took me through a neighbourhood much quieter than those near Sihanouk Boulevard. But despite attempts to stick to the back streets, where most of the houses were hidden behind high-brick enclosures, it was only a matter of time before I ran up against a major intersection. To the untrained eye, the hundreds of motorbikes and SUV's whirring past, unfettered by such impediments as a traffic light, made it appear that crossing the road would be virtually impossible. Fortunately, I'd been in Cambodia long enough to know that the best way to deal with heavy traffic was to ignore it. That is not as foolhardy as it sounds. There was no question one had to be alert. The trick was to not be intimidated. Experience had shown that waiting patiently at the curb for a break in the flow or someone to yield, would literally get you nowhere. Mesh and merge was the key strategy; not in a manner that implied others should back down, but rather with a fine sense of timing. Watch it, gauge it, and join it.

Feeling a little smug that the theory functioned, I stood on the opposite curb, speculating about the tide of over-sized gas guzzlers streaming past. Many tended to look alike, but one brand in particular stood out. That was because owners had adopted the peculiar habit of adhering letters to their side-door panels, spelling out the vehicle's make. Other drivers had yet to succumb to such a boastful urge, presumably preferring more subtle ways of saying "hey, look at me, I'm rich."

Being our last night in Cambodia, pressure was on to make it a memorable one. Options, however, were somewhat limited, as the tumult of the past two weeks had begun to catch up, leaving me somewhat emotionally and physically whacked. Rather than spending a "night on the town," what I really needed was to unwind, a task greatly simplified by Conrad's cancelling plans for a mutual dinner, claiming he had "last minute work to attend to." The idea of merely lounging away the evening in my room sounded less than appealing, and I was mulling over my choices when something Franz had said several days earlier came floating back.

"If it's a 'respectable' place, you won't be asked if you're interested in extras," he had advised.

A quick call to reception revealed that such an establishment was virtually right around the corner. Able to make an appointment, thirty minutes later, I was walking out the front door, nodding hello and good-bye to the passive-young Cambodian who spent most of his waking hours opening and closing the lobby door for hotel patrons. In less than a minute I'd reached a shadow-filled courtyard, and entered a dimly-lit foyer to be greeted by a trio of pretty young women in matching beige uniforms. After selecting a program at the front desk, I was shown to a tastefully decorated waiting room and asked to remove my shoes. Mindful that a week in the heat had turned my hiking boots into near lethal weapons, I'd taken the precaution of switching to runners I'd only worn in the city. What I had failed to take into account was that due to a unique element in their construction, the sneakers tended to retain an odour with the shelf life of plutonium. Although I was the only person present, I nonetheless attempted to disdain ownership by placing the offending footwear on a rack in the furthest corner of the room. Nonchalantly flipping through a magazine I could not decipher, it came as a relief when several casual sniffs offered no incriminating evidence. Just as I was starting to speculate which of the young women intermittently dashing back and forth through the lobby might be my masseuse, one approached with a steaming cup of jasmine tea. But before there was any chance to enjoy the tongue-scalding liquid, I was beckoned to accompany the smallest of the original trio. Following her through a curtain of rustling beads, I found myself in a long-dark corridor, the flip flops I'd received at reception echoing off the tiled floor. Off to my right was a large fountain. Half-buried within a wall of lush green foliage, it was busy bubbling along to the sound of chirping birds so repetitive it could have very well been a recording. On the opposing side of the hallway, a row of curtained doorways, a few of which were open, offering brief glimpses into sparsely furnished rooms. Escorted to the second last unit, I was shown into a dark-panelled room, lit by a single three-watt bulb above the archway. After placing a card atop a desk covered in yellow-and- red rose petals, my guide politely requested I disrobe and position myself face down on the padded bench. Turning my back to comply, I heard the curtain being drawn as she slipped back out into the hallway. With no sheet or towel in sight, I was debating whether local tradition deemed it proper to get down to basics, when the curtain re-opened and I found myself face to face with the most solidly built Cambodian I'd ever seen.

"Sophea," was how she introduced herself, taking a short bow with clasped hands before gesturing that I make myself comfortable on the bench.

"Is okay?" I stuttered awkwardly, pointing to my underwear.

I wanted to explain that I came from a land where old habits died hard, but she simply dismissed my concern with a wave of her hand and pointed again to the bench. Deciding to retain my last article of clothing, I squirmed to find a comfortable position while Sophea produced the sheet that had been eluding me. Laying it over my lower half, she deftly created a series of folds that left my right leg exposed from waist to toe. She then proceeded to peel back one side of my briefs, lodging them in such a way that it felt like I was wearing a string thong. With my modesty now in tatters, I interrupted her preparations long enough to slip out of my underwear, casting them unceremoniously on a nearby chair.

Over the course of the next hour, I was lost to the respective pleasures that come with being kneaded, pushed, pulled, rubbed and covered with warm oil in almost every nook and cranny of one's being. Just when it seemed like I was approaching a level of complete abandon, budding fantasies were brought to a halt by a curt bow and the request that I "rest now, please." Aloft in a glow likely visible from a satellite, I bequeathed myself a full fifteen minutes of tranquility before slowly dressing to the sound of soft music that made me wonder what floor I should get off on.

Feeling at one with the world, I returned to the now-crowded lobby to accept a second helping of tea. Still basking in a peaceful aura, it wasn't until I realized I had yet to reclaim my runners that the spell was finally dented. Fortunately, there was no detectable scent as I tied up the laces, and after settling the bill I wandered back out into the warm nighttime air.

Whatever suburb of nirvana Sophea had dropped me off in, vanished the second I opened the door to my room. In my absence, a well-meaning chamber maid had seen fit to lower the setting on my air conditioner to accommodate a polar bear. Retreating to the more moderate climes of the bathroom, I happened to catch sight of myself in the mirror as I closed the door. Squinting for a better look, I realized I'd completely forgotten about the oil Sophea had applied to my face and scalp, which helped explain the raised eyebrows of the doorman upon my return. Now endowed with puffed-out beard and frizzy hair, I resembled a scrawny Ernest Hemingway, albeit without the barrel chest, smouldering cigar or bullet through the brain; a startling transformation that had been acquired for the meagre sum of eighteen dollars.

Day 12: Tuesday, December 21st.

"It's a plane…What can I do?" she said snappily.

Having just spent two weeks in a country where one of the main Buddhist tenets was to try and become a better person, I was hesitant to resort to the list of suggestions perched on my tongue. Instead, all I could offer to the large woman who'd been leaving imprints of her kneecaps in my spine since take off, was a pained grimace.

Twelve hours earlier I'd been facing another fierce battle, one that involved conquering the pervasive boredom that often precedes a scheduled departure. Unsure as to when or even if I would ever return to Cambodia, I had quickly agreed to Conrad's suggestion at breakfast, to pay a return revisit to the Russian Market. Having become somewhat familiar with the layout and dynamics of the place, it was easier to enjoy the ambience, casually engaging merchants in a friendly duel as I wandered through at my leisure. Sure of what I did and didn't want, within half an hour I'd accumulated enough soaps, balms, oils, spices and peppers to open my own boutique. Following lunch back at the hotel, another hour was killed trying to figure out how to pack all these new found possessions. It was with a combination of relief and anticipation that we finally dragged our luggage down to the hotel concierge in late afternoon and headed off for a farewell drink. Even the Tuk-Tuk drivers seemed to sense the jig was up, leaving us unmolested on the short walk to the bar.

"When was the last time you were hugged by a chambermaid?" Conrad asked, once we were seated on the patio.

"You mean this week?" I answered with a smirk.

No further explanation was needed as I knew what he was talking about. We'd come to expect being greeted each morning by a pair of women in matching burgundy uniforms. Squatting barefoot besides their work trolleys, like permanent live beacons, they waited patiently in the hallway for rooms to be vacated. Upon seeing us round the corner to the elevators, each would break into a broad, toothy smile, before delivering a friendly duet of "good morning."

"Did you notice something different about them this morning?" Conrad continued. "At first I thought they were just sad to see us leaving, but after awhile it almost felt like there was... I don't know...I guess you could call it a sense of desperation."

"Mine did seem a little down, now that you mention it. But I never really gave it much thought at the time."

"The young one followed me right into my room when I came back up after breakfast."

"And?"

"She just plopped herself down on the bed and launched into a speech about how much she hates her job, how badly it pays and how she only get two days off a month."

"I don't mean to be cynical, but was this before or after you gave her a tip?" I asked, hoisting the drink that had arrived.

"It did cross my mind that it might have been a ploy for money, but I don't think so. You should have seen how she looked. She had tears welling up the whole time she was talking."

Despite bouncing possible explanations for her behaviour back and forth over the next few minutes, neither of us had been able to resolve the mystery.

Fortunately for all concerned, aside from the mini dust-up with the knobby-kneed lady, the return to western civilization proved unexceptional. Following the stream of de-planing passengers through the terminal, half of whom already had cell phones welded to their ears, I cast an envious glance to the other side of a plate-glass barrier where expectant travellers were waiting to go through security. Having declined the offer of being picked up, I was glad to see there were no familiar faces waiting to jar me back into European reality when I entered the arrivals hall. Ultimately, it was a gust of winter wind sweeping through a set of automatic doors that did the job. A few minutes later, as my boots squeaked their way across the subterranean train platform, I was briefly transported back to the temple in Phnom Penh. Other images quickly flooded in, ebbing only when the bright light of an approaching train pierced the tunnel. Stepping into the crowded wagon, I took my seat amidst a swarm of grey-faced commuters as the doors closed with an echoing finality. As we picked up speed to re-enter the tunnel at the opposite end of the platform, a circuit breaker somewhere, clicked in long enough to temporarily extinguish the harsh overhead lights. Thrust into momentary darkness, I felt a bittersweet smile spread across my face at the realization that somewhere on the other side of that darkness, lay a return to the "Magic Kingdom."

Intermezzo

According to the American cultural anthropologist, Ernst Becker, "One of the greatest dangers of life is too much possibility... and the place where we find people who have succumbed to this danger, is the madhouse."

I hadn't been back in Germany more than a week, when the "*it's great to be alive*" moments from Cambodia began to resurface en masse. Ironically, South East Asia had never been high on my travel radar, but the two weeks had spurred a longing to explore more of the country if for nothing else than to, "get it out of my system."

The timing for such an adventure however, had not been auspicious, with a thousand and one, real and imagined reasons rallied against a return. The prospect of a self-financed trip meant parting with a fair bundle of cash and work had not been that plentiful in the previous months. There was also the question of leaving my partner with all the obligations of daily life, while I galavanted through Cambodia for three or four weeks. But in the end, it was simply the credo, "what will you do if you don't?" that tipped the scales. A few painless mouse clicks the next morning and I was committed, albeit not in the sense Becker had predicted. And so... a mere six weeks after returning, there I was boarding a plane for Bangkok, trusting the theory that all those who take honourable risks, truly are rewarded.

PART TWO

Day One: Wednesday, February 2nd

From thirty-nine thousand feet, the swirling patterns of sand and sea reminded me of Canadian native artwork. If the route planner on the screen could be trusted, the captivating display I'd been staring at for well over ten minutes, was in all likelihood the shoreline of Bangladesh; at or near where the Ganges river delta empties into the Bay of Bengal. Whatever the actual location, the sight was a welcome distraction from the hulk seated in front of me. Ever since departing German airspace, he had been suffering from some sort of an acute affliction, the self-determined treatment for which evidently involved repeatedly pulling himself forward in his seat, only to thump back heavily enough to shudder my tablet, forcing me to grab on to my juice glass to prevent its contents from splashing across my lap. After several episodes I'd tried asking the stewardess if it was possible to change seats, but she had simply flashed a stiff smile and gruffly informed me that the plane was full, *"of little whiners like you,"* before slinking back up the aisle.

A short while later, Burma made its debut. Deep, dark and mysterious, it appeared to be nothing but trees from one end to the other, with no sign of the six-lane autobahn the ruling junta had reportedly built through the middle of the jungle.

Exhausted from the ten-hour flight to Bangkok, it came

as a pleasant surprise to climb aboard the connecting flight to Phnom Penh to find only fifty people on board. All evidence pointed toward a quiet and uneventful flight; that is until we were airborne. A group of American sports jocks seated in random rows around the plane, took the extinguishing of the seat belt sign as permission to behave as if partying on their own private aircraft. Either too dense or too drunk to contemplate they might be disturbing other passengers, they continued to shout back and forth across the rows of empty seats, under the disdainful gaze of the stewardesses, who despite being visibly nerved by the group's antics, did not appear eager to interfere and disrupt their own unexpected idleness. The staff's lethargy left me in a bit of a quandary as to how to respond. Issuing a polite request to "belt up," was ruled out on grounds of my wishing to go through passport control with a recognizable face, so I simply moved further back in the plane, where the droning engines put them out of earshot and me to sleep. Awakened a short while later by a batch of turbulence, I was surprised to see the culprits had quieted down, thanks in no small part to the subtle generosity of the stewardesses who had apparently not been so idle after all, when it came to handing out sleep-inducing "beverages."

At first, everything looked familiar, as if I'd never left. Same city, same road, even the same time of day; yet somehow, the buzz was missing. Adding to a lurking sense of gloom, rather than a friendly "welcome back" at hotel reception, sincere or not, a familiar face subjected me to a heated conversation over an issue I thought had been settled while still in Germany. With my tolerance level already dangerously low from jet lag, the discussion over a room reservation threatened to intensify until the manager stepped in and resolved it without any weapons being drawn. Not long after, I was on my way up to the room, accompanied by a cluster of doubts over the wisdom of having returned at all. Hoping a diversion might help break the tightening grip of my mood, I postponed unpacking and headed out for a salutatory mojito at my favourite watering-hole. It must have been a slow night as Jerry, the owner, approached me as soon as I entered, greeting me like a long-lost friend, before guiding me to a private table on the patio. Almost immediately he erupted into conversation. Within the span it took to order and finish half my drink, which I was assured was "on the house," he managed to cover a myriad of topics until somehow getting mired on the topic of safety.

"Shit happens man. Things can go down anywhere," he mused. "You just gotta use a bit of common sense. If you're gonna walk around with an expensive camera, hang it over your neck and make sure it's on the side away from the road. Motorbike thieves are as common as friggin' flies around here. Why make it any easier for them?"

"*Why is he insisting on telling me all this?*" I thought, raising my hand to cover a deep yawn. "*And more to the point, why does he think I'm interested in hearing all this? He acts as if there hasn't been anyone to talk to, or at, for weeks.*"

"*It wasn't a mistake to come back. It wasn't a mistake. It wasn't a mistake,*" I kept repeating over and over, after Jerry finally excused himself to attend to a confused-looking waiter. Strongly suspecting that physical exhaustion was to blame for part of my mental erosion, I was about to take my leave when Jerry returned.

"Like I was saying man, keep your eyes and ears open and you should be alright... although, there are a few places in Phnom Penh where even I wouldn't go to at night"

"For example?" I asked, stirred out of my fog by his reference to "even I."

"I was gonna say around Toul Sleng, but come to think of it, a couple of weeks ago a woman got shot just two blocks from here. So there you go. Refused to give up her purse to a robber, so he shot her. Turned out she had sixteen dollars in it."

Almost hallucinatory from exhaustion by this point, I watched in dismay as Jerry, who had obviously mistaken my stupor for interest, switched into high gear, setting his sights on gang violence in the coastal city of Sihanoukville.

"It's mafia man. Russians, drugs, prostitution, the whole ten yards. They got squeezed out of Thailand, so they moved down to Sihanoukville. Toss in the strange vibes from all the ex-pats and old hippies and... well let's just say it's not so cool down there anymore."

In the midst of this verbal barrage, I realized Jerry was not about to cease of his own volition. Struggling to my feet, I tossed several bills on the table and muttered a reasonable facsimile of farewell to my monologist, before stumbling back out into the night. Once back in the sanctuary of my room, the fatigue had become so overwhelming, I dropped to the bed without removing a stitch of clothing. Immobilized by my leaden extremities, I lay there staring at the ceiling, hoping my brain would soon take the hint from my body. Any hopes of easing into sleep, however, were interrupted when a couple in the next room began to argue loudly in a foreign language. While waiting for the battle to run its course, my attention was held by a small gecko on the wall above the television. Fixing it with a frozen stare, I issued a secret challenge as to who would be the first to move. Despite my fatigue, the gecko was victorious, leaving me to finally crash into sleep, aided by the rhythmic whine of the air conditioner and the hope I'd awaken to a better world.

Day Two: Thursday, February 3rd

As paradoxical as it may sound, next morning my mood had improved enough, that I decided the "killing fields" memorial would be a good post-breakfast destination. During the thirty-minute drive to the Choeung Ek Genocidal Centre, the official Khmer name for the "fields," old familiar strains of the fervour that comes with travelling had begun to course through my veins again. The scenery helped. Accustomed to the string of weary-looking proprietors seated out front of their shops in the city centre, it was as we began to pass through the outer-lying districts that I was introduced to a new and unexpected vista - karaoke stalls. Crammed side by side along the road, they were in essence little more than patches of earth covered by rusting metal roofs, each filled with between twenty to thirty plastic chairs out front. Mounted under a canopy behind the chairs, was a television set and a pair of large speakers, out of which music was blasting to lure in passing clientele. It was a sales tactic that appeared to be working, for despite the early hour, most establishments were close to full, a sobering illustration perhaps, of their patrons' reality, not to mention priorities.

The few remaining buildings disappeared altogether as we turned south on to a major thoroughfare; replaced by a landscape of water-filled rice fields behind which rows of stilted houses lay spread out across the distant horizon. Not long after the paddies tapered off, the landscape became a series of dry and debris-filled fields, occasionally interrupted by a decorative arch leading to an unseen temple.

At breakfast, I'd learned from a newspaper article that residents near the "killing fields," had not been pleased when it was announced a Japanese consortium had taken over control of the Choeung Ek site. No specific reasons were given for their discontent. Presumably it was the same consortium I had to thank for the dust-free ride I was experiencing along the newly-paved road leading to the Centre. Oddly enough however, the Japanese had neglected to include the parking lot in their largesse, as evidenced when we pulled into a dusty clearing filled with idle Tuk-Tuks and tour buses. Despite the number of vehicles, there was no line up at the ticket booth, making entrance to the compound both swift and painless. With the temperature already inching into the low thirties, I headed for the air-conditioned museum, having spotted a sign indicating a film on the history of the site was about to start. Removing my boots as requested, I managed to occupy one of the last seats just as the house lights dimmed. I needn't have bothered rushing. The twenty-minute film turned out to be a disappointing bore, peculiar considering how much the "fields," had become a tourist attraction.

Back out in the blinding sunlight with little more knowledge than when I'd left it, I opted to explore the shaded perimeter of the grounds, hoping that some reflection might help close an unsettling gap I felt opening up between myself and the gravity of the events that had taken place here. Following a gravel path that hugged a tattered chain-link fence, I looked out over a plain of scorched-dry paddies extending as far as the eye could see before disappearing in a shimmering haze. The view was a strong contrast to that inside the compound where lush foliage abounded, fed by a large rectangular pond all but hidden in a thicket of long, marsh grass and overhanging trees. Given the circumstances of its location, one couldn't but help wonder whether it had also served as a watery grave. On the far side of the slough, the path led into a sparsely-wooded area pockmarked by what looked to be a number of small craters. A sign near the edge of one crater revealed they were in fact a series of former mass graves, excavated shortly after the Khmer Rouge were overthrown in 1979. Staring at the emptied plots, I felt unable to connect with the past or muster a sense of dread or outrage. Instead, I found myself asking just what it was I had expected to see at the Centre. But before any answer was forthcoming, my attention was diverted by a large group of tourists heading my way. Wishing to avoid them, I veered off towards an obelisk-like structure near the centre of the compound. Resembling a church bell-tower, minus the church or the bell, the column's seventeen windowed storeys rose to a height of nearly twenty metres before being crowned with a pagoda style roof. One of the two glass doors at the sole entrance was locked, resulting in a lengthy queue. Not making life any easier for those wishing to enter, an elderly English couple had stopped in the single doorway to inspect a map and discuss their next move. After easing my way past the befuddled pair, I was suddenly confronted by the sight of several dozen human skulls, cheekbone to shattered cheekbone on shelves behind a pane of smudged glass. While some skulls were bleached as white as porcelain, others appeared more weathered and dirt streaked, often resembling the stitching on a collection of soccer balls when viewed from the back. Logic told me I was looking at the remnants of heinous crimes, yet I felt no affiliation to real people. Somehow, the exhibitions at Toul Sleng had been much more chilling, likely because it was easier to attach a life to a portrait than to a skull.

Given that only the first four levels of the tower's tiers were accessible, all visitors were crowded into the cramped viewing areas. Rankled over the way people were elbowing amongst themselves to take selfies with the skulls, I sought refuge in the shade of a large tree not far from the entrance. Retrieving what was now a rather warm bottle of water from my knapsack, I was attempting to quench my thirst, when I overheard a passing guide addressing a group en route to the tower.

"People brought here from Toul Sleng were beaten to death with bars or shovels, or had their throats slit," he explained matter of factly. "Then they were thrown into mass graves, like the ones you have just seen."

Judging by the non-plussed reactions of most within the group, it seemed I was not alone in feeling that imagined horrors were more ghastly than the actual remnants.

Images of the "killing fields" had begun to fade by the time we were back on the main road heading towards central Phnom Penh. Taking a different route through what looked to be a poorer section of the city, I asked the Tuk-Tuk driver to stop in order to take a closer look at scenes of daily life. By pure chance, he rolled to a halt directly before an opening cut through a solid row of buildings. Looking into the gap, I could see a narrow wooden walkway leading to what appeared to be a lengthy a pier, bordered by houses straight out of a Dickens novel. Just as I was about to disembark, a second Tuk-Tuk bearing two tourists, pulled in and parked directly in front of us. I watched as a tall lanky man with a camera bag slung over his shoulder, hopped out and trundled off through the gap, leaving his bored-looking girlfriend to flip through a dog-eared guidebook.

"I'll be back in ten or fifteen minutes darlin'," he called back in a thick Australian accent. Following several steps behind as we made our way down a creaking boardwalk, I was the first to spot a swarm of children running out of their hut to greet us. Faced with the brunt of the onslaught, the Australian stopped to shoot a photo of the gathering flock, allowing me to discreetly slip past. Somewhat unsettled by the sponginess of the boards beneath my feet, I quickly moved towards the end of the raised walkway, which also served as a terrace for the last house. With several planks missing, it was easy to envision that a false step could end with my plunging to the soggy earth below. But before that could happen, I hurriedly took shots of the strips of green land that jutted out into a labyrinth of muddied channels, as if representing an aquatic version of snakes and ladders.

The Aussie tourist was still being held captive as I made my way back up the gangway, past several residents resting in hammocks on their shaded porches. When and if a glimpse was available into one of the darkened interiors not hidden behind drying laundry or gates of corrugated metal, there was little to see beyond a number of abandoned shoes and flip-flops, darting silhouettes and the occasional small, lighted Buddha shrine.

*

Not normally big on acknowledging ostentatious displays of largely undeserved wealth, after a quick lunch back at the hotel, I nonetheless decided to use the afternoon to venture to one of the capital's top attractions, the Royal Palace. With no intention of wandering through room after room of artifacts of little interest to me, the plan was to concentrate on the ornate, temples within the royal enclosure itself. That plan however, was dealt a severe setback when I entered the Royal Gardens to see a massive throng of Chinese tourists lined up at the ticket booth. With no desire to stare at the back of other heads for the next few hours, I simply returned to the hotel to pass the remaining hours of daylight lounging at the rooftop pool.

Oddly enough, a listless afternoon by the pool proved to be invigorating, prompting me to pay a return visit to the Meta Haus that evening. A German cultural centre Franz had taken us to in December, the two-storey concrete structure was sandwiched between an array of telephone shops and take-away food kiosks on a busy thoroughfare. Sponsored and run by the Goethe Institute, the rooms on the ground floor were reportedly used for language instruction, as well as a gallery for events or /exhibitions. What had lured me back was the prospect of watching a movie with the Cambodian sky as a ceiling. The feature that night at the rooftop cinema was a film titled "What Happened to the Fish?", a British-made documentary that set out to examine the consequences that six major dams would have on residents within the Mekong basin in the coming years. It turned out to be a timely screening as while at the pool that afternoon, I had happened to read an article about electricity costs in Cambodia. According to the report, a single kilowatt hour of power in Cambodia cost fourteen times as much as the same kilowatt hour in England.

Having arrived an hour before the film was scheduled to start, there was time to enjoy a light supper on the rooftop patio, while being entertained by the chaotic scenes unfolding on the street below. If those activities weren't able to hold my attention between mouthfuls, it was the antics of half a dozen geckos clinging to a nearby wall. Although I found both vistas captivating, it was the geckos that ultimately won the upper hand, shifting from their frozen stances as wall decorations, with phenomenal grace and speed.

The film turned out to be an excellent source of information, revealing that the fifty million people residing in what was described as the largest inland fishery in the world, stood to have their major source of nutrition throttled by the proposed dams. It went on to point out that reports prepared under the auspices of such austere organizations as the International Monetary Fund had predicted as much, only to be quietly shelved by unknown forces. If you could believe the film's premise, the instigator, financier and main beneficiary of the dam projects, as well as the least open to compromise, was China. Whether the other five countries affected by the proposed dams could stand up to such an opponent was just one of the questions the film and its director, in attendance for a post-screening discussion, could not fully answer. Fuelled by my second German beer, curiosity compelled me to ask how activists hoped to counter the cost/benefit argument of cheaper power that would undoubtedly be exploited by the dams' promoters. The director acknowledged the point, but unfortunately could not supply a definitive answer. My question did however, bring a sharp response from an elderly British gentleman in the audience. Clearly accustomed to speaking in public, he initially directed his remarks to me before shifting to the crowd, addressing the issue of alternative sources of power available in Cambodia. As interesting as the subject was, an underlying fatigue was beginning to loosen the strings of my concentration. When the discussion swerved to another topic a few minutes later, I used the opportunity to make a quiet exit. Back down on the street, I chose to return to the hotel on foot, hoping not only to enjoy elements of the nightlife, but also to help remove any last resistance my body might still have towards sleep. It seemed hard to believe it was the same day that had started off at the "killing fields." But despite all the memories created over the course of a single day, the dominating thought as I strolled along in the warm evening breeze, was the recognition that the previous night's sombre mood had been thoroughly vanquished.

Day Three: Friday, February 4th.

As much as there is to dislike about the blandness and anonymity of staying in a large hotel, it does have its advantages. For example, the ability to fulfill small needs with minimal stress, at little or no extra charge. Having reached the decision to travel to Siem Reap as soon as possible, a portion of the previous day's pool stay had been spent investigating my options. Told I was facing either a six to seven-hour bus ride, or five hours on what was described as a "speedboat up and across the Tonle Sap," I had opted for the more adventurous method of transport. Within hours of making inquiries at reception, a ticket had been waiting for me at the front desk.

Upon arrival at dockside the next morning, I was immediately accosted by a man offering to organize my reception in Siem Reap. Glancing at the scrap of crumpled paper in his outstretched hand, I declined the dubious deal and lumbered off down a springy metal gangway to the pier. Standing at the stern of the boat, one of the crew was waiting to accept my ticket. But rather than inspecting its validity, he merely crunched it in his fist without so much as a hint of interest, before mindlessly tossing my knapsack into a darkened hole on the rear deck. Any thoughts of complaining were dashed by the fact it was already a fait d'accompli, and a wish for it to still be there when I arrived. Whether the ticket mangler had interpreted my hesitation as potential trouble, or was just plain irritable, he brusquely motioned me to "move please," so he could abuse the next piece of luggage.

It was a bit of a balancing act to inch forward along the narrow gangway, where a misstep would have resulted in being crushed between the pier and the swaying boat. Once I'd reached what appeared to be the only entrance to the lower passenger deck, an inherent survival instinct forced me to stop and assess my current situation. Suddenly it was 1973, the middle of the oil crisis, brought back to life by the image of a phalanx of de-commissioned jet airplanes parked in some distant desert. Noting that both wings had been sheared off and its jet engines replaced by an inboard/outboard motor, it suddenly seemed glaringly obvious as to the origins of this so-called "speedboat."

"There's no way I'm staying in this death trap," I muttered to myself, after working my way down the soiled central aisle of the fuselage. Unable to open a sealed window at seat 22D, I noticed there was no other way out than the way I had just come in. Amazed that none of my fellow passengers appeared at all concerned about the potential danger to their well being, I jostled my way back up the aisle, leaving the more passive souls to their potential tomb. Once back on deck, it was quickly apparent I was not the only one who preferred to at least have a fighting chance should one be needed. Negotiating my way through a jumble of outstretched legs, I managed to secure one of the last open spaces on the cold metal deck at the bow. From this position, I had a clear view of passengers continuing to stream onboard; each new addition increasing the chances of being part of tomorrow's banner headlines.

Fifteen minutes past the stated departure time, there was still no let up in the number of people boarding. With all seats, with presumably the exception of 22D, occupied, latecomers were being directed on to the boat's roof. Grateful to have arrived as early as I had, I felt a small tinge of "Schadenfreude" as I watched them scramble to secure a spot atop something as wide and comfortable as a bowling alley.

A cooling breeze hit my face immediately after the boat swung out into the middle of the river, its captain seemingly oblivious to any other traffic on the water. As the wind picked up with our increasing speed, I slouched back down behind the metal gunnel, mildly cognizant of the sun's burning rays. The first portion of this sheltered existence was spent observing fellow passengers in mutual stages of discomfort. By the time I rose to stretch my legs and survey the surroundings, the river had shrunk to one fifth its size in Phnom Penh, offering a closer view of life on its banks. Amidst the thick foliage lining the shore, it was possible to make out a few thatch-walled huts, most of which were perched upon improbably high stilts. Occasionally, the homes were clustered together, much like buildings on a small farm. It was below one such "community," resting on the upper ridge of a grassy slope, that a family could be seen going about its daily chores. Standing next to a wooden skiff beached on the sandy shoreline, a glistening bare-chested man and his young son were busily preparing their boat for a round of fishing. Not far away, a woman sat squatted next to a pile of wet clothing, raising and lowering garments into water the colour of beige paint. As fascinating as these rural vignettes were, they were repeatedly offset by the futile search for a comfortable position on deck. Tired of twisting and turning amongst my fellow shipmates, it came as welcome news when word spread that we were approaching the city of Kampong Chang. Scheduled for only a short stopover, which I hoped would at least include a chance to awaken my tingling extremities, our stay was shortened even more when it became apparent our designated quay had been blocked by several badly moored skiffs. A large and boisterous crowd, gathered along the shore, seemed to be enjoying the spectacle, offering up periodic cat-calls in Khmer, as they speculated on how the captain intended to handle the dilemma. As for the Cambodian passengers on board, they settled for angrily shouting at a group of youths on the quay, presumably ordering them to push aside the smaller craft. Also seemingly bemused by the goings-on was a group of cyclists marooned on the pier. Clad in identical brightly-coloured Spandex shorts and matching tops, they looked like a professional racing team gone astray, albeit one outfitted with protruding bellies and greying temples,

"They can't be serious," a middle-aged Australian woman sitting nearby grumbled, after realizing the "athletes" in question were actually waiting to board. "Where the bloody hell are they going to put them all?"

Her concerns were justified, for no sooner had landfall been made, then they started to clamber aboard. After leaving their bikes in the rear hold, the few who attempted to enter our domain at the bow were swiftly deterred by discouraging glares and unbudging bodies. With no room below on the doomed passenger deck, most were forced to jam into space begrudgingly freed up on the roof. Only half of the twenty or so cyclists had come aboard when the boat, having reached critical mass, slowly started to tilt to one side. The Australian quickly grabbed hold of what I assumed was her husband's arm, while emitting a muffled shriek.

"I'm not staying on this boat," she groused. "It's not bloody safe. And they're still letting more people on."

Small listings continued to be felt with each additional patron, but it was only when a more hefty arrival caused the boat to dip severely that a shiver of concern dislodged my own ambivalence.

"We gotta say something," I told the Australian woman. The question was to whom. Other than the man in the wheelhouse and the deleterious ticket taker, it was anybody's guess as to who else was actually part of the official crew.

"This is insane," I added to no one in particular, as another sharp list produced the first serious thought of disembarking. At this point, even the prospect of a dreary bus trip was beginning to look better than life at the bottom of the Tonle Sap.

"Look," the Australian woman blurted out. "That man from our boat looks like he's paying off the harbourmaster. Talk to *him*. He can obviously see the boat is overloaded."

Without any real plan of action, I instinctively reached for my camera. By the time I managed to extract it from my bag, the transaction had already been completed. Blocking the man's path as he came aboard, I asked him directly whether he believed the boat was safe. With a look somewhere between ignorance and derision, he raised his hands to plead a mock, "sorry, no understand."

"Look pal," I said, continuing to impede his passage while I snapped a quick shot of him. "If we turtle, those of us up here at least stand a chance. Those down below will have had it. This tub is overloaded and you know it. So just keep this in mind. If something happens, people will know who's responsible," I added, holding up the camera. "So if I were you I'd ..."

The remainder of my two cents was lost when another lurch forced me to grab hold of a railing, allowing him to slip past.

"I think you can forget about *him* doing anything," the Aussie husband advised, when I returned to my place. "This kind of thing happens all the time."

"If you knew that, why are we even on this boat?" his wife interjected. "We could have just as easily taken the bus."

"If it's any solace, love... We happen to be in the best possible position to jump if it goes over. One must simply remain calm and observant."

"Not a terribly consoling notion," I offered.

"Not one bloody bit," she added, echoing my sentiments.

For the next half hour, a quiet nervousness reigned. Those of us on deck and the rooftop gallery attempted to enjoy the passing scenery, but the calm was belied by a chorus of nervous moans whenever the boat listed a little too far for comfort. The Aussie wife, meanwhile, had fallen silent, quietly seething behind a book.

An hour out of Kampong Chang, the river widened again with most of the huts replaced by sporadic, empty wooden platforms, open to the elements save for a thatched roof. The Australian husband, who in interim small talk had revealed himself as a professor and frequent visitor to Cambodia, informed me that the primitive structures were temporary housing used by farmers during the rice season, a prospect that seemed completely inconceivable.

Not long after, we entered the river's delta, a series of channels buttressed by thin, low-lying peninsulas that accompanied us for several hundred meters before ending abruptly. Once land was left behind, the khaki-coloured water with us since Phnom Penh, began to develop a slight shade of green. Marker buoys started appearing off our port side and the man in the wheelhouse seemed to be paying them strict heed. Having yet to earn its moniker of "speedboat," our pace soon slowed even further, insinuating that a certain degree of danger was present. I was in the midst of wondering how *"Caution is the better part of valour,"* might translate into Khmer when we all lurched forward as the boat came a complete and unceremonious halt.

"Now what?" the Aussie wife moaned.

"It appears we've run aground on a sandbar, likely because we're too heavy," the professor said.

"And we're too heavy because we're too bloody overloaded," she added, letting her book slump in her lap.

Fortunately for all aboard, we'd stranded relatively level. Had we stopped at a precarious tilt, panicking passengers might have rushed to the opposite side, setting off a chain reaction that would have certainly sent the boat toppling over on its side or worse. With barely concealed anxiety ricocheting around the upper deck, it was difficult to imagine the atmosphere amongst those below. Assurance that everything was under control was not enhanced when the man I'd confronted in Kampong Chang harbour wove his way forward, peeled off his shirt and jumped into the water.

"I guess going down with the ship isn't part of Cambodia lore," I quipped.

Upon resurfacing, the man shouted something to the captain, who had meanwhile stuck his head out of the wheelhouse to assess our predicament. Following directions barked by the captain, the man swam several meters to his right before raising an arm and letting himself sink. As his hand disappeared below the surface, it was obvious we'd missed the deeper water by only a few feet. For reasons not entirely clear, at this point two more crew members deemed it necessary to join their colleague in the water. Simultaneously, the command was given for all passengers on deck, to move towards the rear of the boat. The plan was a simple one. With less weight at the bow, the better the chances that reversing the engines would free us from the sandbar's grasp. People obeyed quietly, shuffling back as far as space would allow. The re-concentration of weight caused the boat to wobble dangerously, but before there was time to react to the new threat, a huge cloud of black smoke from the revving diesel engines engulfed us all.

"This obviously isn't a first," I said between coughs, as the boat jerked free and the engines were throttled back. Not waiting for permission, passengers began to move forward again, eager to reclaim their positions. Once back in our uncomfortable fold at the bow, amidst recriminations, sighs and laughter, we watched as the aquanauts returned to the mother ship. Aware that this semi-unexpected delay had put us behind schedule, the captain let off steam via the horn and finally allowed the boat the chance to live up to its name.

What followed were two hours of nautical nothingness, leading me to ponder how Columbus and crew managed to handle months at sea. As if on cue, just then someone aboard actually yelled "land ho, mates." Peering over the rim of the gunnel just in time to catch a face full of spray, I was surprised to see a hazy mountain on the distant shore. With a return to "Terra Firma" now a confirmed possibility, a palpable sigh of relief made the rounds, prompting people to start stowing their scattered belongings in the belief our ordeal was nearing its end. Those scouting for signs of a built-up harbour however, were disappointed when we cruised past a renowned floating village and entered a channel alarmingly small for a boat our size. Slowing to a virtual crawl, we plowed through water that shifted from luminous green to light brown, and on to dull yellow in the span of a hundred meters. With no sign of life on the barren shorelines, my attention turned to the young man who had taken over the wheelhouse. Able to pass for sixteen with ease, he wasted no time confirming suspicions he hadn't been long on the job, careening from one shore to the other like some wayward pinball in slow motion. Fortunately, each time disaster looked imminent, it was avoided thanks to the swift efforts of crew members poling us away from the looming embankments.

"Tell me this isn't happening," the Aussie wife said. "After all we've been through, this is the last thing we needed."

"I presume this *is* leading somewhere," I added supportively. "The question is where? I mean wouldn't it have made more sense to have built a dock back out on the lake?"

"The problem is that out here, the lake's shoreline is constantly changing," the professor advised.

As we continued further up the narrow channel, the cool lake breeze that had kept the heat at bay out on the lake, had disappeared, making it feel at times as though we were sailing under a magnifying glass. With both temperatures and tempers approaching critical heights, a final bend in the waterway revealed the object of our desires. Totally out of sync with the surrounding terrain, one couldn't help but wonder who must have owned this particular patch of Cambodia before it was designated as prime territory for an inland harbour. As we inched closer to the dock, one increasingly had the impression that this makeshift haven, gouged like a wound in an otherwise innocent landscape, had been completed within a few days.

With the five-hour journey now nearing its end, the collective yearning for solid ground sparked a perilous scramble to disembark. Once back on dry land, couples immediately parted company, with women heading for the much-needed shade of the terminal building, while men vigorously shouldered each other in a struggle to sort through the pyramid of luggage a bucket brigade of crew members was erecting on the pier. Pleased to see my belongings had survived the trip intact, I hoisted my backpack on to my sun- scorched shoulders with a weary grunt, and trudged up the loading ramp in the direction of the parking lot. There, amidst a mottled group of welcomers, was a man clutching a sign with my misspelled name on it. Relieved to finally be off the water, I collapsed into the back seat of his air-conditioned car, unconcerned by the fact that my sweaty, sunburnt skin was adhering to the plastic upholstery. Nor was I bothered when less than a kilometre from the terminal, we became ensnarled in a lengthy traffic jam. The reason for the delay was a funeral procession. As our cavalcade of buses, Tuk-Tuks, and private cars slowly inched past a long line of people shuffling along on foot through the heat and dust, one almost felt like an intruder. That is until noticing that most of the mourners, dressed in bright, multi-coloured attire, were smiling, chanting, and even waving to the passing crowd.

Once past the flower-bedecked cortege at the head of the procession, we were able to pick up speed, following a snaking road that paralleled a small creek through the jungle. It was not long before we entered a small village set amidst a wealth of exotic looking greenery. Equipped with the standard array of shops and kiosks, it was bustling with activity. What made it even more interesting, was a roadside sign touting a "genuine" crocodile farm. Too tired to investigate what differentiated a genuine one from a fake one, I declined the driver's offer to stop and instead urged him to continue on towards Siam Reap proper.

Although much smaller than Phnom Penh, Siem Reap nevertheless displayed all the hectic pace of the capital. I'd been previously warned about the hordes that descended seeking to bear witness to the splendours of Angkor Wat, and had taken the precaution of booking a hotel outside of town. Just how far outside became apparent when the roadside shops and kiosks soon gave way to untended fields, and the glut of motorized traffic was replaced with bicycles and clusters of pedestrians. Jarred out of my complacency when the asphalt suddenly turned to hard, rippled sand, I was about to ask the driver if he was sure he'd taken the correct route, when we turned off down a side road, following a pink-walled soccer field in the middle of nowhere, before pulling to a stop at the heavily treed entrance of a well-hidden resort.

Within minutes of closing the door to my bamboo hut, I was in sheer delirium, standing in a stone, walk-in shower, ridding myself of the sweat, dirt and memories of the recent speedboat adventure. Once dressed and unpacked, I led myself back up the garden path to the hotel's open-air lobby, where discussions with a pretty young Cambodian revealed that Angkor Wat was only a half-hour bike ride away. Too late in the day to warrant a visit, I decided to make use of the ebbing daylight to explore the area closer to home. To my misfortune however, all of the hotel's better bicycles had been rented out, forcing me to accept a contraption whose non-adjustable seat and jammed gearshift, promised to make riding an ordeal. Slowly but strenuously making my way through the quiet countryside, careful to avoid wheel-snaring patches of loose sand on the undulating road surface, it suddenly came to me that I'd inadvertently managed to land exactly where I'd hoped to; smack dab in the heart of rural Cambodia.

The nearer I got to the last village we'd passed through an hour earlier, the more plentiful small family kiosks started to become, replete with pyramids of coconuts and mangoes abutted by orange-coloured ice coolers. Although I chose to remain on the main road, I couldn't help noticing how enticing the side streets were. Little more than rutted strips of sand, lined with large palm trees and shrubbery as far as the eye could see, each was dotted with residents on foot or bicycle, making their way home in the approaching dusk. Suddenly, I was blindsided by a swarm of uniformed school children spilling out of a walled compound. Forced to stop by a surging sea of bright-white shirts, I watched as the youngsters congealed into pairs or small groups, grinning and waving to me before setting off down the road. Once the exodus had cleared, I pedalled on into the village, coming to rest against a cement utility pole, atop of which an enormous jumble of electrical cables jutted out in every conceivable direction. From there it was possible to observe the dynamics of the day's demise, as dozens of motorbikes, many with three or four passengers aboard, wove through an uncontrolled intersection, effortlessly avoiding the flow of pedestrians crossing from all four corners. Every once in awhile a large truck would rumble through the junction, momentarily cloaking all activity in a trailing cloud of orange dust. Directly across the street, people were lined up at a bright-blue, two-wheeled cart, that somehow reminded me of those old pop-corn vendors with a glassed-in cabinet. A column of whitish smoke was wafting up from a small bent chimney on its roof, and as I eased my way across the road for a closer look, I saw it was coming from a pan of frying shish kebabs, monitored by a lone sweating vendor. Business was booming, with another patient customer joining the end of the line just as payment was accepted from one at the front. Elsewhere villagers could be seen entering and exiting various stores, hurrying to complete last-minute shopping before heading home. It was a scene that unfolded daily in thousands of other towns and villages around the world, yet I stood there in silent awe, grateful to be a witness, pleasantly confounded by what made it all so fascinating.

✻

For those who've never had the pleasure, the jungle at night is not a quiet place. Following a pleasant dinner on the patio, where I'd been assured that the mosquitos constantly buzzing around my head were not *those* kind of mosquitos, the ones that carried malaria, dengue fever and who knows what else, I adjourned early. Lying in bed, lazily watching the wind-blown shadows of a full moon move across the opposite wall, I was startled by the distant howl of a single dog. Right on cue, several other hounds soon joined in, each with its own distinctive resonance. Although the canine chorus was brief, other participants were waiting to take the stage. The first I pegged as a Cambodian cricket. But unlike its foreign counterparts, this one seemed incapable of delivering anything more complicated than a single tone. Normally unappreciative of such disturbances, I made light of the nocturnal concert by adding a few rhythmic thumps on the mattress in time to the cricket's metronomic moan. Ten minutes of this uninspiring melody was about all I could take, and I was just about to throw something at the unseen perpetrator, when it decided to take a break. Any hopes of indulging in the ensuing silence were swiftly crushed by the piercing screech of what sounded to be a rather irked monkey, loud enough to have me think the peeved primate was right outside my shuttered window. No sooner had that its echo faded, than the cricket resumed its monotonic plea, sounding more and more like the plaintive mating call of a lonely insect. If that was indeed its intention, I feared the both of us were in for a long and troubled night.

Day Four: Saturday, February 5th

Asked to hazard a random guess as to the current population in China, most people would answer, "somewhere between one and one and a half billion." A decent attempt, but they would have nevertheless been wrong. The correct answer was half that figure. I happened to know because the other half was lined up in front of me when I arrived at the entrance to Angkor Wat just before nine the next morning. After being stuck there for what felt like an eternity, or at least long enough to have become fluent in Mandarin, I was able to purchase my three-day ticket and pedal away from the teeming masses. Still facing a three kilometre trek to the first of the temples, that task was made less daunting by the fact it wasn't yet scorchingly hot; perfect for cycling, even if my mode of transport barely met that description.

Having looked forward to exploring the multiple sites, my enthusiasm had been rattled by the throngs encountered at the entrance. Matters weren't helped much when a few minutes later, I rounded a corner of a shaded path to see another massive horde, this one streaming across a stone footbridge at the moated entrance to the main temple of Angkor Wat. That there *would* be a crowd came as no surprise, given that the temple is the largest religious edifice in the world. It was simply the sheer size of this one that was so overwhelming. Starting in the bus parking lot and extending over the moat, it was impossible to see the end of a line that was slowly advancing towards a temple still three quarters of a kilometre away. As luring as the iconic towers were that morning, I couldn't face the prospect of exploring the temple in the company of such a crowd. Artfully dodging the stragglers and vendors trying to push their wares in the parking lot, I backtracked into the forest, promising to return when the masses had hopefully gone home.

Baksei Chamkrong and Phnom Bakheng were the first temples on my list. As I'd managed to forget the guidebook back at the hotel, there was no chance to brush up on the history of either temple. Wishing to explore them nonetheless, it was a struggle to ascend the first of what would be many steep staircases over the next three days. Huffing and puffing my way to the top, I couldn't help wondering what it must have been like to have been one of the drones hauling the large chiseled stones in unyielding heat a thousand years ago.

Baksei Chamkrong was smaller than anticipated and it only required ten minutes of snooping before I was ready for temple number two. Ignoring the signposted route for Phnom Bakheng, I followed a path less taken, so much so that I soon found myself lost in a seemingly impassable thicket of prickly underbrush. Forced to re-trace my route past a row of white spider webs, I hadn't seen on the way in, I was able clamber up a hill towards what appeared to be a viewing platform built into the side of a steep hill. Fortunately, there was no one around to witness my predicament, as I clawed and stumbled my way up to rejoin the regular path. Slapping off dust and thistles that had collected on my jeans, socks and shoelaces, I stepped on to the platform to be treated to a spectacular view of the temple

I'd just left. Poking through a canopy of dark green jungle that was slowly smothering its presence, the cloistered temple was a vivid illustration of how nature was reclaiming its rightful place following man's intrusion.

Once having reached the upper level of the second temple, I wandered through a series of squat stone towers, spread out on an area half the size of a soccer pitch. Spaced between the towers were numerous small stone prayer huts, each covered with ornate engravings, and blackened by what must have been a devastating fire. Just how fortunate I'd been in exploring these two temples in the absence of other tourists, was brought home a short while later when I approached the tower gate controlling entry to Angkor Thom. Here, beneath four menacing faces carved into the tower's facade, a lengthy queue of tour buses, cars and Tuk-Tuks had developed, all waiting for a white-gloved traffic attendant to wave them through the single lane archway. The reason for the congestion was revealed a little more than a kilometre inside the gate; Bayon, a sprawling, multi-spired temple that looked like a giant, black-toned postcard set against the brilliant blue sky. Anxious to explore its innards, I locked the bike to a fenced-in compound that was safeguarding a pile of numbered, ancient, oblong stones, presumably waiting to be re-assembled. Scouting around for an entrance not overrun by umbrella-led tourist groups or aggressive souvenir hawkers, I was lucky enough to find a free stairway near the centre of the temple. Scrambling up the stone steps, I slipped into a labyrinth of light and shadow, where darkened doorways led to darkened corridors, linked by stone passageways in various shades of red and brown, all covered in intricate bas reliefs and inscriptions.

Despite multiple storeys of hallways, foyers, and stairwells, there didn't seem to be many actual rooms, an architectural tribute to the adage that the journey is more important than the destination.

Given the sheer number of people mulling about, Bayon was remarkably quiet. Equally astounding was the fact that nobody was controlling where you could and couldn't go. Unlike countless other historical sites around the world, here you were free to examine every nook and cranny for as long as you liked. Totally immersed in the tranquil atmosphere of Bayon, two full hours passed before I was finally able to pull myself away.

Similar encounters followed at the Baphuon and Preah Kahn, two temple complexes, the latter of which immediately made my list of favourites. Glancing at my watch as I left Preah Kahn, I was amazed to discover it was already five o'clock. I'd managed to cover a lot of territory in eight hours, something my muscles attested to as I straddled my bike for the ride home. Cruising back past the main Angkor Wat temple, I couldn't help noticing that the masses from the morning were now pouring over the footbridge in the opposite direction, with many gathering along the outer banks of the moat. Spotting a couple, whose gaudy, logo-filled attire instantly gave them away as Americans, I stopped to ask the reason for the assembled throng.

"The sunset," the man in his fifties explained. "It's the bookend to this morning's sunrise over the spires of the main temple."

Something, however, was not quite right.

"Uhhh... I don't know about you, but in the part of the world I come from," I pointed out. "A sunset shot usually has the sun beside or behind the object of affection."

As the three of us stood there silently gazing across the calm water at the distant temple, I had to bite my tongue to prevent from adding that the sun in question was actually behind us. Meanwhile, hundreds and hundreds of people continued to file out of the main gate in search for a suitable location along the cement embankment. Although the expected event was still some twenty minutes away, the facade of the complex's outer walls had already started to take on a reddish tint. A part of me wanted to stick around to see how it all turned out, but doing so would mean traveling home in the dark, a prospect I wanted to avoid seeing I was dressed in dark clothing and the bike, to no one's surprise, had no functioning light. Once the decision to forego the spectacle was made, a small scuffle broke out amongst the more faithful for my vacated spot as I pedalled away.

Despite the risk presented by the encroaching darkness, I decided on the spur of the moment, to take an untested route I hoped would prove shorter. With no signage to identify it as an alternative back to the entrance, and a road too narrow for large tour buses, I pretty much had the tarmac to myself and could cycle along lost to the world, swerving from side to side as if on some virtual slalom course. It was in such a moment of abandon that I suddenly became aware of a strange high-pitched whine, that conjured up the image of a subway train as it screeched around a curve. With nothing in the vicinity to suggest it was man-made, I tried to focus on its source. It seemed to lose intensity whenever I passed a gap in the trees, so I rolled to a stop alongside a clump of bushes, hoping to investigate. After making my way across a gulley of dead leaves to stare up at a large tree, I noticed that something in the branches was moving. Just as I strained to identify the origin, I was distracted by the voices of two young girls walking along the road.

"Excuse me," I called out, trying to look as non-threatening as possible as I came out of the bushes. "Do either of you speak English?"

The two teenagers shared an awkward glance before one of them nodded. Pointing to the trees, I asked whether they had any idea what was causing the din. This prompted a second exchanged glance as well as a round of giggles.

"Bird," the taller of the two said.

"A bird? What kind of bird makes a noise like that? There must be a million of them for that kind of racket."

"Small bird," the girl told me, clenching her fist to indicate the size of the alleged culprit. "Small bird, big noise," she added with a broad smile.

Showing no interest in answering any further questions, the pair quickly set off down the road, glancing back once or twice amidst a burst of muffled laughter.

"Thank you," I hollered belatedly, turning away in hopes of catching sight of the invisible squealers. Additional attempts at investigation were cut short by the ever-dimming light, and the whining continued to rise and fall as I pedalled on. Strangely enough, once out of the official confines of the Angkor Wat complex, it inexplicably stopped.

Shortly after dinner, it became apparent there wasn't a lot to do out in the the "boonies" at night. Not about to venture out on my bike through unknown territory, or remain in my bungalow to await another midnight concerto, I arranged for a Tuk-Tuk to take me back into downtown Siem Reap. After leaving my driver at an impromptu station with the promise of returning once I'd had my fill of the nightly delights, I followed a leisurely strolling crowd towards what my map indicated should be the "famous nighttime market." Wandering up one street and down another, past the flashing marquees of crowded bars and restaurants, and a cavalcade of souvenir stores that catered to all degrees of desire, I felt as though I'd stumbled upon the midway of a country fair. But a half hour of this spectacle was all I could take before I was pining for the tranquil boredom of my rural abode. In what struck me as a stunning turn of events, I actually had to stir a dozing driver from the back of his Tuk-Tuk to have him drive me back to the lodge, after my original driver was nowhere to be found.

Despite the raised hairs on the back of my neck caused by a sudden rustling in the bushes, I tried to maintain a respectable pace as I made my way up the path to my bungalow. Glad to be away from the glare and blare of downtown Siem Reap, I settled in under the delusion small prey would respect the porous borders of my bamboo sanctuary and refrain from conducting another nocturnal symphony.

Day Five: Sunday, December 6th

Just how demented does a rooster have to be to begin crowing at 4:00a.m.? As detrimental to sleep as the cock was that morning, he wasn't the sole reason for my having to rise long before the sun intended to crack the dawn. Misfortune also came with the arrival of the resort manager with her two, white Terriers in tow. Just as the fowl seemed to be tiring of his own torturous cackle, the pair of four-legged toilet brushes were set loose to terrorize any stray jungle creatures in the courtyard. It must be said they did a commendable job, awakening everything within a five-mile radius. Later at breakfast, when the little beasts tried to suck up to me for leftovers, I steadfastly refused to pay them any notice.

Thirty minutes later, as I left the lodge's bike compound and made my way towards the road, a pair of testy, skeletal cows gaped at me from a nearby field, as if to imply I was to blame for the minuscule tufts of dried grass they had to munch on. Despite the early hour, one could tell it was going to be hot. So hot, that the layer of sunscreen I'd applied, could not prevent my forearms from burning by the time I'd made it as far as the village. With more activity on the street than I expected for a Sunday morning, most notably a parade of rumbling dump trucks, it wasn't long before my face and arms were coated with a sticky film of orange dust kicked up by the passing vehicles.

Another round of temples was on the day's agenda, and

once back inside the Angkor Wat complex, I halted at a crossroads to survey my map. With the bulk of traffic turning left, there was more than enough reason to venture right. According to the map, a four kilometre jaunt would bring me to Banteay Kdei, a temple described as exuding a sense of "elegance, tranquility and finesse." Lost in my own little tropical paradise as I pedalled down an all but empty road, my solitude was suddenly disrupted by the sound of children's voices that seemed to be coming from somewhere in the neighbouring forest. Looping back to a bridge I didn't remember crossing, I peered down at a group of young Cambodians, splashing and churning in the brownish waters of a small creek some thirty feet below the road surface. It seemed an odd place for an outing, particularly since the surrounding vegetation looked virtually impenetrable. Even the sun had difficulty piercing the foliage, gracing the surface of the water with only a few splotches of light. Watching them play under the protective eye of several guardians, barely visible in the dense underbrush, one almost expected Tarzan to come swinging by, bellowing out his distinctive call before disappearing back into the treetops. The scene was a far cry from memories of my own family outings, where weighted down with coolers, lawn chairs, air mattresses and other paraphernalia, my parents, siblings and I would tromp down a manicured beach until staking out our territory for the day. Judging from the squeals of delight echoing through the jungle, it appeared just as much fun could be had without the conglomeration of accessories.

Banteay Kdei lived up to its hype and then some,

surpassing anything seen so far with the exception of my leading favourite, Preah Kahn. Fascinated by its intricately carved bas reliefs, intriguing dark hallways and pleasant, peaceful grounds, it was while wandering through this splendour that I caught sight of my first strangling fig. Instantly recognizable by its absurdly enormous, four-sided base and spindly roots, the tree was first made famous to the outside world in the 19th century, when published photos illustrated their continuing reclamation of Angkor Wat. Add in the bonus of exploring Banteay Kdei's treasures with fewer than a dozen fellow tourists, one can understand why I departed the temple with a combined sense of awe and loss.

The second temple visited that day was completely different, a large four-level edifice with stairways so precipitous, they threatened to keep all but the bravest visitor on "Terra Firma." Making it to the summit of Takeo was a harrowing experience, especially in the heat. As a reward for doing so, I sought shelter in a tiny shrine, where inside, an elderly woman with a wizened face was seated before a small Buddha draped with flowers and banners. Interrupting her meditative chant, she invited me to light a stick of incense and offer a prayer. Once I'd made a donation for the incense, but declined on the prayer, she proceeded to tie a thin, blue, woollen band around my wrist, softly stroking the back of my hand, while uttering a few unintelligible words. She ended the ritual by blowing across my knuckles and releasing me with a smile. Returning the bow with clasped hands, as I turned to leave, she extended a final "good luck" wish in perfect English. Back out on the scorching terrace, I sat in the shade of a pillar, reflecting on the blessing I'd just been given. However well intentioned, it somehow felt superfluous to the gift of simply being there.

The lunch-hour rush had pretty much subsided by the time I rolled into the sandy courtyard of Sras Srang. With fewer targets now to choose from, a group of young girls encircled me the moment I dismounted, each waving a plasticized menu in my face while nattering away in an attempt to cajole me into eating at one of the food kiosks. Getting into the act was an even younger girl, no more than three or four. Upon noticing my arrival, she had instinctively dropped the ball she'd been playing with, to don a small tray full of plastic knick-knacks, and waddle over the join the melee, looking like history's tiniest cigarette girl. Polite but persistent to a flaw, all of them were seasoned vendors, and it was only my prolonged indecision and the approach of another potential customer that prompted them to run off, trailed by the tottering youngster. Freed of the entourage, I moved to a shaded bench on the shoreline of an enormous, rectangular pool the size of a small lake, hoping to take advantage of the refreshing breeze blowing in off the water. In less than a minute however, a petite, middle-aged woman, dressed in a loose-fitting blouse and black pyjama pants approached.

"You eat here," she said, more a statement than a question. "Fish good. Good price. When you eat, you eat here."

Not wanting to encourage her, I simply shook my head while keeping my eyes glued to my guidebook. Clearly it was not enough.

"Best fish here. Make good price... You eat".

Awareness that she was just trying to eke out a living kept my frustration in check, until ultimately concluding the only way to discourage her was simply to leave. Returning to the main road, I cycled past a row of more established eateries before selecting one bereft of customers. Whatever hopes I'd had of dining in peace, however, were dashed when a loud, chugging generator located right next door, started up the second my meal was placed in front of me.

Ta Prohm was a complete madhouse, with dozens of Tuk-Tuks scooting in and out of the central parking area, stirring up plumes of dust which quickly enveloped unsuspecting tourists disembarking from row upon row of tour buses. Adding to the mayhem was the fact that the normal entrance was closed for renovations, forcing those wishing to reach the temple to funnel up and across a narrow bridge of wobbly scaffolding. Uncertain if I wanted to join the lengthy line waiting to cross over, I clambered to the top of a nearby hill to consider my options.

"Why are there so many people here today?" I asked a nearby Tuk-Tuk driver, who was taking in events from the comfort of his back seat.

"Chinese New Year," he answered with a yawn.

"That explains a few things," I nodded, recalling the crowds at entrance and the moat, and envisioning a future where the only place in the world not overcrowded would be China.

Although highly skeptical of whether I wanted to share the features of Ta Prohm with thousands of others, I nonetheless swallowed hard and took my place in line. Ten minutes later however, with the masses having made only minimal progress forward, I was done. Handed an unforeseen, extra amount of daylight, I decided to take a more leisurely route back to the hotel, following a number of groomed pathways through the forest. It wasn't long before I found myself skirting alongside the moat on what appeared to be the rear side of Angkor's main temple. Neither the temple, nor its onslaught of visitors were visible from this point, but in their place was a spectacular fireball sun whose reflection cut a shimmering path across the moat's stilled waters. With plenty of time to dawdle, I secured a spot on the earth embankment to observe the sundown. It managed to put on a spectacular show, turning from a fiery red to a muted pink, and finally a light rosy grey. Other passing cyclists stopped to gawk at the unfolding spectacle during the transformation, and there must have been more than a dozen of us enjoying the sight when a loud rumbling announced the arrival of a tour bus. Fulling expecting its contents to spill out any moment, I glanced back to see that passengers were merely crowding to one side to shoot the scene through dust-caked windows. Within the allotted seconds, the tour guide signalled time was up and the idling bus pulled away, leaving the rest of us to watch the sun slowly drop beneath the tops of the distant trees in quiet solitude.

Dinner that evening at the resort was pretty much a non-event. Finished by eight, I had the choice of either catching up on the latest world news blaring from a nearby television, or trying my luck with an ancient looking computer terminal. Still suffering from the after effects of last night's disruptive sleep, I gave both a pass, hoping to log at least a few hours rest before the dogs were set loose again. As fate would have it though, not longer after getting into bed, something in my bamboo hut began faintly scratching a manifesto into a section of the wall. Taking a deep breath, I waited in vain for the nervy beast to stop, before flicking on the light on the bedside table, and scouring the room for a suitable weapon. Oddly enough, I landed on what appeared to be a local telephone book, a rather useless accessory considering there was no telephone in the room. As far as I could tell, the noise seemed to be coming from directly over the adjoining bed. Whether the resounding thud of the directory hitting the wall knocked the creature from its perch or simply scared the wits out of it, ten minutes of silence ensued before a very slight scratching sound could be heard again. From there matters quickly evolved into a test of wills. Scratch and wait. With no resulting thud, the perpetrator risked another scratch, this time a fraction longer. Too lazy to retrieve my weapon, which had fallen down between the wall and the other bed, the game of nerves dragged on for the next fifteen minutes. Vowing certain revenge if I heard it five more times, my lethargy stretched the count to seven before another thud echoed through the bungalow, this time the result of a flying shoe. But despite this second counterattack, it was only a matter of time before the scratching resumed. As a last resort, I turned to the air conditioner, using the remote control to set it as high as possible in the hope its monotonous whirr would either drive him to distraction or another bungalow. Twenty minutes passed before the thermostat cut in and the room fell silent. I could almost hear my pulse throbbing in my veins as I anticipated yet another outbreak, but as the silence lengthened, I became convinced the creature had either frozen or fled. Rolling over on my side, content with the smug conviction we're not superior beings for nothing, sleep was advancing when a distant bird emitted a series of piercing shrieks. No sooner had that racket faded, there came a gentle tapping at the window above my head. With no desire to identify the latest culprit, I was ultimately forced to surrender to the continuing menagerie of noise. The sole silver lining in the midst of this aural torture was that I did manage to acquire a fragment of sleep before the unhinged rooster began to crow anew.

Day Six: Monday, February 7th

What with it having been my final day at Angkor Wat, I was determined to undertake a tour of Ta Prohm, regardless of whatever crowds might be awaiting me this time. Consulting my trusty guidebook at breakfast, I learned that Ta Prohm meant "power and endurance," somehow fitting given what it might take to suffer the crowds. The best time for visiting, was allegedly mid-afternoon, when one could expect smaller crowds and optimal light conditions. Despite a suspicion that everyone might heed such advice, I adjusted my plans and decided to visit to a lesser-known temple that morning. The problem was, I couldn't find it. According to the map, it should have been somewhere between Takei and Banteay Kdei, but if it was, it was extremely well hidden. In spite of backtracking over the same territory several times, I failed to find a single sign indicating its whereabouts. Finally, out of sheer frustration, I stopped at an isolated kiosk on the main road to ask directions.

"Banay? Banei?... Banlei? It's a temple that's supposedly around here somewhere. Temmmm...pulllll!!", I blathered to four adult Cambodians who had emerged from under an awning. From the looks on their faces, it was obvious they had no idea what I was talking about. As they proceeded to conduct a lively debate, the scene was interrupted by a tiny voice.

"Tanei?"

"Yeah, that's it... Tanei," I said to the small boy stepping forward through a curtain of legs to address me. "I've been looking for it for almost an hour. Can you tell me where it is?"

With the adults still busy exchanging puzzled stares, the youngster simply turned and pointed to a path directly behind them. Somewhat skeptical that a solution had been so close at hand, I nevertheless thanked the group before cycling off down what looked to be an abandoned logging trail. Barely wide enough for a car, provided the driver didn't mind having his paint scraped off by protruding branches, the first hundred metres of the rutted path was beset with numerous jagged rocks. Forced to walk to avoid an untimely flat, I'd no sooner hopped back aboard, when the surface softened to loose sand, causing my front wheel to jam sideways, and nearly send me catapulting over the handlebars. Sensing Halley's Comet was likely to return sooner than someone else I could ask directions of, I set myself a time limit on any further advance. Not long after I came to a junction in the trail. Instinct suggested Tanei was to the right, prompting me to follow. But doubts began to set in as the underbrush thickened, slowing my pace to a crawl. Ducking and weaving between branches as best I could, it suddenly dawned on me I was doing precisely what all the guidebooks had warned not to; that being, travel down an unmarked, unfamiliar, seldom-used path in the middle of the jungle. In an instant, every random log and oddly located rock began to look suspicious. Although logic suggested that officials could not allow tourists into Angkor Wat without having thoroughly checked it for land mines, uncertainty and frustration increased with every twist and turn in the trail.

Finally, I decided enough was enough. Pausing to catch my breath and settle my jangled nerves back at the junction, I looked up to see two Cambodian women emerging from the narrow path I could, and perhaps should have taken.

"Tanei?" I heard myself pant. "I'm sorry. Do you speak English?"

Once the older of the two had echoed the question into a statement, I dug out my map to show them where I hoped I was headed. Both gave it a cursory glance before vigorously jabbing their fingers towards the recently abandoned path.

"You're sure eh?" I asked. "Why are there no signs?"

When the question produced a dual set of shrugs, I added, "How long from here? Five minutes... Ten?"

As they slipped into a lengthy consultation in Khmer, I was about to thank them for their troubles and be on my way, when one held up both hands to announce, "ten meenoots."

But they had been right, and after "ten meenoots," of cautiously edging my way back down the path, there it was, a faded, vine-draped signpost confirming their prediction.

Given the sheer amount of grumbling over the last few days regarding the surfeit of tourists, it came as a surprise to feel myself unnerved at being the sole visitor to Tanei. With no lounging Tuk-Tuk drivers, no swarms of New Year's celebrants, not even a random water vendor, the sudden chill of isolation briefly threatened to let a wave of groundless worries send me scampering back to civilization. Having come this far however, I felt committed to stick it out. Exploring the grounds proved slow going, thanks largely to numerous oblong blocks of stone strewn about in a post-earthquake style. Jutting out in every conceivable direction, and covered in slippery green moss, they created a challenging obstacle course in which both hands and feet were needed to make headway. As if that wasn't enough, one also had to be careful not to step into any darkened cubbyholes just in case a snake, spider or crazed animal might be lurking inside. On the rare occasion it *was* actually possible to reach a recognizable doorway, I was usually disappointed to discover that access to the inner core of the temple was blocked by more collapsed masonry. Reluctant to spend less time at the site than it took to find it, I gave up trying to explore the temple's inner core and opted instead for a peripheral tour. After navigating through more fallen pillars and lintels, I reached what the sun told me was the temple's southern wall. As I started to make my way along a lengthy terrace, I couldn't help noticing a long line of small, white nets attached to its side wall. On closer inspection, I suddenly realized I'd trampled right into the middle of a tarantula colony. Rather than panicking and fleeing like any sensible person would have done, I succumbed to the urge to count them, and was up to thirty before Conrad's comment of their potential aggressiveness and speed halted the spontaneous poll. Having had quite enough adventure for the moment, I decided it was time to show Tanei my back, the route out taking considerably less time than the journey in.

As far as my visit to Ta Prohm is concerned, despite numerous attempts, I found no words that could adequately capture the experience of visiting the compelling, other worldly, sanctum of that temple. One must simply see it first hand.

Following several hours at Ta Prohm, traffic was sparse

on the road heading home.

"What the hell is that?" I asked myself, pulling over to the side of the tree-lined alley to get a better look at the approaching vehicle. At first I took the distant figure for a nude body strapped on to the back of a motorbike. But as the gap closed, it became apparent that the body in question happened to have eight legs, all of which were pointing skywards. As the motorbike finally sputtered past, the extraordinary cargo revealed itself to be a pair of ex-pigs, stiff as boards, with their pink derrieres exposed for all the world to see. Standing there with my mouth draped open, regretting that I had not thought to take a photo, it took a honk from a passing car and a backseat of mocking children to snap me out of my momentary trance. By that time the former swine had shrunken to nothing more than a tiny pink dot on the horizon, stranding me with an image that no one would ever believe.

One of the primary aims in having returned to Cambodia, was to explore and experience as many aspects of rural life as possible, to get a truer sense of "real life." Back at the hotel earlier than expected provided the perfect opportunity to continue that quest. Although I had planned to make use of the remaining hours of daylight by heading to another nearby village, I was only halfway there when I was sidetracked by a sandy road too inviting to pass up. From the second I entered the street I could feel an "end of the day" tranquility. People on foot or bicycles were heading home in what seemed to be graceful slow motion. Women with baskets of groceries balanced on their heads would occasionally wave to neighbours tending to chores in their front yards, while further along, shoppers gathered at thatch-roofed kiosks, loading up with necessities for the evening meal. Here and there, children chased each other around like tiny whirlwinds in the dusty sand amidst a soundtrack of squeals and laughter. So different yet so similar to everyday life in Germany, the captivating vistas drew me into a momentary fantasy of what it might be like to actually live here.

Not long after, as the few remaining houses gave way to scrub-filled countryside, I found my path blocked by a vehicle from the district telephone company. As I attempted to ease past the parked van without tumbling into a dried-out culvert, I was treated to the sight of three uniformed men struggling to make sense of a colossal jumble of wires atop a concrete utility pole. Two of the men were hunched over a fluttering blueprint spread out on the hood of the truck, intermittently shouting instructions to a third man perched on a ladder amidst the tangle of cables. None appeared to have a firm grasp of the situation. Although I enjoyed watching the theatrics for a few minutes, I left them to their Sisyphean task upon realizing they might be there for days if not weeks.

With little in the landscape to now hold my interest, I was about to turn back when my focus shifted to the arched roof of a pagoda sticking out from a cluster of trees. As there were no signs to indicate entry was restricted, I made my way to an open, weathered gate and walked through into what appeared to be another temple complex. Too lazy to remove my hiking boots to enter the large building that dominated the centre of the grounds, I selected to circle the perimeter. Ringed by at least two dozen tall, orange pillars and set atop

144 |

a raised concrete platform, the temple's outer walls were covered with colourful murals depicting a Buddha-like figure in various stages of his life. It was while I was admiring this artwork that I spotted a smaller shrine at the rear of the grounds. Unlike the multi-tiered arches so common to temples elsewhere, this building had a bulbous, onion-shaped spire that looked like some sort of stylized chimney. Equally intriguing was a large black cube directly adjacent, resting beneath an open-walled dome. Just as I was moving in for a closer look at this peculiar structure, I was distracted by a group of young, orange-robed monks huddled nearby.

"Excuse me," I said, walking over to introduce myself before gesturing towards the black box. "Is that what I think it is?"

"It is a crematorium," one monk replied.

"Really?" was the extent of my somewhat foolish reply. Stuck for a follow-up, I was scrolling for a more fitting response when four women in off-white lab coats, each carrying a small bowl and towel, emerged from an adjoining building and moved across the parking lot in close formation. Anticipating my next question, the young monk informed me, "They are body washers. They have prepared a body for cremation tomorrow. The body will be burned and the ashes given to the relatives of the deceased if they so desire. Otherwise they will be placed in the pagoda."

I watched the solemn-faced body washers in silence until they disappeared into yet another building, before respectfully bowing my appreciation to the monks and taking my leave, hoping to get home before darkness set in.

It was shortly after 9:00 p.m. when I locked the door to my bungalow and made my way along the darkened path, accompanied by a chorus of crickets, a few of which had managed to expand their repertoire to more than a single tone. Slipping past the becalmed pool pierced by beams from underwater lights, it was only a few steps to the site of the night's self-imposed treat, a session with the resort's resident masseuse. With no door to knock on, I carefully parted the mosquito netting draped around the outdoor cubicle, and was greeted by a young woman who introduced herself as Rahum. Showing little interest in engaging in small talk, she quickly instructed me to disrobe and relax on the bench. Although the first task was accomplished with little fanfare, the second took considerably longer. That was because the cubicle lay directly alongside a large commercial refrigeration unit that was busily humming away. Initially distracting, the white noise eventually faded into the background as Rahum got down to the business at hand, gently guiding me towards an oblivion where all I could think of was how much a tiny brain can absorb in the span of a single day.

Day Seven: Tuesday, February 8th

Faced with an early morning temperature of thirty-two degrees, I briefly reconsidered the wisdom of fulfilling my pledge to visit a temple complex known as the Roluos Group. It wasn't so much the formidable heat that had threatened to scuttle my plans, but rather the twenty kilometre bike ride it would take to get there. Despite that daunting prospect, I set off in a good mood, a disposition that lasted until reaching a residential section of Siem Reap. Much more upscale than anything seen to date, the disproportional display of wealth in the form of huge, luxurious villas set in a quiet, leafy neighbourhood was disquieting to say the least, and a stark contrast to the tumultuous conditions that awaited me only a few blocks away. As I pulled on to a busy, main artery heading south, I was overwhelmed to see hundreds if not thousands of people on motorbikes, or in Tuk-Tuks and cars, all doing their best to clog what was left of a four-lane street. Adding to the chaos were huge, diesel-spewing trucks, overcrowded buses and rusting long-haul freighters manoeuvring through traffic with little regard for their lesser counterparts, including cyclists like myself. I was starting to have second thoughts about subjecting myself to such conditions when a large sign, barely visible through the brown haze, indicated that the city limits were only two kilometres away. I was right to persevere as shortly after passing that border, the congestion quickly dissipated. As far as scenery was concerned, there was not a lot to see amidst the flat, baked countryside other than several random warehouses and an occasional factory. Although the dull landscape tended to make my mind wander, I was quickly snapped back to the task at hand, namely that of staying alive, by the strong gusts of winds created by passing trucks and buses. Between the bike's frozen odometer and the usual dearth of signage, I had no idea how far I'd travelled and how much further there was to go. After a good hour, both mental and physical exhaustion were starting to make themselves apparent, when I risked following two large tour buses that had turned off just ahead of me. Wrong decision or not, it was relief to be away from the stressful pace of the highway and find myself in a quiet channel of palm trees bordered by thick green foliage. A short ways up the road, houses began to appear with even an occasional kiosk or two. The downside of this renewed civilization, however, was that local traffic was soon backed up, exacerbated by two ox-drawn carts hauling a load of cut bamboo. Given the slowed progress, it seemed the perfect time to replenish my dwindling supply of water and try to establish my exact whereabouts. Stopping to converse with a roadside vendor, I learned I'd inadvertently happened upon the first of the three temples at Roluos. Located literally a stone's throw from where I was standing, I strolled across the road to investigate. Mirroring my footsteps on the opposite side of a fence, a uniformed security guard muttered, "Ticket please," as we jointly arrived at the entrance gate.

"I need to buy one," I told him, reaching for my wallet. "How much is it?"

"You not have one?" the man said, with a slight hint of

irritation.

"No, I've just arrived, so I need to buy one."

"You cannot enter without ticket, sir."

"That's why I want to buy one," I repeated. "How much are they?"

"Twenty dollars for day, sir."

"Twenty dollars? For three temples? That can't be right," I insisted. "I only paid $40 for three days at Angkor Wat."

"You have ticket for Angkor Wat, sir ?"

"Yes," I acknowledged with a glimmer of hope. "But my ticket is back at the hotel"

"Angkor Wat ticket good for Roluos."

"That's great, but like I said, mine is back at my hotel," I told him, neglecting to mention it had expired the previous day.

"You must have ticket sir."

"Yes, I know. We've covered that already. Okay look. I can't go all the way back to the hotel in this heat, so how much is a ticket just for this temple... just for today?"

"Not possible, sir. You must buy ticket in Siem Reap."

"What?" I said, my wallet still at hand. "You mean I can't buy a ticket here?"

"No sir."

"That crazy... I mean that's crazy," I grumbled. "I've come all the way here to see these temples, and you're telling me I should have bought a ticket in Siem Reap. How the hell was I supposed to know that?"

"Sorry, sir, What is hell?"

Despite the urge to tell him it was where I currently found myself, I didn't take the bait. In hindsight I don't think it really would have mattered. With his folded arms and frown it was clear he had no intention of relenting. As a result, the pair of us simply stood there for a moment, stewing in a silent standoff.

"One question," I said finally. "If I can't buy a ticket here, why did you tell me one costs $20.00 for a day?"

"I want make you special deal. That price for three temples."

Convinced the money from any "special deal" was destined to end up in his pocket, I glanced over his shoulder at the ruin in question. As the site didn't appear to be particularly spellbinding, I settled for thanking him through gritted teeth and walked off to retrieve my bike.

As taxing as the encounter had been, the silver lining was that traffic had cleared in the interim. After a virtual free run up to the end of the road, I looped through a makeshift roundabout to follow a stone wall just high enough to block my view of what lay beyond. Curious as to what could be lurking on the other side, not long after I glided to a stop where the wall dipped low enough to reveal a glimpse of a river the colour of pea soup. A quick check of my map confirmed that the spire poking out of the forest on the opposite shore was in fact a part of Roluos' main temple, Bakong. Figuring my chances of gaining entry without a pre-ordained ticket were nil, I decided to at least shoot a photo of the temple from the wall. Doing so however, meant climbing up on a marvel of construction, whose red-stone blocks were fitted together so seamlessly, that even after a thousand years they offered little in the way of a foothold. Once on top, I crept along the narrow stones until I had an unobstructed view of the Mayan-like pyramid, its black steps rising up from a thick green mantle of vegetation to tower over the surrounding forest. From this new vantage point, I also caught sight of a colonial style building on the banks of what I'd originally taken to be a river, but could now see was a moat. Surrounded by palm trees and lush foliage, the building instantly conjured up images of some remote tropical outpost in deepest, darkest Africa, where ex-patriots named Nigel or Cecil, clad in khaki uniforms and pith helmets, sat on a terrace with frilly-frocked wives named Hillary or Beatrice, sipping their gin and tonics while being fanned by natives in white jackets. Needless to say, it was disappointing to later learn it was merely a monastery still in active use.

Rather than trying to bluff my way past the guard at the entrance bridge, I resorted to the tried and true strategy of touring a temple's perimeter. Once underway, it came as a bit of a surprise to discover that despite the fact there was no water anywhere to be seen, with the exception of the moat, many huts in the surrounding forest had been built on stilts. What I wasn't aware of at the time was that the ever-changing shores of Tonle Sap were only a few kilometres away. Leisurely cycling past one of the thatched-walled homes that offered only a ground floor existence, I spotted a young woman in black pyjamas, stoking the fire beneath a large steaming pot. A bored-looking teenage boy was watching her closely from a doorway, as two dogs lay sprawled under a bamboo table laden with various pots and cooking utensils. Hoping to snap a photo of the bucolic scene without being taken for the intruder I essentially was, I stopped a short distance away and pretended to focus on several neighbouring buildings. It was only when the woman briefly turned to look in another direction that I quickly took the shot and moved on. A little further up the path, a group of small children came running out from one of the huts to greet me with howls of "hello, hello, hello." I stopped to return the greeting, prompting a young girl about nine or ten, dressed in the familiar white and black school uniform, to step forward from the quartet and shyly offer me a small flower. Perhaps because I could not envision safely transporting it back to the hotel, I politely declined, a "faux pas" I instantly regretted. Hoping to assuage any feelings that may have been bruised by my refusal, I pointed to my camera and asked if it would be okay to shoot a picture. After mugging for the camera, the group seemed delighted when I showed each of them their own cropped faces. But the thrill proved to be short lived and within seconds of having viewed themselves, the entire troupe ran off in a burst of laughter.

Half an hour later, back at the moat bridge, I was digging out my map to consider my options, when I looked up to see a flock of young girls advancing towards me from a trio of kiosks across the road.

"A coke and a bit of advice," I announced before anyone could pepper me with offers. "That's all I need."

Emerging from a den of puzzled looks, one girl reached into the bag on her shoulder and withdrew a droplet-covered can. Holding it aloft in her small bronze hand, for a moment she looked like a miniature Statue of Liberty before setting it down on a nearby table where I had spread out my wrinkled map. Now that the temples were no longer part of the day's agenda, I was hoping to gain directions to the floating fishing village I'd seen briefly from the "speedboat." After posing the question to the young girl, I watched as her soiled finger traced a line across the printed terrain before arching up to point to an opening in the trees some fifty meters away.

"You must go that way," she said with a smile, accepting my money before running off to join her retreating friends.

What followed was a twenty-minute ride down a secluded trail teeming with plant life and the sounds of birds, insects and unseen animals. Eventually, the trail passed under an archway of tall trees fused together at their crowns, serving as the entranceway to a small village. As I soon discovered, it happened to be market day, complete with familiar kiosks, open-doored workshops and mobile food carts. Unfortunately, the setting for this bustling bazaar also included an enormous amount of trash strewn everywhere you looked. Especially plentiful on the banks of a small, muddy creek that divided the village in two, had it not been for the overpowering odour, one could have almost mistaken it for a perverse display of modern art. Luckily for me, a strong breeze was blowing in from the direction I wished to travel, so that by the time I reached the village's western limits, the air had more or less cleared.

"*Nah...there's no way. It can't be,*" I thought, having noticed the distant sound of rhythmic thumping that was piggybacking on the breeze. "*It's only early afternoon.*" But sure enough, as I rounded a sharp bend, there it was in high gear, with dozens of guests decked out in their Sunday best celebrating a wedding under a pair of colourful open-walled tents. As I approached, I could see people under the left tent waiting patiently in line to stack their plates with a broad assortment of foodstuffs. Those beneath the right one had remained seated, engulfed in clouds of cigarette smoke as they casually conversed to the accompaniment of a blasting soundtrack. Given that the road ran straight through the middle of the banquet, it was difficult to remain inconspicuous as I walked the bike past the milling herd. Barely had reached the midway point when a man, acting like a grade-school patrolman, stepped forward to block my way. Turning to what I assumed was the male contingent of the bridal party, he gestured them to move forward under a flower-bedecked archway displaying the names of the happy couple. My curiosity piqued, I moved to the far side of the tents and positioned myself several meters from where the bridegroom and his ushers, in matching pale-blue, rather ill-fitting suits, had assembled. Once the "patrolman," who turned out to be the official photographer, had succeeded in capturing his less than attentive subjects, their female counterparts were quietly ushered in. In regards to sartorial splendour, the women seemed to have fared considerably better than their male counterparts. All four bridesmaids were dressed in matching bright, yellowy- orange outfits, made up of an intricately brocaded satin. Perched atop each head of thick, dark hair, which showed signs of having been dipped in henna once too often, sat a small shiny tiara. Not wanting to be outdone by members of her own wedding party, the bride's two-piece garment was something to behold, looking as though it might have been designed by the same person who created Elvis' gold lamé stage outfit. Up to this point, I'd had no reason to think that my presence had ruffled any feathers. It was only when the bridal party had returned to the centre of celebrations that I happened to glance over to a small group to see them staring and pointing in my direction with what could only be described as less than welcoming looks. Not wishing to hang around to witness the repercussions of a shifting mood, I quickly reclaimed my bike and headed further west.

Most of the musical revelry had been lost to the continuing wind by the time I rounded another bend and found myself on a treeless plain stretching as far as the eye could see. Now at the full mercy of the blazing sun and uncertain as to whether the single lane dirt road was even the right route, I began to weigh the merits of venturing further. Pausing to re-check the map, I was in the midst of trying to determine my location, when a fast-approaching cloud of dust suddenly appeared on the horizon. Visible for at least a kilometre before it zoomed past, the tourist couple on board the speeding Tuk-Tuk appeared far too busy trying to maintain their occupancy to pay me any attention, let alone supply me with directions. Although logic suggested they were likely returning from the fishing village I was seeking, with no assurances and a nose-full of the featureless terrain, I was about to re-mount my scaldingly-hot saddle to head back when another cyclist rode out of nowhere. Loaded down with an impossible amount of kindling affixed to his rear fender, I watched as an elderly man wobbled past with barely enough momentum to stay upright. Mystified as to where he had come from and why I hadn't seen him coming days in advance, I dismissed the urge to have him confirm my location, for fear that the slightest interruption might send him and his lopsided cargo toppling into the ditch.

Having abandoned the search for the fishing village, the return trip was deceptively swift, slipping back through the wedding, past the reams of trash and alongside the moated temple in no time at all. On the go now for nearly eight hours, I thought it a good idea to stock up on some energy before subjecting myself to the kilometres of heavy traffic still ahead. Just before reaching the main highway, I eased down off the asphalt and coasted to a stop on a plateau of hardened sand directly across from the temple overseen by the adversarial ticket taker. With no wave of young salespeople waiting to greet me, I selected a beverage from a kiosk of my choice and wandered over to a small shop displaying leather goods on its patio. In no dire need of a hair clip, watch band, address book, decorative wall hanging or any other article with the outline of a gecko stencilled on its surface, I was browsing through the premises when I spotted a number of artisans near the back of the store. Busy cutting, hammering, stretching and of course stencilling leather with patterns of geckos, a good many looked no more than ten years of age. Having noticed me, one stopped work long enough to hold up a nearly completed toilet paper cover for my inspection. Adopting a friendly frown, I simply smiled and shook my head, before making good my exit.

That night I fell into bed utterly exhausted, reflecting on the spirit of simplicity so appealing about rural Cambodia, and asleep before the inevitable midnight concertos could commence.

Day Eight: Wednesday, February 9th.

I don't know why I even bothered looking at the forecast. It wasn't likely to be anything other than blisteringly hot. The air was already nudging towards sweltering when at breakfast, it dawned on me that I'd been in the country for a full week and had yet to give much thought to actualizing a half-baked plan to include Laos. With no firm items on the morning's agenda, the logical choice fell to visiting a tourist agency in Siem Reap. Three-quarters of an hour later, I was sitting on a saggy sofa, the back of my thighs sticking to the leatherette upholstery, as I absently flipped through a series of tattered magazines I could not decipher. Adding to the moment, a squeaky ceiling fan was straining its way through another erratic revolution when one of the three young agents finished with his customer and signalled me to approach.

"Am I just getting old, or does this guy look all of twelve?" I thought, as I sat down across from what to date had been that rarest of animals, a stern-faced Cambodian. Ardently tapping away at his keyboard before I had even uttered a word, it didn't take long to determine that getting to Laos could be an ordeal. Speaking in a perfunctory monotone, the agent informed me that two levels of prices existed for flights. My head was already starting to ache as he droned on about the logic behind the differences, but fortunately he picked up on my irritation and abandoned his speech long

enough to suggest an indirect flight via Thailand.

"When you want go?"

"Would fifteen minutes be okay?" I answered, rubbing my throbbing brow. "Doesn't matter, what's available?"

"Direct flight have seats but no does fly for day or two."

"What do you mean a day or two? Don't they know?"

A lengthy silence followed while the youngster focused on his computer screen, all but confirming that Laos was looking more and more like a future endeavour. Taking advantage of the fact I was there, I decided to ask about booking a bus to Kampong Thom, the best location, so I'd read, from which to explore the nearby pre-Angkorian temples of Sambor Prei Kuk.

"Sorry, you must speak with colleague," he said, pointing to a young woman two terminals further along. Not bothering to ask why *he* couldn't answer the question, I slid over, pleased to see she was at least smiling.

"So if I've understood you right," I began, while inspecting the sheet she had printed. "I have to pay the same price to get to Kampong Thom as I would to Phnom Penh, even though it's only half the distance? How does that work?"

Presumably having understood my query, she nodded without looking up from the screen.

"And?" I asked, when a moment had passed "Why is that?"

"Seat not booked Phnom Penh. You pay."

It took a moment to register that if no one else requested a ticket from Kampong Thom to the capital, I would have the dubious pleasure of paying for the entire trip.

"Okay, I get it. But what happens if I buy the ticket today, and between now and when I leave tomorrow, someone in Kampong Thom wants to go to Phnom Penh? Will I get a rebate?"

As the word "rebate" bounced off her glazed eyes into the stratosphere, I swallowed hard and handed over my credit card, fully convinced that a visit to a second agency would prove equally futile.

"Normal or deluxe?" she asked, typing again before I could answer.

"The difference?... besides price."

"Deluxe better."

"You don't say. How many dollars better?"

Throwing caution to the wind, I spent the extra dollar, hoping to be pleasantly surprised by what "deluxe" entitled me to.

"Can you at least make sure I get a seat up front if I'm paying for the deluxe ticket?" I asked. After another flurry of typing that could have rivalled translating the contents of War & Peace, she handed me a small piece of paper with a handwritten address.

"Excuse me, but what am I supposed to do with this?"

"You go here tomorrow. Get ticket."

"But why can't I get my ticket now? I just paid for it."

"Ticket tomorrow," was all she seemed capable of saying as she handed me another slip to sign.

"*Oh, oh...This does not bode well,*" I murmured, before thanking her and returning to the street. Eager to escape the city before my disposition soured any further, I rode off down a nondescript alley, intending to head for a temple not far from the Tonle Sap harbour. Not long after leaving the outskirts of Siem Reap behind, I abandoned the main road to follow a sandy trail into a small village.

Grateful for the intermittent patches of shade provided by the patterned shadows of overhead palms, I continued past huts, houses and villas sequestered behind bamboo fences or dense walls of vegetation. Occasionally, gaps would open up to reveal that I was paralleling a small river. River perhaps, is an exaggeration. The guidebook may have granted it such a status, but given a decent start, I could have leapt half-way across its murky waters in a single bound. Despite its meagre girth, living space along the waterway seemed to be in great demand. Dwellings built on high stilts were tightly wedged in along its shoreline, their laundry-draped porches jutting out over the brownish water. Beneath many of the porches, flat-bottomed gondolas tethered to wooden pilings, could be seen shifting lazily in the barely detectable current. As the path pulled away from the river, I decided it would be a good idea to take a break from the stifling heat before any wheezing set in. Stopping at a kiosk to enjoy a cold drink under a large, tattered umbrella, I also thought it an opportune time to read up about my intended destination.

Prasat Phnom Krom, a 9th century temple built atop the 140 metre mountain Phnom Krom, apparently consisted of three "spectacular" towers dedicated to the Hindu gods, Brahma, Shiva and Vishnu. According to the guidebook, despite having been exposed to the elements for eleven hundred years, the temple was in remarkably good condition. Although the accompanying photos made it look very appealing, it was less of a thrill to read that said towers were still another ten kilometres away. Having decided to ignore the guidebook's suggested route, which would have taken me back into traffic, I trusted my inner compass and set off on an unmarked route, on the assumption it would eventually lead me to today's nominal target. As was to be expected, the narrow lane was lined with a continuing series of small wooden huts. What came as a complete surprise however, was the sudden emergence of a large temple. Puzzled as to why a temple had been erected in such a location, I decided to stop and investigate. After locking my bike to a nearby tree, I was strolling through the park-like grounds, when a group of young boys dressed in brownish, purple robes, hurried past and entered the pillared temple. Wanting to know what these "mini-monks" were up to, I followed the group inside. As my eyes slowly adjusted to the darkened hall, I saw that the young monks had joined another group near the front of the temple to listen to a lecture being delivered by an older monk. Sticking close to the outer wall where a thin carpet muted my advance, I edged forward to take several photos of the brightly-coloured murals before retreating to the rear to enjoy a few minutes of the tranquil atmosphere. No sooner had I seated myself on the cold, marble floor, a member of the group rose up and headed over in my direction. Clasping his hands in greeting, he proceeded to politely request I not come closer than one meter to any monk in prayer. Suppressing, albeit with some difficulty, the instinctive urge to protest that I hadn't gone anywhere near the group, I chose to accept his dose of preventive medicine and assured him I had no intention of disrupting them any more than I may have already.

"Hello. Where you from?" I heard a voice say, as I crouched down to tighten my bootlaces on the outside steps. Shielding my eyes from the sun, I looked up to see an orange-rimmed silhouette hovering directly above.

"Canada?" he repeated with what sounded like practiced enthusiasm. "Ohhhhh, that very nice country. I like go there someday maybe. How long you stay in Cambodia?"

Suddenly, it was December 1986. I had just disembarked from a bus at the central market in Fez, Morocco and was about to collect my backpack from the under-carriage, when a young, self-proclaimed student stepped forward out of the crowd to ask if he could practice his English for what he assured me would be no cost. Despite repeated attempts to discourage him, he had followed me around the old market for nearly an hour only to act miffed when I later refused his request for a "donation."

"Three weeks," I told the young monk, before turning the tables.

"I here for five years."

"And how much longer will you stay?"

"Two years more."

"And then?"

"And then I am monk."

"What happens then?" I asked. "Will you be sent somewhere else?"

"That not up to me. Perhaps I stay here, perhaps I go other place to help people."

Despite genuine interest in learning more about what had inspired him to want to be a monk and what was required and expected of a full-fledged monk, his body language intimated that his own two questions had all but exhausted his interest in me. As a result, the young man simply bowed his head with clasped hands and quietly slipped into the temple before there was a chance to make further inquiries.

It took nearly an hour to traverse the long, steaming strip of asphalt that was my only option when the trail I'd been on abruptly ended. After striving to get past acres of scorched earth, dried up rice paddies, and a small village crammed with people and fume-spewing buses, I finally found myself at the bottom of a steep staircase carved into the base of Phnom Krom. Glancing up at what the guidebook claimed was the sole route to the "wondrous" temple, I was not elated at the idea of having to climb two hundred or more steps. Before tackling that daunting ascent, there was still the chore of finding a place to leave the bike where I could be relatively certain it would be there when I came back. It was during that search that I happened to come upon a woman washing her laundry by the side of a building. Dressed in a full-length sarong and waist coat, she seemed impervious to the magmatic heat, as I watched her methodically lift each article of clothing from a pile at her feet, rinse it under a rusted tap and toss the dripping garment into a plastic basket. Occasionally she would look up to audit two children chasing a half-inflated soccer ball back and forth across the garbage-strewn field, shooing them away with a hand full of water whenever their dust threatened to make her work in vain. Purposely dawdling as I locked my bike to a pole several yards away, I watched her balance the full basket on her head before taking the hand of the smallest child and walking off towards a row of distant huts, the other child following along close behind.

Back at the steps, I took a deep breath and started upwards, silently counting each step until reaching the decorative archway at the top. It was only when my heart had ceased pounding and the threat of nausea subsided, that I could begin to enjoy the view. Beyond a panorama of red and grey rooftops in the village, the terrain was a patchwork of varying hues of green. It was a remarkable display of colour given that everything I'd encountered in the last hour had looked as though it had been burned to a crisp by an unforgiving sun. Suddenly it came to me that the fickle Tonle Sap, only a mile or so down the road, was to blame, and what I was looking at was simply vestiges of last year's floods. By the time the last of my own water had found its way down my parched throat, I'd mustered as much resolve as I was ever going to, to begin the final slog to the still unseen temple. Fifty metres further on, the path merged with a paved road, suggesting there may have been a less strenuous way of reaching the temple after all. Just up ahead, a man in a lean-to stirred from his hammock.

"Ticket?" the uniformed gentleman asked, while I was still several meters away.

"Oh yeah, like this is what I need," I thought, observing his outstretched hand. *"Go ahead, tell me I should have bought a ticket in Siem Reap."*

"How much?" I asked.

"For temple $5.00," he said, his wrinkled palm remaining stationary.

Although not exorbitant by any means, somehow the mere mention of money, combined with the heat, approaching exhaustion, and a dash of temple overload, was enough to have me abandon my quest.

"Excuse me," I said a short while later, interrupting a trio of Cambodian women on the veranda of the store I'd come to seeking aid for my sun-burned arms. "Do any of you speak

English?"

Two of the women, each of whom was holding a wide-eyed infant on her lap, shook their heads in unison, while the third merely turned and bellowed for someone in the back. Following the clattering of sandals across the warped wooden floor, we were joined by a young girl.

"I take it you speak English?" I asked with a hopeful smile.

She nodded, as I grimaced and pointed to my reddened arms.

"I need some lotion. I have a long ride in front of me and as you can see, I need..."

I halted my dispersal of unnecessary details when her eyes darted to the adults for reassurance. But instead of waiting for them to confer their way through a series of pantomime gestures, I decided to snoop on my own, hoping to confirm that I'd come to the right place. The question was where to start, as every conceivable square inch of space was jammed with merchandise, some of which looked as though it hadn't been touched for years, if not decades. As I made my way through one section filled with beach balls, which struck me as rather odd, garden tools, and magazines, I spotted a small sprinkling of cosmetics. But before I could explore any further, the woman who had earlier bellowed for help, walked over to a cabinet of murky glass, opened it from behind, and removed a small yellow bottle with Chinese lettering on it. Realizing I couldn't read the label, she flipped it around to reveal a cartoon figure in the throes of a bad sunburn.

"Goot," she announced with a toothy smile as she handed it over for inspection. A familiar brand name would have been more reassuring, but I was desperate, especially given that this was the first sun lotion I'd ever heard splash when shaken.

"How much?" I asked, pulling out my wallet.

"One dollar," she replied, more a question than a statement.

Handing her an old, 5,000 Riel note a few days shy of disintegrating, I didn't wait for change before liberally dousing myself with what smelled like lighter fluid. Pleased at having at least rid myself of the burning sting, I proffered my thanks and rode away to yet another fading chorus of giggles.

Back at the resort, re-visiting the cavalcade of travel agents, vendors, monks and vistas, from under a cleansing, albeit painful shower, I emerged to discover it was only four p.m. Too whacked to consider another tour of the local surroundings, it seemed as good a time as any to check out the long-neglected pool. Save for a couple ensconced on a pair of lounge-chairs, both pool and patio were empty. Slipping noiselessly into the water so as not to awaken the slumbering male of the species, I began swimming slowly from end to end, occasionally breast-stroking away flotsam blown in from nearby trees and bushes. With no jabbering hotel guests, distant barking, or humming generators to disturb the tranquility, I was drifting along to the soundtrack of twittering birds and my rippling wake, when the recumbent gentleman suddenly started to snore. Taking her cue like some partner in a vaudevillian act, the woman gently set her book aside to deliver a staccato burst of high-pitched coughs. The choreographed display of snorting and hacking might have almost been comical had it not been so annoying.

Convinced that a loud Austrian yodel, or a well placed cannon-ball would do little to resolve the situation, I retreated to a distant chaise lounge, hoping to simply be out of earshot. But no sooner had I laid down and closed my eyes, a squawking English couple with extremities as white as feta cheese, tumbled in to join the cast. To make matters worse, after an initial survey of the dozen or so empty chairs scattered around the pool, they chose to occupy the two right next to me. Whether it was merely a stroke of bad luck, or karma for the misdeeds in a previous life, I had no choice but to accept defeat and return to the bungalow, dead certain that my sensitivity to noise was a curse I was destined to take to the grave.

Day Nine: Thursday, February 10th.

Not particularly bright-eyed, nor bushy-tailed early next morning, I was seated in yet another airless travel bureau, waiting for the predicted bus ticket fiasco to unfold. But despite all expectations to the contrary, it only took several well-placed glares to convince the new agent to forego the mistakes of her counterpart and produce a valid ticket in time to catch the seven-thirty bus to Kampong Thom.

To no great surprise, in spite of having requested and paid for a deluxe seat at the front, I climbed aboard to discover I'd been assigned one in the eighth row. Unwilling to fan the flames that had been narrowly averted in the office, I simply heaved a sigh, stored my knapsack at the rear and took my allotted place. Fortunately for all concerned, it was not as bad as envisioned. Not only was the seat beside me vacant, but so far back that the terrible music emanating from a tinny speaker above the driver was muted enough to bear. Once settled in, it dawned on me that the last time I had actually been on a bus was 1983; a thirty-one-hour marathon that had taken me from Winnipeg to Toronto, en route to Germany. Seeing as that trip had been made long before the advent on in-house videos, it was virgin territory when an overhead monitor flickered to life shortly after we hit the open road. I suppose I should have considered myself lucky when the first program up was an episode of Mr. Bean, for in spite of having seen it a dozen times, it was multiple notches higher in calibre than what came next. Having borrowed a tattered page from Japan's so-called funniest home videos, this program was about as deranged as you could possibly imagine, showing people in precarious situations that inevitably turned out bad for them, all with an underlying sound track of raucous laughter.

"Spare me," was all I could think of when it ended.

As if that hadn't been enough cruel and unusual punishment, the third program turned out to be a re-run of the old US series, Starsky and Hutch played with no sound, leaving viewers to read lips or guess at the thickening plot. Seeing as that was not an exercise I wished to partake in, I reverted to my favourite pastime of peering out at the passing scenery. But unless one happened to enjoy looking at mounds of garbage piled along the roadside, the panorama was not much of a diversion. Much more disturbing to witness was the number of unsupervised little kids playing in ill-advised proximity to the passing traffic. If there had been a pleasing feature to the two-hour journey, it was the lotus fields. I'd seen some from a distance on the trek to Phnom Krom, but here they ran right up to the edge of the road, offering an excellent view of the blossoms in various stages of development.

With no sprawling suburbs or industrial parks to warn of an impending city, Kampong Thom central bus terminal arrived with scant notice. Little more than a dusty parking lot, the "terminal" was located next door to a large concrete structure prominently billed as the KT Market. Keeping with tradition, I had barely set foot off the bus, when deluged by a drove of Tuk-Tuk drivers, each pushing the availability of a "top line" hotel. Knowing the one I'd booked the previous evening was too far to walk to, yet too close to part with a hefty fee, I asked one driver if he was familiar with the hotel. Nodding ferociously, he started dragging me towards his vehicle before we'd settled on a price.

"Hey, hang on a minute," I said, refusing to relinquish the belongings he so desperately wanted to stow in his carriage. "How much?" Feigning nonchalance for a moment, he briefly looked away before suggesting three dollars.

"Close... try again," I said. "It's less than a kilometre from here."

Several minutes later, and for half the quoted price, we were pulling up to a hotel entrance that overlooked the banks of the Stung Sen river. Once checked in and assigned a bungalow that was not only huge and clean, but also embarrassingly reasonable, I decided to take advantage of the good weather by accepting the hotel's offer of free bikes.

"*It must have something to do with Asians being so short,*" I griped, while wrestling to adjust the rusted seat of one of the hotel's contraptions for someone taller than four-foot-two. As the struggle continued, the first drops of sweat had begun to trickle down my forehead when I was distracted by shouts coming from the opposite side of the river. I looked up to see two teenagers in a flat-bottomed skiff, pushing off from a broad amphitheatre of sand into the toffee-coloured water. In what had to rate as one of the most authentic-looking jungle motifs seen to date, my attention remained riveted to the pair as they slowly poled their way downstream before ultimately disappearing around a bend in the river. With the bike's seat now as high as it was ever going to get without risking impalement, I headed off in the same direction, passing houses considerably more upscale from what I'd seen in other rural parts of the country. No more than five minutes from the hotel, the dwellings gave way to open countryside filled with brilliant green rice paddies. After being cooped up on the bus, it was a relief to be pedalling through a landscape with no domestic activity or traffic anywhere in sight. So pervasive was the silence, the tires of my bike could be heard scrunching the hardened sand. Not long after, as the road swerved away from the river to enter a thick forest, modest homes began appearing again. In what was now almost an expected event, it wasn't long before a band of laughing children stormed out of a yard, waving and shouting welcome to the passing novelty. Several kilometres on, the road rejoined the river spurring me to pull off on to a small plateau that offered an astonishing view back up the waterway. From this vantage point, the vertical drop from the upper edge of the embankment down to the water's edge, looked to be in the neighbourhood of eight to ten metres, making it appear as though a giant hoe had gouged out a long, jagged trough in the landscape. The sheer biblical amounts of water needed to fill that trough, made it clear why the distant houses had been built on stilts.

Back at the hotel that evening, I sauntered in for dinner on the balcony restaurant only to discover all the tables occupied. A quick scan landed on a couple at a table for four. As they didn't appear to be ax murderers in waiting, I asked if they would mind my joining them. It didn't take long to strike up a conversation. Both were from Sweden, the outskirts of Uppsala to be more precise, and as it happened, had spent the better part of their day visiting the very temple ruins I had come to visit.

"Sambor Prei Kuk is where I'm off to tomorrow" I told them, wincing at the first sip of what could have ranked as the world's worst mojito.

"You must go by car," Bjorn advised. A distinguished looking grey-haired gentleman in his early fifties, he went to inform me that the road was currently under construction. "Believe me, it is very dusty and bumpy. You would not enjoy going there in a Tuk-Tuk. You can try organizing a car through the hotel like we did."

"Thanks for the tip. The Tuk-Tuk driver who brought me here this morning was trying to sell me on the idea of going with him, but he never mentioned anything about a bad road."

"That's not surprising," Bjorn continued in studied English. "He wants your business of course."

"My problem is I'm here on my own, so a car could be kind of expensive."

I wouldn't have minded hearing more about their visit to the temple but a single glance at the body language Bjorn's wife was emitting, convinced me she at least, would prefer their dining alone. Just then the scraping of chairs announced that another table was being vacated, so I excused myself and moved to no objections.

That evening dinner received and deserved the same rating as the mojito. After skipping a nasty-looking dessert, I was on my way back to my bungalow when I decided to stop at reception to inquire about a car. Forced to wait for the receptionist to complete a call, I passed the time observing a half-dozen geckos glued to the office walls. So stock-still were the creatures, my first inclination was that they were fake, rubberized ornaments meant to decorate the blank wall space. Slowly inching forward while avoiding any sudden movement, I managed to get close enough to see the translucent, webbed cups on their feet, which explained how they were able to cling so casually to the vertical surface. The largest in the ensemble, approximately ten inches from nose to tail, was roosting above a cluttered filing cabinet, while the tiniest, no more than two inches long on a good day, was barely visible above the telephone jack. Given their close proximity, I suddenly felt the urge to stroke them. But the second I started to raise my hand, off they scurried at a speed that would have put Superman to shame.

"Thirty-five dollars seems a bit high," I replied, once my question about a car rental had been answered.

"You alone sir. Perhaps he do it for thirty."

Still considerably more than I wanted or intended to pay, I thanked her and exited with plans to seek my own transport in the morning. Listening to my sandals scrunch the loose gravel as I walked across the courtyard, I was looking forward to getting a good night's sleep free of any animal or insect concertos. But no sooner had I shut the door and pulled the heavy drapes closed, the sound of voices coming from the bathroom caused me to freeze. Remaining motionless for a moment, I could make out random words of a conversation between a man and a woman. My initial reaction was that the hotel had somehow managed to double-book the room, but that theory was quickly discarded after a look around revealed no unfamiliar luggage or possessions. Coughing loudly to indicate my presence and avoid being shot as a burglar, I opened the door to an empty bathroom. As the discussion continued unabated, I peered up through the dim light to see a rather sizeable gap between the top of the plastered wall and the wooden rafters of the tiled roof.

"Bloody hell, "I said out loud, thinking *"If that guy snores as loud as he talks, one of us is done for."*

What made the situation even more irritating was that I had taken time at check-in to recite my boring litany of requests for a quiet room. Kitchen fans, ice machines and connecting rooms had all been listed as negatives, but somehow I had neglected to mention gaps in bathroom walls. Fortunately, I simmered down on the jaunt back to reception, making it easier to accept the offer of moving me to another bungalow with an empty adjoining room. Moving me, however, did not mean helping me. It was a bit of a chore to gather up all my scattered belongings and schlep them across the courtyard in the dark, but I figured it well worth it if it was going to mean a quiet night. Or so I thought. Within minutes of having laid out my clothes, arranged my toiletries, and crawled into bed, a lone howl broke the silence. Seeing no point in cracking open a book, I released the mosquito netting suspended above the mattress, convinced that a dog, unlike a terminal snorer, would sooner or later give it a rest and we'd both get some much needed sleep.

Day Ten: Friday, February 11th.

It was just after eight a.m., when my Tuk-Tuk driver spotted me in the large crowd milling around outside the central market. I'd walked into town to see about arranging transportation to the temples, and after rejecting his assurances that the road in question was indeed "fine," had agreed to the hire of a private car and driver for a fee of $20.00. Within the hour, a tumbledown sedan was waiting outside the hotel entrance. Having become somewhat accustomed to Cambodia's youthful energy by now, I was not surprised to see that the driver looked all of fifteen, five times the number of English words he appeared to know.

Half an hour later, it was obvious I owed the Uppsalers, Uppsalites, or whatever they call themselves, a huge debt. The "fine" road cited by my Tuk-Tuk driver was actually an on-going disaster. The first twenty kilometres may have been paved, but often reduced to one lane by on-going construction. Especially disconcerting was that the warning signals and plastic barriers you'd normally expect to see in sections under repair, had been replaced with branches, making the idea of nighttime travel a particularly interesting prospect. Judging by the company logos on the menacing trucks passing us, China appeared to be a big player in road construction in the region. I'd heard rumblings about Chinese investment in Cambodia before, and word had it they were there to stay, a theory bolstered by the fact that nearly every road built, reportedly needed repairing within a few months of the end of the rainy season.

Shortly after leaving the main road, our pace picked up considerably, largely because we were the only vehicle in either direction, not such a bad thing considering the solid tube of dust trailing our car. Another advantage of the increased speed was less time spent shunning the mundane landscape, which may have been pleasing to the eye during the rainy season, but had since become a victim of a scorched-earth policy run amuck. Everything in sight was dry and brown, as if some gigantic magnifying glass had recently passed through, leaving a swath of lifeless devastation. Fifty minutes after leaving the hotel, we were rolling up to the entrance of the temple compound. My driver's English had remained pretty much an unknown quantity during the trip and continued to do so as he accepted money for the attendant in the gatehouse and gestured to a shaded area of the empty parking lot.

"I wait here."

"What? In the car?" I said. "But I have no idea how long I'm going to be here. Wouldn't you rather meet me back here in a few hours?"

Whether he had fully understood me or not, he was not about to be talked out of waiting in the car. The only tourist in sight as I turned away from the ticket booth, I was about to be declared open season by a group of uniformed guides, when a woman stepped out of the pack to introduce herself as Sodani.

"*Pleasant enough name,*" I thought, shaking her hand, "*Even if it does conjure up the image of a second-rate TV hypnotist.*" The name, however, was where any comparison ended, as Sodani quickly revealed her knowledge of Sambor Prei Kuk to be encyclopedic. For the next hour, as we traipsed along leaf-covered trails connecting the various sections the temple ruins, I was inundated with details of the Chenla empire under the reign of King Isanavarman. Regrettably, I couldn't appreciate her expertise as much as I would have liked, as something from last night's dinner was cramping my style in more ways than one. Luckily, back in the days when cars had chrome bumpers, I'd inadvertently learned that cola was capable of removing rust spots. Amazed that something I was regularly putting in my stomach could accomplish such a feat, the phenomenon had stuck with me over the years to the point where I'd gotten into the habit of bringing an emergency can along whenever venturing far from the beaten track. True to form, it wasn't long before the magic liquid had worked its wonders on whatever was still lurking in my abdomen. Although not altogether cured, I could at least now stand back in "relative" comfort, and listen to Sodani expound on yet another Sanscript inscription. Judging by the sheer scope and intensity of her presentation, it was clear she didn't get the chance to strut her stuff very often. Whereas an archaeologist or historian would have revelled in the nuanced information she could supply about the ruins, statues and ceremonies dedicated to Shiva, Vishnu, Rama, and Hari Rama, *I* was just glad not to be doubled over.

Careful to moderate my sigh of relief when she announced we'd reached the end of our tour, I invited Sodani to join me for a drink at the outdoor canteen. With my stomach finally acceding to demands to behave itself, there was a chance to ask some of the questions that had been accumulating during the tour. Eager to answer, she explained how Prasat Sambor, Prasat Yeay Peau, Prasat Tao and all the other names that hadn't fully registered the first time around, had been built as a tribute to Hinduism in the 6th and 7th centuries, making them a full two to three hundred years older than their counterparts at Angkor Wat.

"So why is it so empty here then?" I inquired, offering a sweeping papal wave to indicate the void.

"It too far from city. Many tourists don't come. We hope it get better."

Nodding in agreement, I didn't have the heart to tell her that unless aliens chose to land near Kampong Thom, or someone had a religious sighting nearby, equivalent to that of Fatima or Lourdes, things were unlikely to improve any time soon. Aside from the deterrent of the drive from Kampomg Thom, the lack of tourists could also be explained by the fact that once exposed to the marvels at Angkor Wat, most people would find the crumbling temples at Sambor Prei Kuk, a poor second cousin. Unlike the mysterious, labyrinthine edifices further north, many of these ruins were simply one-room, chimney-like towers rising as high as six stories. Wall panels, doorways, and chapel interiors may have been steeped in elaborate bas reliefs and inscriptions, but simply lacked the awe-inspiring grandeur of a Ta Prohm or Preah Khan.

"How many tours do you do on an average day?" I asked as our drinks arrived.

"In high season, maybe three."

"Three a day? That's not a lot eh? And when is high season?"

"Now." she answered, with a furrowed brow of

resignation.

Hoping to lighten the mood, I asked how Sambor Prei Kuk had come to be chosen as the site of a temple complex in the first place, when it seemed so far from a main artery, then or now. The answer was Ishanapura, an ancient city that had once been home to over 20,000 people.

"The ruins of Ishanapura are completely gone," she added. "That part of history no one can see."

"But why did they build Ishanapura here in the first place?"

"Mainly because of water," Sodani explained. "Here land is higher. It does not get flooded in rainy season."

Recalling the drive, it seemed inconceivable that any part of the region we had travelled through was significantly higher than the other. Sodani was in the midst of delivering another historical fact, when she stopped to briefly acknowledge a uniformed man walking past our table. Small in stature, with a wrinkle-free face and a head of thick black hair, what caught your attention about the man was the neatly folded shirt-sleeve fastened to his epaulette by a shiny metal clasp. Once he had moved out of earshot, I asked Sodani if that was her boss.

"Yes. He is park ranger."

Watching him out of the corner of my eye as he took a seat near and lit up a cigarette, the follow-up question was already in my throat when Sodani offered a clarification.

"Khmer Rouge cut it off," she said. "He not want to talk about it. It happen long time ago."

"I don't mean to pry Sodani but…"

"Excuse please. What means pry?"

Stuck for an answer, I told her it meant to ask questions

that maybe shouldn't be asked.

"I no understand."

"I wanted to ask you why so many Cambodians don't seem to want to talk about the Pol Pot period?"

"It bring back sad and bad memories. Old people don't like remember."

"You told me earlier that you're from a small town near here. What was it like living under the Khmer Rouge for people so far out in the country?"

Taking a long sip of her drink, she glanced over to make sure the ranger's attention was focused elsewhere before answering.

"Nearly every family in village lose somebody. My uncle killed by Khmer Rouge."

She seemed hesitant to continue and I didn't press, but after a minute or two of reflection, she continued. "My father was teacher. He interrogated by Khmer Rouge. They give him book, but my father smart. He hold book upside down. They suspicious but he convince them he can no read and they leave him alone."

"So the people who interrogated him weren't from your village?"

"No, they come from Phnom Penh. They bad people... But not all Khmer Rouge killers. Local leaders say they Khmer Rouge, but they also try help farmers. Khmer Rouge from village know life of farmer hard. They try help. Some bad, some not. More trouble when people come from outside."

"Higher officials you mean? From Phnom Penh?"

Having noticed that the ranger had stubbed out his cigarette and risen from his chair, Sodani stopped in mid-sentence, resuming her explanation only after he'd entered a nearby building.

"Not only Phnom Penh. Other places too. When they come, local Khmer Rouge people obey. When they go, same people help friends and neighbours again."

I still had many questions, but sensed Sodani felt she had talked more than she would have liked. Visibly relieved when I shifted the subject to current life in the village, she told me with detectable pride that she still lived at home with her parents and siblings, and worked at the park to help support them.

"Have you ever been outside of Cambodia?" I asked.

"No," she answered sheepishly.

"And if you had the chance? Where would you like to go? Canada? Germany?"

"Thailand," she said, breaking into a beaming smile.

"Thailand? Why Thailand? It's not a lot different there than here is it?"

She was about to explain the reasons for her choice when the air was pierced by a series of rapid, high-pitched screeches. Both of us looked over to see a group of small monkeys come racing across the courtyard and hop up on a table several feet from our own. We both watched in silence as the sad-faced primates artfully peeled open some sort of melon a waitress had left for them. Noticing their Spock-like ears twitch as they dined, I was somehow reminded that my driver was still waiting in the car.

There was a bit of an awkward lull in conversation as Sodani walked me to the parking lot. Having learned a little about her personal life, it was hard not to wonder whether she was happy here or if there was a longing to leave, muted by the knowledge she must remain for the sake of her family.

Not wanting to be maudlin, I was searching for something beyond a simple goodbye when she took hold of my arm.

"I forget show you Nagu," she said with a look of urgency.

"Nagu?"

Following her back across the compound, we climbed several steps to a bamboo porch where four young Cambodian women were busy weaving a straw-like material by hand.

"They members of Nagu," Sodani explained, before telling me Nagu was a non-profit organization established to train local women in trades that could help supplement their incomes. Examples of their work, including plates, cups, bowls and baskets of various sizes were on display on shelves along the back wall of the porch. All items showed a meticulous devotion to detail, but as much I would have liked to support the project, travel space limited my purchase to two small plates. Told the price, I was convinced Sodani had erred until she pointed to a handwritten number on the attached tag. The price seemed patently unfair in terms of the work involved, so I asked Sodani to have them consider the extra several dollars as a donation, a gesture that was met by a succession of clasped hands and smiles.

As the car pulled out of the parking lot, I looked back for a final wave goodbye, only to see Sodani had already turned away. Once underway, grateful there was no need for small talk with the driver, I had been deep in thought about Sodani's future, when the car braked sharply to avoid slamming into a slow-moving van in front of us. Forced to yield to a number of on-coming cars before we could pass, I was in the process of rolling up my window when the van unexpectedly pulled over to the side and five tourists proceeded to spill out and scramble down a shallow embankment. Twisting in my seat to see what they were up to, I caught sight of a dozen or more water buffalo immersed up to their necks in the muddied waters of an adjacent pond. Off in the distance, another group stood grazing on exposed patches of land, searching for what scarce nourishment they could find. After asking my driver to pull over, I walked back and positioned myself a meter or so above the water from where I had a clear shot of black, wet faces that looked like a series of bovine water lilies afloat in a sea of brown mercury.

Forty minutes after the meeting with the water buffalo, which the guidebook later informed me can actually be quite dangerous when irked, we were back in the bustle of Kampong Thom. Still early in the day, I asked to be dropped off at the central market. It was as I was climbing out of the car, that the man who'd arranged for the morning's transportation, broke off from a nearby group of Tuk-Tuk drivers and walked over.

"You like the temples? You need Tuk-Tuk? Go to hotel now?" he said in a single breath.

"No, not right now, maybe later."

"Where you want go? I give you cheap price."

With "cheap price" still ringing in my ears, I suddenly recalled a brochure I'd picked up at reception that morning.

"How much to take me to the silk farm south of here?" I asked.

"Ten dollars," he answered, in a manner I'd come to interpret as an opening shot across my bow.

"I'll give you eight if you first take me to the hotel so I can change. We can go from there."

Patiently awaiting his deliberation, feigned or not, my attention was aroused by the sight of a large feathered object cruising past on a motorbike. Presumably unable to afford other means of transport, the driver had taken to attaching a stack of fifty or more dead chickens to the seat behind him, giving him the appearance of a giant motorized peacock. As if that wasn't enough, another dozen former fowl had been arranged in a bouquet across his handlebars. Completing this bizarre picture was a poultry necklace of eight or nine specimens hanging from his neck.

"Okay. We have deal," I heard the driver say as the feathery mirage turned off and disappeared down a side road.

A hypnotizing whirlpool of wet dust was slowly draining into the basin, as I dried myself off, leaving a faint orange imprint on the damp towel. Grabbing a clean shirt and a fresh bottle of water before heading out, I couldn't resist a quick stop in at reception.

"Excuse me," I said, pointing to the brochure. "This silk farm. The Santuk silk farm. How much would it cost to take a Tuk-Tuk there?"

Shuffling through some papers for no apparent reason, the woman behind the desk looked up to tell me, "Twenty dollars."

"Twenty dollars? There and back?" I said with a tone of possible interest.

"That correct, sir."

Dying to tell her what the man waiting outside was charging, I let her off on the assumption she'd been told what to quote.

"I'll think about it," I mumbled as I shuffled off, freeing

her to get back to whatever she wasn't doing.

The trip to the farm was anything but inspiring, with the exception of the village of Kakaoh. Little more than two rows of houses paralleling each side of the highway for a few hundred meters, what made it so memorable was the assortment of masked men in every yard, hammering and chiseling away at blocks of stone, amidst clouds of white and sand-coloured powder. Although intrigued by the spectacle as we drove through, I held off asking the driver to stop, in the knowledge we would be returning via the same route. A few miles east of Kakaoh, we left the highway and continued for another half mile on a dirt road, before arriving in the front yard of a large farmhouse. Having read a little about the history of the farm on the ride out, I had been looking forward to touring the production facilities behind the elegant scarves they had advertised. Thus, it was no small letdown to discover the doors to the main showroom locked. Hopes of salvaging some sort of tour were briefly fanned when I heard muted laughter coming from a neighbouring glassed-in enclosure. With hands cupped to my eyes, I peered through the grimy window of what could have been mistaken for a greenhouse, to see several women lounging around a table. The look on the face of the one delegated to respond to my tapping suggested I was not a welcome interruption.

"Clozedd," she said, showing no intention of opening the locked door.

"I know, but can you tell me when you'll be open again? There's no sign with your hours anywhere."

"Owner no here. Phnom Penh," she answered, turning to go.

"Is it at least possible to buy something?" I asked, pointing to a table of scarves not far from where the others were watching with disinterest. "I've come all the way from Kampong Thom."

Following a short discussion with her colleagues, she reluctantly let me in.

"Owner back evening," she admonished, blocking any attempt to explore an area of the workshop where a number of wooden looms stood idle. Under her constant surveillance, I felt rushed to make a selection, which in the end was not such a bad thing. Had I not been faced with her impatience and scrutiny, I might have ended up exiting with far more than just two of the finest quality silk scarves I had yet to see anywhere.

Back on the outskirts of Kakaoh, I asked my driver to park so I could conduct an inspection of the wares and works-in-progress. Slowly working my way up the road, I couldn't help thinking that for souvenir-hungry tourists seeking locally-made products, you couldn't get much more local than this. First impressions were that both discerning and not-so discerning tastes were being well served, with dozens of Buddhas, lions and multi-headed creatures of varying sizes filling the canopied tables in each yard. Business however, was anything but brisk, not surprising considering we were in the middle of nowhere. In spite of the plentiful stock on display, there was nothing in the repertoire that came close to sparking my interest. Climbing back aboard the Tuk Tuk after I'd completed my circuit, I couldn't help wondering how these artisans subsisted. If the smaller carvings were slow movers, how likely was it that anyone would ever shell out for one of the two metre giant Buddhas that were being carved in a number of yards?

Had the silk farm been open, chances are we wouldn't have returned to Kampong Thom much before dusk. As it was, it was only 4:30 when we arrived back, prompting me to be let off at the central market again. It wasn't a matter of having been in a buying mood, especially for scarves or Buddhas, I was simply curious to compare the inner workings of a provincial market to those in Phnom Penh.

As I wandered in a side entrance, dreary was the first word that came to mind. I suspect that may have had something to do with the glaring lack of patronage. After all, Kampong Thom itself wasn't exactly overrun with tourists, and that dearth had simply been translated into low attendance at the market. The plus side was that I was able to move through the narrow, musty aisles pretty much unhindered. One might have thought that with so few customers, those present would have been prime targets. Instead, most of the vendors appeared listless, with anticipatory smiles and sales pitches replaced by silence and looks of solemn resignation.

"What must it be like being cooped up in one of these tiny booths day after day?" I thought, as I continued my tour. With most booths buried deep within the market's entrails, their occupants were virtually cut off from the light of day, all day, which no doubt affected morale. At least the Russian Market had an occasional skylight or two, that could provide a welcome glimpse of the outside world, even if it was through a greasy spattered window. Here everything was illuminated by row after row of dim, humming neon bulbs. Perhaps the most striking contrast between the KT market and the venues in the capital was the number of children working.

Youngsters who had clearly not yet reached their teens, could be seen tucked away in minuscule cubby-holes, toiling over antiquated, foot-powered sewing machines. Others sat huddled over poorly lit benches, tapping out decorative designs into jewelry and brass plates. I'd witnessed similar scenes in the souk in Morocco in the mid 1980's, but there younger labourers had for the most part been hidden from view.

Despite all its differences with Phnom Phen markets, there were commonalities to be found in the KT market. For example, in one grease-coated aisle, where my boots literally stuck to the painted floor, a gaggle of squealing teenage girls were busily painting each other's finger and toenails in all the glossy colours of the rainbow. Halfway down another corridor, several young women were gathered around a hairdresser's chair, chattering incessantly to a friend lost beneath a steaming towel and head of shampoo. Elsewhere a couple lingered above a glass vitrine full of jewelry, agonizing over a favoured bauble while a vendor patiently waited alongside. As had been the case in the Russian Market, the most hectic commerce was underway in the food section. Here customers heartily jostled with each other amidst reams of fruits, vegetables, meats and fish, some of which appeared so fresh, it was not uncommon to detect a last wobble of life as a transaction unfolded. Compared to other areas of the market, the mood here was buoyant, especially amongst merchants who'd sold out their wares and now lazed in hammocks suspended above empty platforms. One couldn't help but get caught up in the spirit of the moment, reversing the image of a community that seemed to be in a downward spiral, resigned to wiling away its hours, days, and lives.

I missed the Uppsalers sorely that night at dinner, at least the one who had talked. The absence of Bjorn and his wife, who had left that morning for sites unknown, was made even more pronounced when a group of Belgian and English cyclists invaded the hotel restaurant en masse. Clustered around three tables they had pushed together, they all but sealed themselves off from external conversation. With other couples also off in their own spheres, there seemed little hope of finding anyone to trade anecdotes with. Half-way through a meal that matched the standard of yesterday's, I left to return to the bungalow for what I hoped would be an evening of quiet reading. What I failed to take into account was the toll of the day's activities. Tucked in with good intentions, within three increasingly blurry pages, I was sound asleep.

Day Eleven: Saturday, February 12th.

I'd been sitting in a wobbly, plastic chair at curb-side for over twenty minutes, stewing over the belated arrival of my Tuk-Tuk driver and the suspicion I'd been had... again. But I only had myself to blame. Despite the near fiasco at the travel agent in Siem Reap, shortly after leaving the KT market the previous evening, I had cautiously agreed to purchase a bus ticket to Kampong Cham from a sidewalk kiosk recommended by my driver. I admit that the idea of shelling out money to someone whose "office" consisted of a two-wheeled cart and a pair of kitchen chairs had seemed somewhat dubious at the time, but the driver had insisted there was no reason to worry... that "everything was fine." Truth be told, there really wasn't any reason for fretting about the ticket or the tardiness. What with it only being a two hour ride to Kampong Cham, I was sure that the people from the "homestay" I'd reserved, would have told their driver to wait in case the bus was late, not an uncommon occurrence.

"Morning sir. Bus come soon," my grinning Tuk-Tuk driver announced after screeching to a halt directly in front of me.

"I certainly hope so, Ollie," I told him. "Any idea when it's supposed to get here? Yesterday you said something about eight o' clock."

Raising his hands in mock surrender, he cast an expectant

glance up the empty road.

"One other thing… Which type of bus is it? You know I don't want to travel on one of these," I said, pointing to a ripped poster pasted to the front of the "office." "I've heard some unpleasant things about them."

"Yah sir. That it," he answered with another broad smile.

"What do you mean that it? That's what I *don't* want."

"Bus come now sir. You bring backsack."

Before there was a chance to argue the point, he sped off to meet the vehicle that was approaching a crowd of people across the street.

Cambodian bureaucracy turned out to function much better in Kampong Thom than it had in Siem Reap. Within minutes of the bus's arrival, we were hurtling back down the same highway that had taken me to the silk farm. Although I'd booked a window seat, I took advantage of the empty space beside me to avoid the strong rays streaming in. Given the lack of scenery witnessed from the Tuk-Tuk the previous day, that wasn't exactly much of a sacrifice. In fact it was my familiarity with that considerably less than breathtaking landscape that had prompted me to come equipped with an MP3 player. Kakaoh came and went unnoticed while I was lost in a musical interlude, and it wasn't until we were a few kilometres past the turn off to the silk farm, that trees started to become more plentiful, eventually resembling a virtual army of soldiers at parade rest. Scouting around for some sort of signage, I heard a voice from somewhere in front of me, mumble something in German about a rubber tree plantation. But no sooner had that information been registered, the trees disappeared and the terrain opened up to expose fields with a high concentration of cattle. I wasn't sure if cows in Cambodia held the same revered status as they did in India, but these specimens certainly seemed to enjoy laying down on the job, looking like carefully arranged figurines in a 3-D storybook. A vague and mindless attempt at counting them ended abruptly when we entered another channel of foliage and palm trees, coinciding with a sudden and sharp reduction in our speed. Leaning into the aisle, I could see that our progress was being slowed by a smoke-belching truck. With on-coming traffic spaced timely enough to thwart several attempts at passing, when we did finally pull out, our sluggish pace allowed for a closer look at the tightly packed group of farmworkers standing in the open truck bed. Beeping his horn as a warning or a greeting as he passed, the driver's gesture prompted a flood of smiles and vigorous waves in response. Why the driver had even bothered to overtake at this point was a bit of a mystery, as several hundred yards on, he eased the bus off the pavement and rolled to a stop before a jumble of outdoor kiosks. As the engine shuddered and died, it was announced that passengers bound for Laos needed to disembark to await their connecting bus. For a brief moment, the idea of spontaneously altering my plans and heading for Laos pushed its way to the forefront, only to be deflated by the knowledge I'd already committed myself for three nights at the "home-stay" near Kampong Cham. Declining the offers of numerous mobile-melon vendors as I got out to stretch my legs, I decided to approach a young woman I'd noticed sitting several rows ahead of me.

"Excuse me, you're German aren't you?" I asked in German. Looking somewhat defensive, she nodded without speaking.

"What part of Germany are you from?" I continued.

"Frankfurt."

"Really?" I said, genuinely surprised. "Me too... well not actually Frankfurt, but not far. Between Hanau and Gelnhausen."

"I know them," she answered with a slight smile. "But I have not been there."

Although it had just begun, the small talk was about to stagnate when I thought of asking whether she was amongst those who would be switching buses.

"No, no," she answered. "My friend and I just returned from Laos a few days ago," an admission that caused her speech to become notably more animated.

"Have you been there?" she asked eagerly. "It is such a cool place. Much more peaceful and laid back than here. If you like Cambodia, you would love Laos."

"*More laid back than here?*" I thought, recalling how sedate some villages I'd visited had been. I was about to ask for more details concerning Laos when we were joined by her travel companion. With communication skills that seemed to consist of little more than suspicious, accusatory glances while sipping on a soft drink, there seemed no point in trying to break or fall through the ice with the second woman. But before I could continue my conversation with the first woman, a short toot of the bus' horn signalled our imminent departure. Side-stepping a raucous group of tiny, Cambodian kids flogging souvenirs, we all climbed back on board. Apparently mutually interested in continuing our discussion, once back on board, the first young woman switched to the row directly ahead of me so we could talk over the headrest. Travel remained the primary topic, laced with anecdotes of other countries she had recently been to. Although those mostly involved destinations in South East Asia, I was surprised to hear that Namibia and Mozambique had also been two of her recent favourites.

"You're kidding me. You have been to Namibia?" I echoed with envy.

In what has to rate as a case of exceedingly bad timing, just as we had scratched the surface of our mutual fascination with Namibia, the driver's squawking voice interrupted to announce we were about to arrive at the Kampong Cham station. With no stopover scheduled, it was a rush to extricate my knapsack from the pile at the rear, leaving no chance to exchange addresses or even names. After a quick swap of friendly smiles and a hint of mild regret, as I made my way to the front of the bus, we disappeared from each other's lives.

Imagined images of Namibia were still lingering as the Tuk-Tuk rattled over the bridge spanning the Mekong river. Settling in as much as anyone can "settle in," in a Tuk-Tuk, thoughts eventually turned to the prospect of spending the next three days in a bamboo hut without such amenities as electricity and running water. That scenario had sounded adventurous, even appealing back in Germany, a logical goal for anyone wishing to experience Cambodian rural life "up close." But now that I was less than ten kilometres from my destination, a level of uncertainty had begun to creep in.

A somewhat less exuberant welcome would have been fine. Commencing the second the Tuk-Tuk pulled into the driveway, the yelping continued non-stop all through my introduction to the "home stay's" manageress, Kannitha.

"This is getting off to a good start," I thought. *"Why doesn't she just tell this dog to knock it off?"* I asked myself, as Kannitha showed me to my hut and attempted to explain how the battery lamps functioned. Finally, with the dog's barking virtually incessant for a full ten minutes after she had departed, I felt compelled to say something.

"Nimol... quiet now," Kannitha belatedly ordered, as I approached her in the yard. "It will pass," she told me, scolding the dog with a stiff finger. "Not to worry. He always does this with new arrivals. Can I make you a pot of tea before lunch?"

Placated for the moment, I returned to the porch of my one-room hut, hoping to read up on the region I now found myself in. But as much as I wanted to focus, I was soon staring absent-mindedly out into a veil of lush greenery so dense my vision couldn't penetrate beyond three or four meters. In the midst of that limbo, I was suddenly aware of an audience.

"Hello, you," I said to a wide-eyed boy peeking around the corner of a stilt support below me. "What's your name?"

"Rith," he answered shyly, as an even younger sibling stepped out from behind him.

"And you?" I asked, setting aside my guidebook to give them my full attention.

"Nuon," she replied, coming forward to offer me a flower blossom.

"Thank you Nuon," I said, reaching down to take it. "Rith and Nuon. Sounds like a comedy team. I take it you're Kannitha's children?"

Nodding in unison, the pair swivelled nervously as their mother arrived with the promised pot of tea. Taking this as a signal, both of them jumped up on the porch and plopped themselves down in the two remaining chairs.

"I don't want you bothering our guest," Kannitha warned, as she filled my cup, "There will be plenty time for that when we go for our walk." Scooting them off towards the house with a winking smile, her tone turned more formal as she began to explain a walking tour that was part of the "home-stay package."

"If you like, we can start at three. It will only take us two hours, so we will be back in plenty of time for dinner."

"Sounds fine."

"I make us lunch now. We will eat in half an hour. I hope that is okay with you," she said, turning to make her way back to the house without waiting for an answer.

Kannitha, the children, and I had already taken our places under the roofed patio when a rust-spotted motor bike drove into the courtyard. On board was a tall man, whose greying temples placed him in his mid-sixties. He appeared to be wearing a grey blanket draped around his lower half, but as he dismounted, one could see that it was actually a loose fitting, ankle-length skirt. Stooping briefly to reproach a restless Nimol for an unseen crime, he then walked over to introduce himself.

"Nice to meet you," he said, extending his hand across the table while nodding "hello" to the children. "Name's Ron. I see you've arrived safely and met the family. I'm sure we'll have plenty of time to talk over the next couple of days, but if you'll excuse me, right now I should go and drop off these papers. Won't be long," he said before disappearing through the back door of the house, leaving me to continue making inquiries about Kannitha's background. Having already described herself as a multi-generational Cambodian, she explained how she and her English husband had first met while working for the same agency in Phnom Penh. Although she seemed prepared, almost eager to expand on her story, further discussion was prevented by Ron's return. Patently pre-occupied with other concerns, he took a seat at the table and maintained an awkward silence throughout much of the meal. With lunch finished, I thanked Kannitha and took my leave, hoping Rith and Nuon would not follow so I could grab a short nap before the walk.

It was just after three when the first leg of what would soon come to be known as my pleasurable disaster got underway. As had been pre-arranged, it was to be a group effort with Rith, Nuon and Nimol tagging along. Ron meanwhile, had returned to the village to ostensibly take care of some urgent business "online." Setting off from the rear of the property, the four of us followed the rock- strewn trail of a dried-out creek bed for several hundred metres before turning off on to a smaller footpath. Several minutes later we squeezed through an opening in a tangle of chest-high bushes to enter an unexpected world of rich and brilliant greens.

"This is the winter rice crop," Kannitha explained, as we edged our way along a narrow, mud dike that separated two large rectangular ponds. The water in each appeared to be no more than a foot or so deep, but I nonetheless treaded warily, in no mood to be saddled with wet boots for the rest of the tour. Not nearly as efficient as the more practiced walkers, it wasn't long before a significant gap had opened up between us.

"The dikes are not solid," Kannitha called back with a grin, pausing to let me catch up. "In the rainy season the high water washes them away and they must be re-built each year."

"That must be an incredible amount of work," I said, wiping away sweat from my brow with my forearm. "Do the farmers at least own their own fields?"

The question must have hit a nerve, as for the next ten minutes, Kannitha offered a detailed description of how the farm system functioned. much of which I instantly forgot. Meanwhile, the children continued to race up and down the intersecting dikes, oblivious to minor miscalculations that occasionally sent them tumbling into the warm, muddy water. More aware of their activity than she let on, Kannitha merely called out to them to be mindful of the plants. As we continued on, the rice paddies eventually tapered off, to be replaced by flooded fields filled with the broad, green leaves and pink and white blossoms of lotus plants in various stages of development. In contrast to the relatively compact rice plots we'd just come through, these fields were enormous, stretching all the way back to a hazy bank of trees along the horizon. Rising up from this watery plain were numerous small wooden platforms, which Kannitha said served as accommodation for workers during the growing season. Having said that, she then pointed to several people labouring in a nearby field. All were dressed in what looked to be heavy garments, acting as if they were in the midst of a cold snap despite the thirty degree temperature. As our route took us directly alongside, Kannitha stopped to chat to one woman kneeling in the water as she worked. Clad in a long-sleeved shirt that was soaked right up to her chest, she looked as though she'd been deliberately dipped in a pot of brown paint, when she stood up to change position. Masking her face was a red bandana, held in place by the cinch of a wide-brimmed hat that protected her head from the sun. Virtually motionless as she spoke, it struck me that she could have easily be mistaken for a scarecrow. Unable to understand a word of their conversation, I left the two women to their discussion, navigating my way down a more solid path in hopes of gaining a closer look at one of the platforms. Beyond a thatched roof, a floor of wooden planks and makeshift walls of stretched plastic sacks advertising the products they once held, there wasn't much to see. Vacant for the moment, the only signs of habitation in this model were a pair of straw mats and several cooking utensils.

"We go to my parents' field now," Kannitha suddenly announced, having crept up behind me while I was snapping a round of photos.

Underway once again, I purposely let some distance develop between myself and the on-going chatter between mother and children. With the trio still in sight but their voices gradually fading, I stopped to enjoy the moment, increasingly off in my own little world. Standing there, beneath a solid blue sky bleached white by the time it met the horizon, I glanced back to see the workers silhouetted against a shimmering heat, rising and falling like stringless marionettes as they continued their harvesting. With all of my senses on high alert, I couldn't help noticing how devoid the air was of any scent, with the only sound coming from the pulsating flap of the walls of a nearby platform as gusts of wind struggled to free the sacks from their moorings.

Thoroughly immersed in the moment, I tried to imagine what my current location would be like under a nighttime sky, undisturbed by artificial light and stars at arm's length.

It was a faint yell that pulled me back from the edge of oblivion and I looked up to see a tiny arm beckoning me to follow. As I rejoined the waiting troupe, I felt the urge to share my thoughts.

"I can't tell you how much I'm enjoying this, Kannitha," I confessed, watching a slight frown form. "This is why I came back to Cambodia. Most of what I got to see on my first trip was through a van window or a camera lens. I wanted to experience rural life up close and this... I mean... how much closer can you get to it than this?"

My little sermon finished, I noticed that Kannitha hadn't really been listening, distracted by the children who were cavorting on an adjacent pathway. It didn't really matter. It was my dream and I was there living it. A witness was not necessary.

Tramping off in the direction the sun indicated was south, we passed through another series of rice fields before entering a forested area where the path widened enough to let us walk parallel. Kannitha decided it was a good opportunity to inform me how her parents had come to align their fate with lotus blossoms.

"They had rice fields for many years and could make a good living, but the price of rice has gone down. There's too much on the market, so last year they decided to switch to lotus blossoms."

The uneasy tone with which this was revealed, prompted me to ask if she thought it had been a good decision.

"It is too soon to tell. Their first harvest will start in

several weeks. The problem is... what I worry about, is that many other people from the village also made the same move."

"So you think they'll be a glut on the market?"

"Glut? I don't know this word."

"Too many blossoms on the market at the same time."

"Yes. That is my worry. Then the price goes down."

Shortly thereafter, we'd arrived at her parents' field. Here the raised dikes seemed even more precarious, making me feel like a high-wire artist as I followed the trio along the dissecting ridges towards the parental platform. Finding it empty, Kannitha pulled two straw mats from the floor and laid them out on a rare patch of ground for us to sit on.

"Would you like some water," she asked, lifting the lid on a smaller version of the orange coolers I'd seen all across the country. Despite the fact we seemed miles from any source of ice, the water was welcomingly cold.

"Do your parents sell their blossoms at the local market?"

"They do not sell the blossoms. They sell the seeds," she corrected, turning towards her daughter who had just waded into one of the ponds.

"Nuon... Bring Mama some pods," she said, before shifting back to me. "They sell through a sales... agent I think you say in English. He comes to inspect the seeds and gives them a price."

"It sounds pretty risky, if this agent can set the price as he sees fit."

"He sets his price by how much he thinks he can sell them for. If the end customer won't pay the price he asks, he will pay less to my parents."

Just at that moment, one of the parents emerged from a

clump of bushes at the far end of the field. After a brief introduction, Kannitha's mother's attention quickly focused on her daughter. No longer part of the discussion, I could observe the woman without appearing to gawk. Looking nowhere near the sixty-four years Kannitha had given her, she possessed none of the facial wrinkles most people her age were used to disguising. Had I not already known of another of the "home-stay's" features; that being the opportunity to meet and query local residents on any subject of interest, the urge to bombard her with a thousand questions then and there would have been irresistible. Such eagerness was placated by the fact that when making my reservation, I had asked if it would be possible to speak with someone about life under the Pol Pot regime. Prior to my arrival, Kannitha had arranged for her mother to join us for dinner. In the middle of the current conversation, Nuon ran up panting, with the requested lotus pods clutched in her wet hands.

"They work in the fields every day, weeding and picking ripe seeds which they dry in the sun," Kannitha said to me, when her mother moved off to putter around the platform.

"These are the seeds," she explained, popping open a light green pod the size of a fist and pointing to the small black dots that blanketed the flat inner surface.

"Try one," she urged.

"What do you mean try one?" I asked, accepting the small cream-coloured bulb she had extracted. "Do you mean eat it? It looks like some sort of fat Mexican jumping bean."

Nuon giggled at my hesitation, before provocatively tossing several bulbs into her own mouth. Wry smiles passed between the generations as I cautiously probed the bulb with my tongue before biting down.

"It tastes like some kind of nut," I said with relief.

"Lotus flowers need very much water," Kannitha continued. "There is water here, but it must be pumped from the well to the fields and electricity for the pump is very expensive. Rice can go without water for a short while, but not the lotus. A day or two without it and they will die."

"So your parents stay here during the season?" I asked, gesturing towards the platform.

"My father stays each night but my mother goes home. It's only one or two kilometres to the village from here. Sometimes she stays with him. If not, she brings food and ice the next morning."

The notion of living under such spartan conditions for any length of time seemed incomprehensible to me and I could only stare at the wooden domicile while Kannitha continued my education.

"They will work here until they no longer can," she said with no hint of melancholy. "Maybe it will change in the future but right now there is no social network to speak of for farmers, and no pension plan unless you work for the government. So she will probably work until she drops or is too ill. Then she will stay at home. My sister and I will take care of her, and take over her work in the fields."

I was still trying to grasp the reality of such a lifestyle when a loud popping sound brought me back to earth. I looked over just in time to see Nuon banging a second seed against her forehead.

"It's what children do with the empty seeds," Kannitha said with a laugh, mimicking Nuon's actions with a loud pop of her own.

With the sun starting to sink behind the trees, Kannitha's mother indicated her desire to resume working. Parting with clasped hands and a nod, we headed off back along the dike, promising to meet again at seven.

Hot and sticky after almost three hours on the trail, meant a shower and fresh change of clothes were mandatory before dinner. Normally such tasks do not require a great deal of concentration or stamina, but they take on a different light, so to speak, when you are forced to search for a clean shirt, pants and underwear under three watts of light emitted by the hut's battery lamp. The second challenge facing me that afternoon surfaced when I opened the door to the bamboo "bathing" hut, to discover there was no shower head, no hose, no basin and no tap. The "shower" I was hoping for sat in a large red plastic barrel in the corner. Half-expecting to see an array of exotic insects scramble to safety when I raised the lid, I was relieved when all I was met with was a solitary wooden bowl bobbing on the dark surface. *"No running water really does mean no running water,"* I thought, as I cast a second cursory glance around the room to make sure I hadn't somehow overlooked something.

"Refreshing," I kept repeating, as I scooped up bowl after bowl of coolish water, shivering with each splash until done. Towelling off quickly in the fresh evening air, I decided it prudent to take care of another necessity before the fading light made it all the more difficult. The receptacle itself looked pretty standard. It was only on closer inspection that I noticed there was no flush mechanism, merely another lidded barrel of water, this one blue, with a small sign requesting that toilet paper be deposited in the adjacent

closed yellow container.

Twenty minutes after duties had been completed and remnants of the day were dissolving into darkness, I followed the feeble beam of my flashlight across the crunchy yard to the patio to find my moccasins coated with small sticky seeds of unknown origin. Taking a seat under a swaying lamp whose powers of illumination barely allowed me to see the empty plate in front of me, let alone the other side of the table, I was in the midst of imagining life with no electricity when Kannitha emerged like a ghostly miner, guided by an LED lamp attached to her forehead. Seconds later, Ron followed, using his own headgear to help assist Kannitha's mother to her chair. As difficult as they were to see, the table settings indicated the children would not be joining us for what looked to be cooked noodles and vegetables.

"How was the walk?" Ron asked, handing me a can of cold beer as Kannitha dished out the meal.

"Amazing," I answered, hoping for a glass or a napkin. When neither was forthcoming, I surreptitiously used the edge of my shirt to remove any dust or unwanted residue any inconsiderate dogs or rodents may have left on the rim of the can. "And very informative. I learned a lot about rice fields and lotus blossoms that I never knew."

"That will no doubt come in handy back in Germany," Ron quipped, before sitting down.

The remark ended up being the sum total of Ron's conversation during the course of the meal. As it was, it already felt strange to be conversing in almost non-existent light, unable to see how your comments were being received. As a result, much of the meal was passed in silence. It was only after Kannitha and her mother cleared away the dishes and disappeared into the house that Ron moved to the fore.

"So you're from Canada but you live in Germany," he asked, dispensing a second beer without asking. "I spent time there in the 60's. Part of the army. Went back to England after I got out, but we're talking a long time ago."

"How long since you've been back?"

"To England? Oh, it's gotta be fourteen or fifteen years."

"That beats my record. The longest I've been away from Canada at any stretch is four years. Are there things you miss, even after such a long time?"

"Don't miss a thing," he answered straight away. "Except maybe being able to speak your mind."

"I'm not sure what you mean," I said, halting my beer midway in an arc I hoped would end in my mouth.

"Exactly what I said. Free to speak your own mind. Things are a lot different here in case you haven't noticed. You're not well looked on if you criticize the government, especially if you're a foreigner. Say the wrong thing to the wrong person and you'll end up on somebody's watch list."

"Are you serious?"

"Believe me, I wish I wasn't, but that's the way it is. It's not so bad in the cities, but out here on the land, or in a small village, you can't complain about anything without getting into some sort of trouble."

Sensing I was about to be dragged down a venue of lengthy tirades, I attempted to steer the conversation in another direction.

"You know, talking about different cultures, I can remember when I first moved to Germany, it took quite awhile to adjust to all the weird customs. Having to register with the police everywhere you live, for example. That was a hard one to swallow. I also found it tough to develop meaningful, lasting friendships. My limited German had a lot to do with that, but even later when my language skills improved, it still wasn't easy."

Pausing to reflect on my own comments and take another sip of beer, I asked Ron how long it had taken him to gain Cambodian friends. A grunt, followed by a lengthy silence, suggested it was not a question he relished or planned to answer. Just at that moment we were rejoined at the table by Kannitha and her mother.

"May I ask why you have come to Cambodia alone?" Kannitha asked, once they were both seated.

"Short version or long version?" I replied, waiting for a laugh that didn't come. "Basically because my partner couldn't get away at short notice. I'd like to come back with her to experience the rainy season, but the chances are probably pretty slim because she's not big on heat... How long have you two been married?"

Although the question had been directed at Kannitha, Ron made his disinterest in the subject palpable, pushing back from the table and walking off in the direction of the house without uttering a word.

"Fourteen years," Kannitha answered when he was out of earshot. A twinge of nostalgia was detectable in her voice as she went on to describe the lifestyle she'd been living in Phnom Penh before they met.

"Being so independent was something out of the ordinary for a Cambodian woman at that time. I was twenty-nine when I met Ron. In this country that is ancient when it comes to getting married. Things did not always go smoothly for us, especially when we were in Phnom Penh."

Although I was listening to her story, a part of me kept wondering why Ron had suddenly made himself scarce.

"After we married and I became pregnant," she continued, "there were situations where we would be walking down the street and some people would make nasty comments about my state."

"I'm not sure I know what you mean by 'your state'."

"Comments that I was married to a foreigner and pregnant."

"They would call you names? Ron doesn't strike me as the kind of guy who would take kindly to that kind of thing."

"At the time he didn't speak Khmer so he didn't know what they were saying, and I didn't tell him because I thought it would cause a bad reaction in him."

"What kinds of things were they saying? "

"In Khmer we have two words for pregnancy. One is for humans and one is for animals. The people on the street used the last one."

It was next to impossible to discern the expression on Kannitha's face in the dim light, but her tone was telling. Left speechless by her comment, all I could do was shake my head, thinking that some Cambodians had a lot to learn about basic decency. During the brief interlude, the faint sound of music could be heard off in the distance.

"Speaking of weddings," I remarked, hoping to ease things towards a more positive note.

"Yes, as you can tell, you will hear one tonight." Kannitha said with a small chuckle, extending an arm in the direction of the music.

"It's alright. I know all about them already. I had more than my share of them when I was in Battambang."

Spurred by that memory, I asked why it was people felt obliged to conduct such rituals as renting huge tents and playing loud music, night and day.

"The size of the tent and the music is a status thing," she explained. "The bride's family is responsible for the wedding costs. The groom's family gives the bride's family a dowry when the wedding is agreed upon, and a part of that money is used to pay for the wedding. Sometimes there is money left over and sometimes not."

"What do you mean agreed upon?"

"When two families agree upon the terms of the wedding."

"You mean the wedding is arranged through the families?" I asked with genuine surprise.

"Yes. That's quite normal. Fifty percent of marriages in Cambodia are arranged marriages. A girl can refuse twice, but on the third time she must agree."

"Or?"

"She must agree," Kannitha emphasized, acting as if the question was academic.

"Wow. That's really... I didn't realize that still happened here."

"My parents' marriage was arranged between the two families but she was lucky. Over time she learned to love my father. She was nineteen when they married and even that was old, so imagine what they thought of me at twenty-nine. I was almost a lost cause. Today, it is not unheard of for a girl to marry at fifteen."

Kannitha left me to digest such a scenario, turning to address her mother who'd been sitting quietly at her side the entire time.

"My mother will talk with you now," she disclosed after they had exchanged a few sentences. "What would you like to ask her?"

"I guess I'd like to ask how life was for residents in this area under Pol Pot and the Khmer Rouge."

Kannitha was in the middle of translating my question, when Ron lumbered back to the table carrying another round of beers.

"My mother says King Sihanouk was the favourite of rural people," Kannitha began, after her mother had completed a lengthy answer. "Times were good. People could farm, make money and enjoy life. Then King Sihanouk became too friendly with the Communists. General Lol Nol took over, war started and things got worse. The Khmer Rouge promised to fight Lon Nol and restore King Sihanouk to the throne so many people supported them. The problem was it was a lie. Even Sihanouk believed it for awhile, encouraging people to support the Khmer Rouge because he thought it would lead to his return. Then came the American bombs during the Vietnam war and many people were killed. The Khmer Rouge took over parts of the country, but by 1972 the people realized they had been tricked, but it was too late. The Khmer Rouge took over in 1975 and things became even worse. Many people starved or were killed by the Khmer Rouge."

Added to what Sodani had described of her own village, this latest glimpse of personal history kept me riveted to my seat for the next twenty minutes. Her story however, created as many questions as answers, so it came as a big disappointment when in the midst of refining my next question, Kannitha interrupted the flow to announce her mother had to leave because of the hour. Grateful that she had shared her experiences so openly, I slipped a folded ten-dollar bill into her hand, accompanied by a smile and several heartfelt "Okuns." It didn't go unnoticed, at least by me, when Ron, who'd been standing off to the side during our discussion, made no attempt to bid his mother-in-law "adieu."

Kannitha chose not to return to the patio after accompanying her mother to the main road, providing an opportunity to find a comfortable, common denominator with Ron. It's fair to say that neither of us found it easy going, but aided by yet another beer, Ron began to open up about the route that had brought him to Cambodia. The trail had started in Indonesia where after getting out of the army, he had gone to work as an engineer. At the expiration of his contract, he had accepted similar work in several other Asian countries before ultimately landing in Phnom Phen. Throughout the variety of topics covered, there seemed to be a strong degree of frustration and anger just below the surface, especially whenever the subject of the village government was touched upon. But even the fiery responses he had towards local politics seemed muted in comparison to what he had to say about his own family background.

"My mother was bigoted, plain and simple," he fumed. "I only talk to her once or twice a year. Not much point... You want to know what she said to me once?" he asked, clearly not expecting or wanting a reply. "She told me she felt sorry for my kids. Can you believe that? Said she felt sorry for them cause they weren't English, and they weren't Cambodian. What can you say to that?"

The question hung in the air for a moment, kept aloft by

his simmering bitterness.

"In the beginning it wasn't always easy with Kannitha's family either," he added. "It took awhile. They didn't jump for joy at the news their daughter was marrying a non-Cambodian, but they came around... especially when Rith and Nuon arrived on the scene. So if you ask me again what I miss about England, I can tell you one thing. It's definitely not my mother."

With that statement, the evening ground to an end. Downing the last drops of his beer, Ron pulled himself up from the table with a loud grunt before basket-balling his empty can into a large cement tank already half full of empties. Brusquely wishing me a good night's sleep, he shuffled off into the dark leaving me to reflect on the day's events. It was hard to believe that it was still the same day that had started off curb-side in Kampong Thom. But despite a motherlode of anecdotes to ponder, thoughts kept circling back to Ron's diatribe. Having only known him for a few hours, it seemed unfair to offer a strong critique. Nonetheless, I couldn't help feeling that the streak of curmudgeonliness, as well as an aspect of arrogance were simply part and parcel of who he was, exacerbated by his current circumstances.

A half hour later, with the mosquito netting as secure as it was ever going to be, thoughts turned to my current circumstances. More primitive than either of its predecessors in Siem Reap or Kampong Thom, the bamboo bungalow had also come with a sense of vulnerability; as if some inaudible frequency in the universe had carried the message to all creatures large and small, that a new resident was now available for abuse at the "home-stay." Such, at least, was my state of mind when a light breeze started up, bringing with it the muffled strains of not-so-distant wedding guests hitting their stride. In between the snippets of white noise, which kept switching from sharp to muddled on the shifting wind, I could hear Nimol scratching at something out on my porch. Too lazy to unseal my carefully arranged cocoon and shoo the bothersome animal away, I rationalized that as long as he was there, other potential intruders would feel disinclined to probe for entry.

At some point during the night, sounds from the wedding party ceased. It was only the howl of a lone dog, echoing off the walls of the bungalow, that kept me from taking full advantage of the silence. But when my luminous dial of my clock confirmed the yelping had been going on for a full half hour, I reluctantly pulled myself free of the netting and fumbled my way across the room. What I hoped to accomplish in this groggy state was unclear, but whatever it was, it flickered and died as rapidly as the lamp battery. Half-way back to bed, I realized that the light wasn't the only thing that had vanished. Convinced the silence was only a lull, I sat on the side of the bed for a few minutes, waiting for a bellowing that didn't resume.

"Now what?" I groaned, after being woken up out of a much-needed slumber an hour later. "*It sounds like someone is using a bloody pneumatic drill,*" I thought in disbelief. "*But who changes tires at four-thirty in the morning?*

When attempts to push the rattling out of my mind proved impossible, I again briefly debated the sense of stumbling through the darkness to investigate. Just as I was about to make my move, the racket suddenly stopped. Laying there in the darkness, it struck me that if there was one thing I'd learned about Cambodian nights so far, it was that silence couldn't be trusted. Sure enough, less than a dozen sighs later, a single bark cut through the renewed calm, followed by another, and another. Waiting for a sleep I suspected would never come, all I could think of was what I had done to deserve such a paragon of bad karma.

Day Twelve: Sunday, February 13th.

In spite of the wedding, the dogs and the insomnia-plagued mechanic, I somehow survived the night to end all nights, albeit not unscathed. Mentally and physically drained by the ordeal, the only thing that had kept me sane was the firm conviction I would be leaving right after breakfast. Up before the first slivers of light had started to penetrate the walls of the hut, I dressed, packed and sat on the porch in the cool morning air, wondering when it would be safe to approach the house. What little luck fortune was prepared to grant me that morning, showed itself when I looked across the courtyard a little before six to see Kannitha setting the table. Struggling to keep my frustration in check while walking over to the house, I was about to step up on to the patio when Nimol lunged out of his hideaway and nipped my leg just above the boot. Although it was not a serious wound, it somehow seemed a fitting end to a less than perfect stay. I was still inspecting the reddening mark when Ron emerged from the house with a pitcher of fresh orange juice.

"I'm afraid your dog just bit me," I announced.

"You're kidding," he said. "No blood is there?"

"None that I can see," I answered, waving off further discussion to take my seat at the table. Figuring there was no sense in wasting time, I broached the subject of last night's torment.

"I have to apologize," Ron interrupted. "It's not always

like that around here. We didn't sleep well either."

Relieved to find him empathetic, I felt free to expound.

"I could handle the wedding. I got used to them in Battambang. Even the dogs were tolerable. But what really broke me was the drill. It felt like it was boring right through the back of my head. I mean, what was that all about? Who fixes cars at four in the morning?"

Ron and Kannitha, who had joined us with a pot of tea, exchanged glances before the task of explaining fell to Ron.

"There's a bit of a problem with the village chief," he began tentatively, speaking in a tone I had not heard before. "He lives right across the main road. He owns a twenty-four-hour auto repair shop and sometimes they like to start early."

"A twenty-four-hour garage? They don't even have those in Europe. What's the rationale behind that? There's not exactly a surplus of cars around here. Haven't you complained?"

"Oh yes," Kannitha inserted. "Often... and he knows we have lost customers because of his noise. But he doesn't care. He is chief of the village and he can do what he wants".

"So in other words, one inconsiderate neighbour can ruin the quiet existence for everybody without fear of consequences, if he happens to be the village chief?"

"I'd say that's pretty accurate," Ron nodded, blowing on his steaming cup.

"So then, the natural question is how does one get to be village chief? Better yet, how does one remain one if so obnoxious?"

"Welcome to Cambodia son," Ron sighed. "Welcome to Cambodia."

"He's appointed by the ruling party," Kannitha

continued, hoping to curb Ron's cynicism.

"Members of which just happen to live far enough away not to be disturbed by his antics?" I suggested.

"You're learning lad, you're learning," Ron snorted, refilling my glass with orange juice before ceding the floor to Kannitha.

"We tried to have something done but so far it has been useless."

"God, I wouldn't last a week here," I told them, inadvertently creating the perfect segue to my intention to leave. "You know, I hope you won't take this personally, but with all that went on last night, I literally couldn't take another episode without losing it. I'm sorry, but I'll be leaving after breakfast."

Getting no discernible reaction, I pressed on.

"I know it wasn't your fault, and I'm willing to pay for the days I booked for."

"That won't be necessary," Ron interjected. "This is a guesthouse. We don't take prisoners here. I'll be satisfied if you just pay an extra five dollars for the food we purchased for your stay and that will be enough."

With my decision announced and a settlement agreed upon, the rest of breakfast passed in silence before Ron excused himself, promising to arrange for a Tuk-Tuk before heading into the village. Following a last gulp of tea and a quick handshake, he was gone. Given the awkwardness of the situation, I was glad Kannitha felt comfortable enough to remain at the table.

"Can I ask you something totally unconnected?" I asked once she'd finished refilling my cup."

"Yes, of course."

"This is probably going to sound kind of weird, but can you tell me why so many Cambodians build their houses along the main road. There hardly ever seems to be any side streets. At least I haven't seen very many around here."

"It's because Cambodians are *stuporstitious.*" she answered after a moment of thought.

"You mean superstitious."

"I did not say that?"

"No, but what you did say fits. So how does being "stuporstitious" affect how they build their houses?"

"People believe building close to the road brings good luck. They often compete over the height of houses and distance to the road."

"Are you serious?"

"Yes, it is true. One family will build a few feet or even a few inches ahead of their neighbour. It is a dangerous practice because the government owns the land for the first 25 meters from the road."

"But a lot of the huts or houses I've seen aren't that far back."

"I know. But the government can come along and do what they want, if they choose to. "

"Like run the road right through your living room?"

"If they would want to, yes."

"And the residents have no protection? Not even those in these fancy villas?"

"Many of those villas are owned by people in the government or connected to it. In Cambodia, government and business go hand in hand. Unfortunately, there is also much corruption."

I was mulling over this latest information in relation to

last night's noise, when Kannitha returned to the theme of *"stuporstition."*

"Cambodians like to consult astrologers about many subjects. They ask for advice on the right time to marry, where to build, and how to keep bad spirits away. Did you not see the scarecrow at the end of our neighbour's driveway when we started our walk yesterday?"

I had noticed, but had not bothered to question her on it.

"One other thing I should tell you," she added. "If you see an accident on the road, do not go and help them if they are badly hurt."

"What kind of sense does that make? Why wouldn't I help someone who needed it?"

"Because if they die, they will think you have brought bad spirits. As a foreigner you could be held responsible."

As interesting as I found these subjects to be, any further enlightenment was cut short when Rith and Nuon came running up with news the Tuk-Tuk had arrived. A few minutes later, in the process of loading my backpack on to the carriage, I couldn't help thinking that the three of them looked a trifle sad standing there. Hoping to avoid departing on a downcast note, I asked Kannitha if she was expecting other guests that week.

"No. There are no reservations, but perhaps that will give us time to do some repairs," she said, struggling to maintain a weak smile.

Although the Tuk-Tuk driver had signalled his impatience by starting his motor, I chose to ignore the hint to ask what they had planned.

"Ron wants to add another bungalow but we are too poor."

Whether she meant to be so blunt or not, her words echoed across the yard like a gunshot. Even both children gave her a puzzled look. Not wanting to embarrass her, I remained silent, expressing my gratitude and regret with a bow and a handshake. Turning back to wave goodbye until a curve in the driveway lost them to the trees, warranted or not, I felt sorry for them.

For reasons difficult to fathom, the short return trip to Kampong Cham, set me back more than the bus ride had from Kampong Thom, a distance of over a hundred kilometres. There was no time to argue the point with my driver. As soon as we jerked to a stop on the edge of a crowded plaza, he pointed to a paint-chipped billboard showing that the next bus for the capital was scheduled to leave in two minutes. With the next bus not due for ninety minutes, I quickly hopped out of the Tuk-Tuk, hauling the driver to the ticket booth to increase my chances of catching the earlier bus.

The sigh of relief as I slumped into a seat in the first row, was nearly enough to flutter the window curtains. In comparison to the trauma of the last eight hours, the prospect of spending the next few anywhere but where I'd been, seemed positively thrilling. Even the fact that the bus had seen better days and left thirty minutes later than scheduled didn't disturb the moment of bliss. On the route out of the city, signs of the French influence were visible, as old colonial-style buildings slid past, many looking as though they'd been left to battle the elements ever since the French departed Indochina in the mid-1950's. Beyond the standard fare of crowded markets, and bustling street activity, the most memorable feature about Kampong Cham was the size of the Mekong. At the point we crossed it heading south, it could have easily been mistaken for a lengthy lake rather than a river.

Once the city limits were behind us, the landscape turned into a seemingly endless parade of pastel plains, whose deeper colours had been nearly bleached out of existence by an incessant sun. According to the ticket agent in Kampong Cham, arrival in Phnom Penh was scheduled for noon, early enough to leave open the idea of catching a second bus for the coast. Doing so however, would entail another five-hour trip. Although the possibility of being in Sihanoukville that same evening did have its appeal, I couldn't envision being cooped up in another bus for so long, especially given that dust had begun to seep in through this one's overhead air vents. I was not the only one to notice the sudden decrease in air quality. A Cambodian woman across the aisle, had pulled a tissue from her satchel to cover her mouth, lowering it only long enough to shout something unintelligible, and hopefully insulting, to the driver. I was about to voice my own opinion about the contaminated air that was now starting to coat the inside of my nose, when through no visible change in road conditions, the air mysteriously cleared.

For the next hour or so, the miles slipped by in relative peace. It wasn't until we were within several kilometres of Phnom Penh's central bus station, that we got caught up in heavy traffic. At this point I concluded that any further travel would rate as cruel and unusual punishment and cast my vote for a day of "R&R." When we finally arrived at the terminal an hour or so later, I disembarked in such an upbeat mood, that even the barrage of Tuk-Tuk drivers and hotel hawkers couldn't put a dent in it. Things only started to go awry after I realized that the money I'd given Kannitha's mother, the five dollars to Ron, and the sum handed to Kannitha in appreciation of her informative walk, had left me temporarily financially embarrassed. With the idea of lugging my heavy knapsack on foot a non-starter, and no bank automat in sight, the only alternative seemed to be a round of expert bargaining. Slipping away from the flock working the parking area, I found a less ambitious driver snoozing in the back of his Tuk-Tuk further up the street. A light tap on the metal frame snapped him to immediate attention.

"Sorry to wake you. Do you speak English?" Although multitudes in Phnom Penh did, I'd stumbled across one who didn't. Gesturing that I shouldn't move, he scrambled out of the seat and signalled for the aid of a colleague nearby.

"I have a bit of a problem," I began to explain to the second nodding head. "I need to get to the Golden Hotel, but I've only got one dollar. I need to know if he will take me there for that, and if not, how far will a buck get me?"

Following a translation and a quick debate, assurance was given that everything was "okay, okay, no worry," as the first driver relieved me of my knapsack and beckoned me to climb aboard.

"You're sure he understood I've only got one dollar," I repeated to his colleague. "Just tell him to take me as far as that will get me if that's not enough. I'm not trying to cheat him."

With a final nod, and an echoing "is okay, is okay," we were soon weaving our way through familiar chaos. Several minutes later, we were pulling into the hotel courtyard. Just as I was handing my driver the promised fee, one of the Tuk-Tuk drivers Conrad and I had regularly used in December, recognized me and came over to say "hello." Further conversation however, was interrupted when my current driver issued a loud grunt of displeasure. Turning to face him, I pointed to my open wallet.

"Look, no money. Sorry, but the deal was for a dollar. I don't know what your friend told you back there, but I told him you should only go as far as a dollar would take me."

Attempting to resume my conversation with my former driver, I was hit with an outburst of Khmer.

"Hey, hang on," I snapped back in a octave higher than normal. "I told you that's all the money I had. It's not my fault if you and your friend didn't understand. "

Having understood none of this of course, the man continued to squawk, waving his meagre fare to broadcast his dissatisfaction, a gesture that managed to turn a few heads of other drivers hovering nearby. Theoretically, it would have been possible to have gone into hotel reception for more money, but any incentive for doing so was dulled by the fact I'd gone out of my way to make my situation clear at the terminal. To everyone's good fortune, the former driver chose to intervene, nodding me in the direction of the hotel as a sign he would handle his ruffled colleague.

Once inside, the assistant manager, having apparently forgotten our little scuffle at check-in ten days prior, acted glad to see me again, going so far as to dismiss the need to sign the register, before handing me my key and wishing me a pleasant stay. Within minutes I was in it up to my neck again, this time in the cooling waters of the roof-top pool. Too relaxed to glance over the balcony to see what had become of my irked driver, I spent a good half-hour paddling around in the water before heading back to my room to gain some much needed rest and a meal I would actually be able to see.

Day Thirteen: Monday, February 14th

Thirteen hours of uninterrupted sleep was pretty convincing evidence that the decision to remain in Phnom Penh had been a wise one. As refreshed as I felt the next morning, I nevertheless chose to make the day's agenda a light one. How a return to Toul Sleng came to be considered "light" was difficult to explain, but just past ten, there I was walking through its newly-opened entrance into the crowded courtyard. Although relatively certain there wasn't much I hadn't seen in December, I elected to visit each and every room of the complex. The rooms in Building A were virtually identical; abandoned dark spaces framed by mould-stained walls and grimy, brown-and-white checkerboard floor tiles. Aside from the photo gallery on the main floor, Building B threatened to be more of the same until I wandered into a section that contained a series of wooden cells. Unlike the open-brick stalls witnessed weeks earlier, these "cages" appeared somewhat larger. Each of the enclosures had the added "feature" of a heavy metal door with a bolt latch that controlled access from the outside. Peering in at the tiny cubicle through a viewing slot, it was sobering to realize people had been forced to spend indeterminate amounts of time under such conditions. The question of what had determined whether an occupant was confined to a stall or a cell, remained unanswered. Feeling the need for some fresh air, I exited and found a seat on a bench under a group of soaring palms. Just how close "normal daily life" had been to the prison became obvious when I happened to glance up to the balcony of a nearby apartment building, and saw a woman methodically carrying out the chore of hanging laundry. I would later read that prison officials had often played loud music to smother the sounds of prisoners being tortured. If that wasn't insidious enough, they also occasionally lowered the sound of the music to remind nearby residents outside the compound that they could be next.

With no desire to re-visit the grisly paintings in Building D, I brought the tour to an end and returned to the street, rejecting the advances of a half dozen Tuk-Tuk drivers, in favour of grabbing a drink and plotting my next move. Catching sight of a faded logo advertising souvenirs, I sauntered into a small store just up the street, curious what kind of trinkets would be sold next door to a former prison. I was browsing through rows of the same tacky mementos I'd seen in the Russian market, when an over-attentive clerk approached with the offer of a wooden Buddha for a "special price." I declined as diplomatically as I could, which wasn't that diplomatic, and retreated to an outside table with cola and sandwich in hand, to scour my city map. The fact that nothing seemed to corner my interest, briefly raised doubts as to whether I *should* have hopped yesterday's bus for the coast. Following a pit stop at a grocery store to stock up for tomorrow's planned trip, I returned to the hotel just in time to be mobbed by a lobby full of young European women. While the dominance of blonde hair and northern accents suggested their origin, it was ultimately the flags on the knapsacks piled by the elevator that gave them away as

Norwegians. Lingering as long as I dared before looking could be misinterpreted as Nordic gawking, I went up to my room, glumly accepting that I felt a bit lost, not to mention ancient.

Considering the hectic pace of the last two weeks, some sort of downward slide was to be expected. But rather than succumbing, I decided what was needed was a special treat. All it took was a quick call to reception and the threatening cloud was lifting within minutes, boosted by the knowledge I had an appointment to undergo something called a "Monsoon Special." But with several hours until my treatment, I resisted the urge to hang around the pool observing the bevy of frolicking young Norwegians, to pay a return visit to the Central Market.

"*What was I thinking?*" was my first thought, as I trudged into the musty hall that was as dull and dreary as the last time. The booths seemed even tinier than those of Kampong Thom, which perhaps explained why many vendors looked as thrilled to be there as me. Quick to admit to a severe error in judgement, I was back at the hotel within thirty minutes, only to witness a regrettable silence at poolside.

An hour later I was submerged in other waters, this time a tub of warm, foamy "aqua," daubed with floating rose petals that had a way of attaching themselves to my face. Housed on the opposite side of the walkway from last December's treatment, this evening's inner sanctum came with a noticeable absence of cloying muzak, as well as a dozen or more flickering candles placed on the tub and overhead shelves, creating a subdued, romantic setting, unless of course you happened to be viewing it on your own. According to a brochure I'd skimmed through in the lobby, one was expected to remain immersed in the rose bath for fifteen minutes. But with my glasses out of arm's reach on a nearby table, the clock over the doorway might as well have been on the moon. Squinting didn't do much to improve my vision, so I chose to err on the side of caution and climbed out earlier than necessary. I was already dried off and on a neighbouring bench by the time a thin woman entered and introduced herself as Dari. Even without the aid of my still dormant glasses, she looked awfully petite to be a masseuse. But a masseuse she was; requesting that I turn over to lay face down before covering my back with a sheet and anointing the back of my right leg with a warm liquid. It wasn't until she had moved to my back that I realized the fluid contained small particles which were randomly adhering themselves to my skin. But rather than spoiling the moment by asking what it was, I simply surrendered to a forty-five-minute excursion through the rotating pleasures of a tea-leaf scrub.

"Scrub finish, shower please," Dari ordered as she clasped her hands and disappeared through the cloth partition. Standing under the soothing shower, I was grateful her work had not included my face and scalp as the strong spray from the shower head had difficulty removing the flecks of tea leaves glued to my body.

I'd been in the midst of the "Monsoon" for a little over an hour when the curtains parted again and my next masseuse entered. Shorter than her predecessor, Nareth made up for her lack of height with her girth, although chunky is not how I would describe her, at least not any time she had her hands near my vital organs. But she turned out to be much gentler than expected. Already familiar with the order in which extremities were usually oiled, stroked and kneaded, I was a bit confused when after finishing with my face and scalp, she returned once again to my feet. Although reflexology treatments were nothing new to me, it never ceased to amaze me how pressing on a specific point on a foot could send a devastatingly sharp pain to a seemingly unrelated part of one's anatomy. Fortunately, any slight discomfort induced by Nareth's treatment, subsided as quickly as it arose, leaving the last half hour to be spent lolling in a warm glow.

"Hey man, you're back again. What's happening?"

Following the "Monsoon, I decided to end off the evening with a visit to my favourite restaurant, and was well into my second mojito by the time a familiar grey ponytail negotiated its way to my table.

"Just for tonight," I told Jerry. "I'm planning on heading to the coast tomorrow, which reminds me, I've got a few questions if you have a couple of minutes."

"Can do my man, if it doesn't take too long," he said, glancing around to telegraph that his time was limited.

"When I was here the last time, you sounded like you weren't terribly impressed with Sihanoukville. Can you be more specific? I just came back from a "home-stay" up near Kampong Cham and I'm not much in the mood for another bad experience."

"I think I know the place," Jerry interrupted.

"What... you mean the homestay?" I answered, assuming he was mistaken.

"Tall, English guy in his sixties... Married to a Cambodian."

"Uhhh... yeah," I replied hesitantly. "But it's not exactly

around the corner, how do you know him?"

"You'd be amazed how news travels in the ex-pat community man. I don't remember the dude's name but it's gotta be the same guy. He used to live in Phnom Penh and I met him at one of the ex-pat meetings a few years back. I heard later he had moved up north with his old lady. Also heard he had trouble with people in the village 'cause he was always complaining or demanding things, stuff like that. You can't do that here, man. You gotta play by their rules. Don't know if it's true, but I heard they even cut off his electricity because he was nagging and slagging 'em so much."

"That explains a few things," I said. "But how can you cut off someone's power unless they don't pay their bill or something? Then again, I guess the same way you can change tires at 4:30 a.m.," I mumbled as an afterthought.

"How's that?" Jerry asked, casting another glance at nearby tables. Sensing the meter was running, I reverted to the subject of Sihanoukville.

"Not important, but like I said, after what happened up there, I'm not looking for any surprises. Would you recommend giving Sihanoukville a pass?"

"No man, I like the place. It's got a weird vibe though. Just depends on what you're lookin' for," he mused. "But you wanna stay away from Victoria Hill. Especially at night."

"Why's that?"

"Trust me man, you just do... Lots of strange people hanging out there. You're better off staying at one of the other beaches."

As Jerry segued into the familiar saga of Russian mafia and drugs, the idea of putting in an appearance in Sihanoukville was starting to look doomed.

"You know anything about a place called Kampot?" I asked. "The guidebook paints it as a 'quaint village with colonial architecture' and ..."

"Yeah. I've been there. It's not a bad place, but it's on the river man. No place to swim. It's fifteen klicks to the sea, but the beach there is not so great cause the river flows in and..." he said, his voice trailing off as he monitored a group of arriving customers.

"But Kampot's cool man," he said, getting back to me.

"And Kep?"

"Quiet place. Not much happening. Great food at the crab market though.If all you're looking for is some quiet down time, Kep's the place... Sorry man," he said, once again distracted by the arrival of still more customers. "Sorry man, duty calls. Another mojito? Okay, my man, stay cool. If you make it to Sihanoukville, try Tanners. Nice people." he added, breaking off his own train of thought. "Take care man."

I watched his ponytail jounce its way towards a table of boisterous businessmen, before realizing I'd forgotten to ask how recent these coastal impressions were. Left to my own devices and a final mojito, what had begun as a distant option, had now risen to a distinctly potential destination. To some it might have appeared peculiar to have travelled thousands of kilometres only to visit a place where there was "not much going on," but at that moment, I had to admit that "quiet and laid back" had its appeal.

Day Fourteen: Tuesday, February 15th

Despite a departure time that had long since come and gone, boredom and impatience were still being held in check. That feat could in part be attributed to the inadvertent entertainment Phnom Penh's central bus station provided for all in-coming and out-going passengers. Located in a narrow cul-de-sac, the station demanded that all drivers display a unique set of skills when navigating their forty-seat behemoths amidst a large and constantly moving crowd. I had the benefit of observing the show from the comfort of my bus, lazily noting that it took a departing driver an average of four-to-five moves, forward and backward, until his vehicle was clear to leave. Things tended to get particularly interesting when two or three drivers attempted to negotiate the pencil-thin margins of error simultaneously. The mere fact that the plaza was free of squashed luggage and travellers, implied that most of those in the on-going pageant knew what they're doing.

Shortly after completing our own series of vehicular pirouettes, we eased out into what could only be called claustrophobic traffic, able to put only three kilometres behind us in the first half hour. Making matters worse, our driver had insisted on only driving 60 kph.   even after the congestion had finally cleared and we'd hit the open road.

"Is it just me, or did someone set the air-conditioning to minus ten?" I asked a North American-looking passenger seated across the aisle. Glancing up over the top of his glasses, he simply nodded before twisting slightly in his seat to indicate he did not wish to be disturbed again. In an attempt to remedy the situation, I discovered that both air-control nozzles above my seat were defective. One came off in my hand when I tried to close it, while the other was simply welded open, allowing frigid air to blast unhindered into the passenger compartment. I was not the only one bothered by this climate change. Two rows up, a Cambodian woman, swaddled in bulging shopping bags, struggled to adjust her own rampant flow with equal success. Calling out to the driver would be of no avail above the racket of the engine, so I clambered out of my seat and jostled up the aisle towards his cubicle. A firm tap on his shoulder elicited nothing more than a momentary scowl.

"The air-conditioning is too cold," I told him. "Would you mind turning it up or off? People back there are freezing."

When that request produced nothing beyond an indifferent shrug, I returned to my seat, intent on finding my own solution. No sooner had I plunked myself down, there it was staring me in the face. Reaching up, I tore open the velcro strip holding the window curtains in place and started stuffing the loose material into the vents. A full third of the curtain had disappeared before the air supply was finally blocked, but it did the trick. Settling back in my warming space, it was not long until other passengers began to mimic my efforts, making me wonder just where all of the diverted air was going and whether some poor unsuspecting sap in the rear might innocently open his vent and be blown out an open window.

It started with a three second jingle that was barely

audible over the road noise. As the musical interlude, which wouldn't have been out of place in a laundry detergent commercial, continued to play, passengers began glancing around for its source. It didn't take long to determine that it was coming from someone's cell phone. Curiosity shifted with each unanswered ring, until the entire bus was rubbernecking to identify the deaf owner. Amongst those looking for the culprit, I felt a shiver of dread pass through me when I happened to look up at the overhead mirror above the driver and see him fumbling to retrieve something from a jacket hanging directly behind him. Just at the moment he succeeded in extracting the phone, the bus swerved sharply to the left to avoid an unsuspecting cyclist, followed by a hard right to avert oncoming traffic. Both rapid actions produced a round of mocking cheers from passengers, that were unfortunately lost on a man now in deep conversation.

Once that excitement had fizzled out safely, the next few hours were spent morphed to my I-Pod, blankly staring out at mile after mile of arid land that was occasionally broken up by a line of palm trees that resembled targets in a hazy shooting gallery. With still an hour to go before reaching Kep, I concluded it as good a time as any to brush up on my knowledge of my approaching destination. According to the few pages Kep warranted in my guidebook, the origins of the coastal town could be traced back to the beginning of the twentieth century when the French elite, having presumably grown bored of their pampered lifestyle in the capital, had established a resort at the seaside. After the French departed in the mid 1950's, the area had become a magnet for wealthy Cambodians, complete with casinos, fancy hotels and luxury villas. The growth in popularity however, ultimately made the town a prime target for the Khmer Rouge, who once in power, made sure it was thoroughly trashed and abandoned. Remnants of that era were evident as soon as we entered the outskirts of Kep, passing street after street of deserted or burned-out villas as we continued to follow the coastal road towards the centre of town. It didn't take long to sense that Jerry had been right. The place was definitely laid back. Other than a few predatory Tuk-Tuks trailing the bus, not a single person was anywhere to be seen. Even the beach we were paralleling seemed barren of life, housing only a long row of empty beach cabanas that overlooked a vacant, rock-strewn shoreline. The singular noticeable activity was a small fishing boat bobbing in the turquoise waters off-shore. It was only when we pulled into the main bus station, a patch of gravel flanked by two forlorn looking kiosks, that things livened up. A cool off-shore breeze was blowing as I alighted into the inevitable band of eager Tuk-Tuks drivers. Waving them off, I strolled across the road with my backpack for my first close look at the Gulf of Thailand. Standing on a pebbled beach, gazing out on a carpet of choppy white caps, I could just make out the dark-green silhouette of a forested island. Proving that there wasn't only life on Mars, a pair of young Cambodian mothers materialized, seating themselves under a clump of severely angled palms on the boardwalk to chat, while keeping a close eye on their cavorting children. Back on the same side of the road as the station, I noticed a group of tourists gathered under a thatched gazebo, sipping on colourful cocktails when not raucously laughing. Knowing there would be plenty of time to explore the beach area over the next few days, I crossed a sandy plaza cluttered with abandoned booths and benches and selected a Tuk-Tuk driver. Handing him the address of the hotel I'd booked, I climbed aboard his garishly-painted chariot and settled back for what I hoped would be a short ride. Within meters of leaving the dusty plaza, the road unexpectedly turned into a four-lane asphalt highway, split in two by a manicured grass strip that gave the surroundings the aura of a Las Vegas country club. As the Tuk-Tuk strained to make it up a steep incline, I couldn't help wondering whether this modern thoroughfare was an example of a prophesied future, controlled by Chinese investors.

Passing over the summit of what appeared to be Kep's lone mountain, we continued to head inland, cruising alongside a forest dotted with affluent-looking houses and modest hotels. Not long after the highway narrowed to two lanes, we turned off onto a rutted path, snaking our way up towards the base of a smaller forested peak.

The man stooped over a laptop at the bar was definitely not Cambodian. Deeply absorbed in whatever it was he was doing, he didn't appear to have noticed my arrival. I was about to tap a bell on the counter when he suddenly looked up and jumped to his feet.

"Hi. Welcome to Kep Inn. I'm Eric. How was your trip? Hope you didn't have any problems finding us? Thanks for booking with us, you won't regret it," he spouted in a single breath.

After engaging in a short round of small talk, I left Eric to enter my essentials into the registry and stepped out on to the patio to take stock of my new surroundings. It was immediately clear that I'd once again landed "in the bush," with three sides of the open-air reception/ bar/ restaurant enclosed by a wall of dense vegetation. What the fourth side

236 |

had to offer was the view of a kidney-shaped pool, beyond which a terrain of various shades of green, sloped down to meet the blue sea, eventually disappearing into an indistinguishable haze of water and sky.

"You are in Bananaland," Eric announced, key in hand.

"How'd you manage such an accurate observation after only a few minutes," I thought to answer, but instead resorted to a more polite response. "I'm what?"

"You're in Bananaland. It's the double bungalow I put you in. Up the path and to your left."

With memories of Kampong Thom still fresh, I felt compelled to belatedly inform Eric of my existing curse, briefly describing the repercussions it had produced a few days prior.

"Not to worry," he assured with a toothy grin. "The other guests... Canadians too by the way, have gone to Phnom Penh for a couple of days. They won't be back till tomorrow night, so you'll have the place to yourself."

I'd just finished unpacking and was in the process of arranging my possessions, when there was a knock at the door.

"Excuse me sir," a young Cambodian man apologized when I opened the door. "I must put food for mouse in room."

Puzzled, but certain of what he had just said, I let him in with no questions. Pulling a bamboo chair to the centre of the room, he reached up to retrieve a small box resting on an open cross beam. He then took a small pouch from his pocket and proceeded to fill the box with what looked like rice. I waited until he had re-placed it on the ledge before speaking.

"Can I ask what that was all about?" I asked, as he climbed

down and set the chair back in front of the desk.

"Sir?"

"The box. What did you put in it and why?"

"For mouse sir. There is mouse in room at night."

Quietly closing the door behind him, I thought, "*It's the jungle*. I'm the trespasser. As long as it stays out of my bed, and doesn't snore, it's more than welcome to share the room."

Day Fifteen: Wednesday, February 16th

"So wait a second. Run this by me one more time. It says here insurance is not included, but that it is recommended and can be purchased extra... see right here," I said, pointing to a section of the contract the perspiring agent had handed me to sign. "So what I need to know is how I go about getting some extra insurance?"

"I write contract. No insurance," the man answered, unaware of the cloud of frustration forming over our heads in the lodge's tiny parking lot.

"I know there's no insurance," I repeated. "That's why I want some. I'm not going to rent a scooter without any. It says right here that if something happens, I'll be liable for $700. So where and how can I get some insurance and lower the deductible?"

"Deeduckable?"

"Forget it," I replied, turning in desperation to a passing staffer loaded down with a stack of towels.

"Is Eric around this morning? Yesterday, he said he would see about booking me a motorbike," I explained to a blank-eyed stare. "But there seems to be some confusion about the insurance. Could you try explaining to this gentleman what it is I want."

"Eric no here," she said. "He go early to Kampot. Come one, maybe two hour."

With no intention of waiting for Eric's projected return, I

handed the helmet back to the agent, bidding him adieu before skipping back up the steps to reception.

"Bicycles here are free, right?" I asked a befuddled receptionist, handing over the unsigned contract as she watched the moped owner ride away through the trees. "I'd like to have one for the rest of the day. When Eric gets back, can you ask him if he can straighten out the confusion with the insurance?"

After signing for a lock and helmet, and grabbing a bottle of water from the fridge in my bungalow, it was back down the garden path to the lean-to where a row of beat-up looking bikes awaited.

Whatever flair Kep may have possessed during its golden age as a seaside haven for the rich and decadent, you wouldn't have known it from the portion of the ocean drive I was cruising along. Save for the hodgepodge array of kiosks and outdoor restaurants clustered at one end of the Crab Market, the rest of the curving coastline was void of any signs of civilization, past or present. Nonetheless, I was enjoying a warm breeze that was mine and mine alone as I cycled past palms and shoreline rock formations. I couldn't help thinking how lucky I was to be experiencing Kep now, as opposed to back in its so-called "headier" days, or for that matter, an uncertain future. Halfway along this stretch of seaboard, I paused to observe a fisherman trying his luck with a small hand-held net, when the tranquil scene was interrupted by the sound of approaching motorbikes. Prepared at first to watch what looked to be two tourists pass undisturbed, a sudden last-minute thought spurred me to flag them down.

"Good morning," I greeted the first rider. "Do you speak English?"

He did, with what sounded to be a thick London accent.

"Can I ask you where you got your motorbike?" I said, noticing a familiar-looking scratch running down the side of the front fender.

"In town... uuh, rather, back at our hotel."

The hand-painted number on the cross bar, presumably meant to pass as a license plate, confirmed my suspicion that he was astride the very bike I had turned down an hour ago.

Sparing him the finer details of this morning's saga, I briefly explained the source of my interest.

"Sorry, I don't know anything about no insurance."

"You didn't have to sign a contract that said you'd be liable for up to $700 if you get in an accident?"

"Never signed nothing," he said with a hint of bravado.

During this exchange, my eyes kept drifting to the second rider hidden behind large sunglasses and a helmet, out of which tumbled a healthy mane of blonde hair. With no introductions in the offing, I thanked her partner for his time, nodding a polite goodbye as the pair sped off down the road.

The wind started picking up the moment I came around a sharp curve, turning the slight uphill climb into an unwelcome chore. To no one's surprise, only one of the bike's three gears functioned, naturally the one needed the least. By the time I reached the top of the incline my heart was pumping heavily, prompting me to stop at one of the kiosks slotted amidst a row of empty beachside restaurants. Ordering a much-needed bottle of water presented me with the opportunity to ask how far it was to Angkaul Beach.

According to information Eric had dispersed at reception the previous afternoon, Angkaul was allegedly one of the area's most scenic highlights; an abandoned beach, "not to be missed," as he had put it. Unfortunately, the hand-drawn map he had provided didn't include anything as useful as distances or directions. The young girl serving me, nor the friend lazing in a nearby hammock could provide an answer, forcing a stop at a second kiosk further up the road. By this time the merciless heat had already made me start to question the wisdom of heading for a beach I had no idea was located. Armed with a vague description supplied by the second kiosk, I set myself a limit of ten kilometres, a plan quickly handicapped by the discovery the bike's odometer had been frozen for eternity at 614.8 kilometres. In what was either a profound stroke of luck or an indication that broken odometers were a common occurrence in Cambodia, once back on the road I saw that some astute traffic official had sanctioned that distance markers be painted on the asphalt surface every half kilometre. The first number to pass under my wheel on what had to be the straightest, least-shaded road in the country, was ten-point five. Squinting into the sun, I guesstimated that number would climb to at least fifteen before I would reach a tiny speck of trees visible through the distant haze. Adding to the discomfort of the incandescent heat, was an increasingly brisk side wind which tended to create a vacuum every time a truck streaked past. Under such conditions, five kilometres began to feel more like five hundred. When the first bend in the road was finally conquered, the reward was merely the view of yet another long, empty stretch of heated tarmac. As depressing as that was, turning back seemed pointless, so on I pressed through the broiling air, confident there had to be a sign sooner or later. There just had to be.

Much to my amazement, not to mention ever-lasting gratitude, the twenty kilometre mark coincided with a junction in a small town. According to Eric's crude map, the raised hooves of a white stallion statue, poised forever in the middle of a roundabout, indicated a road leading north in the direction of Kampot. That meant any hopes of finding Angkaul required turning east towards Vietnam. Although both destinations were clearly signposted, neither came with a distance, presumably because there was no point in a country where all the odometers were broken. Standing there in the scorching heat, suddenly the whole idea of searching for "the lost beach" seemed patently absurd. After checking the position of the sun with what I thought should be Prey Thum, the mountain behind my lodge, I abandoned the quest to follow a route that hopefully would not only offer shade, but also return me home before heat prostration set in.

My calculations turned out to be correct. Within forty minutes of having waved goodbye and good riddance to the lonesome stallion, I was sliding the bike back into its rack. After a quick purge of sweat and dust under the shower, I was down at the pool in record time. I needn't have hurried. Quite possibly because at the height of the midday heat, I had the place to myself, swimming in water as refreshing as warm tea. As a result, I soon found myself back up at the patio bar, sipping on an ice-cold drink and luxuriating in the shade as a squeaky overhead fan feebly attempted to swat away the heat.

"Nobody buys insurance," Eric announced, surfacing out of nowhere to lean on the chair across from me.

"I take it you heard," I said.

"Unless you have a serious accident, a small dent or scrape would only cost you $20.00. You don't have to sign anything. I'll talk to him."

A man of his few words, he did so much faster than anticipated. Despite being knackered from the failed tour to the "lost beach," forty minutes after Eric's overture, I was back in the parking lot, this time receiving an impromptu lesson on how to ride a manual shift motorbike, something I had never done. Donning a tight-fitting helmet that felt similar to sticking one's head in a heated oven, I proceeded to jerk and brake my way down the narrow trail leading to the paved highway, all the while wondering if I was going to end up on You Tube. After a few kilometres, I'd mastered the fine art of changing gears and was giddily streaking through the countryside at what must have been close to sixty-five kilometres an hour. I say "must have" because much like the bike's odometer, this speedometer was also lame.

The world looked and felt completely different from onboard the moped, creating one of those "it's great to be alive" moments. Swayed by the momentary elation, I concluded there was still enough time to resume the search for the mysterious beach in spite of the sun's burning rays. No longer having to rely on internal power, I returned to the white stallion in record time, and headed towards the border with Vietnam, some twenty kilometres distant.

With no speedometer or street markings to gauge how far I had travelled, I began to look for indications of a turn off around what I assumed must have been the ten kilometre mark, extremely grateful I had not tried to cover this distance earlier on my own steam. Shortly after passing a sign written in Khmer, an inner conviction told me that the orange-coloured gravel road it heralded had to be what I was looking for. Backtracking to the junction, I stopped at a small kiosk, hoping to obtain more precise directions. Nobody appeared to be on duty, but just at that moment I was lucky enough to spot a woman coming out of a nearby house.

"Angkaul Beach?" I asked, no doubt mangling the correct pronunciation, while pointing to Eric's map. "Is this the right direction?" I added, with a look of expectation.

Relieved to learn that it was indeed the right route, I was somewhat deflated when told in broken English, that it still lay another ten kilometres. At least the wind had shifted, meaning that any trails or whirlwinds of dust kicked up by on-coming trucks would now be blown away from me.

From a distance, the perfectly aligned mounds looked like a collection of miniature white pyramids, each no more than a foot or so high. Set in rows within numerous shallow Olympic-sized "pools," their reflections in the glass-like water, created the illusion one was looking at a field of white diamonds afloat in the azure blue of a reflected sky. Hoping to get a closer look at the salt lagoons that were separated by intersecting ridges of earth that doubled as walkways, I guided the motorbike down a slight incline, coming to rest in the shade of a long, wooden building. Several of the dozen or so workers, all of whom were women, halted work to briefly observe the interloper. One worker, dressed in a loose flowing long-sleeved shirt, black-peasant pants, and a Lawrence of Arabia style cap with flaps that hung to her shoulders, paid me no heed as she flip-flopped along the narrow rim of the dike. Suspended on each end of a bamboo pole she carried across her shoulders, were two open-wicker baskets, making her look for the moment, like an Asian version of Themis, the Greek Goddess of Justice and Law. While the other women resumed their work in the ankle-deep water, I remained at a respectful distance, watching this woman step into a dried-out pond, before bending down next to a pyramid. Holding a small, flat piece of wood in her gloved hand, she then deftly scooped a portion of the salt into the open basket, repeating the procedure until both baskets were full. After adjusting the pole behind her neck so the weight would be evenly divided on her shoulders, she then stood upright, and trotted off with the load in the direction of the building near the road. At the same moment, another colleague arrived with empty baskets to continue harvesting the fifty to sixty pyramids still left in the dry lagoon. By the time the second worker had filled her baskets, the first woman was already on her way back, her two empty containers dangling in rhythm to her jaunty pace. As spellbinding as it was to watch, not to mention photograph, the heat and bright reflections off the water were starting to make me light-headed. Rather than keeling headfirst into the brine, I headed for what I assumed was the warehouse, hoping to find some shade and perhaps beg, borrow or buy a bottle of water. None of the young men loading large sacks of salt on to a nearby flatbed trailer seemed interested in acknowledging my presence. For a moment I considered asking whether one could purchase some of the harvested salt, but as there didn't appear to be anything smaller than the 100 kilogram sacks being stacked, there seemed little point. By now my parched tongue was threatening to swell to the size of an inner tube, but with no drinkable water in sight, I decided to press on towards the "lost" beach, hoping a kiosk would surface somewhere along the way.

The wind had gained in strength by the time I turned off and passed under an arch supposedly marking the way to the missing beach. With the wind now behind me, I hadn't cycled more than fifty meters up the road when a car suddenly raced past, engulfing me in a cloud of choking dust. Noise of its approach had been concealed by the wind and rustling leaves, leaving no time to prepare for the deluge. Forced to stop to shield my mouth and nose, I peered ahead through the trees to see the perpetrator racing across the horizon like a lit fuse. Finally, after several wrong turns, one dead end, and a continuing storm of small children running out to welcome me, there it was.

"*This is it?*" I thought, as I stared down a long strip of leaf-infested sand, abutted by a barricade of palm trees no more than five meters from the water. "*This is the place not to be missed?*"

It may have been lost, but paradise it was not. Granted the sand looked nicer than what Kep had to offer, but that hardly rated the place as outstanding. At a loss to understand what had possessed Eric to recommend it, I had to admit he had been right in at least one aspect. Void of any swimmers, sunbathers, nude volleyball fanatics, or strolling souvenir vendors, it certainly did look abandoned. The only visible sign of life was two fishermen mending their nets alongside their beached boat. Convinced they would not be able to clarify whether I had wandered on to the dud end of the promenade, I started towards a small collection of huts where a group of locals were busy watching toddlers annoy a grizzled-looking dog. The closer I got however, the more the wheels of my moped sank into the loose sand. Finding it too strenuous to maintain control, I was forced to dismount and push the bike on foot, much to the amusement of those watching me. Able to finally purchase a bottle of water, I gulped it down in seconds before waving goodbye to my audience and driving off in search of a better memory.

Back at the lodge bar, refreshed and rehydrated after a shower and cola, I was online searching for just how cold it was in Canada that day, when a voice with a thick German accent drifted into earshot.

"I spent the whole day on Rabbit Island. Es war wunderbar," a woman in her late forties was telling the young Cambodian bartender. Vaguely familiar with the place she was referring to, I felt emboldened to ease my way into the conversation when the bartender moved off to serve another customer.

"Excuse me but what is there to do for a whole day on a remote island?" I inquired in German. "Aren't you stuck there for eight hours?"

Visibly pleased at the opportunity to converse in her own tongue, she extended her hand, introducing herself as Melissa before adding, "You can swim, go for a walk, read a book... just relax."

For the next half hour, the two of us engaged in small talk, comparing mutual experiences in Cambodia as well as sharing opinions about life back in Germany. As light as the banter was, it was enough to have us agree to meet for dinner at a restaurant in the Crab Market.

"The shrimp is out of this world," Melissa raved, once we'd been seated that evening. "I had it last night and I've never tasted anything better in my life."

"Uh huh," I said, scanning the main menu for the third time. "I'm not really a big seafood fan but..."

"Believe me. This is like no other shrimp you've ever had. It's fresh beyond words. It was probably swimming out there somewhere an hour before it landed on my plate."

With nothing else to lure me in another direction, I agreed to give the shrimp a chance. Once our orders were placed, attention turned to the setting we found ourselves in. Having pegged us as a couple, the hostess had placed us at an intimate table with the sea literally at our feet. A fiery-red sun was slowly disappearing behind a ridge of flattened clouds, darkening the encroaching waves of high tide as they proceeded to reclaim the damp sand. A warm breeze was fluttering ribbons and clinking halyards aboard several pink-tinted fishing boats moored offshore. For no extra cost there was even soft music playing from a neighbouring terrace. The potential for romance was palpable and both of us could sense it. There was only one slight problem. Despite being attractive, intelligent, and easy to talk to, Melissa was simply not my "type," nor I, hers. With the prospect of possible conquest or surrender not a factor, we were free to have a very enjoyable evening, and that is exactly what we did, ending it at eleven with a drink, a nod and a handshake back at the lodge bar. Back in the confines of "Bananaland," my head spinning from one too many mojitos, I felt myself drifting back to the events of late afternoon. In the two hours between the conversation at the bar and dinner, I had decided to squeeze in another short tour on the moped. Following the same coastal road I'd taken that morning on the bike, I pulled off where I'd first asked directions to

Angkaul. The sole patron amongst dozens of empty beach cabanas, I settled into a salt-encrusted hammock to enjoy the view and fresh sea air. A hundred yards offshore, a fisherman and his wife could be seen reeling in their nets as their boat dipped in and out of sight in the increasingly large swells. The scene was somewhat hypnotic and I was well on my way to sliding into a late afternoon doze, when a voice interrupted the journey.

"You like drink sir?" Shielding my eyes from the sun, I raised my head to see a young girl hovering above me.

"Okay, sure why not." I said. "How much is a cola?"

"Three thousand Riel, sir."

"Okay, but all I have is a five thousand note."

"No problem, sir."

Several minutes later she was back with the drink, politely relieving me of the bill before running off in the direction of the kiosk. Staring out at Rabbit Island through the haze, daydreaming about whether I might want to devote a day there, I was coaxing out the last few drops of my drink when I realized the girl had still not returned with my change. I let several more minutes pass before going to investigate. None of the four young people hanging out at the kiosk looked familiar.

"Excuse me. You haven't seen the girl who served me by any chance have you?" I asked.

"Sorry sir, English not good."

"This drink," I added, holding up the empty can. "She didn't bring me my change."

A round of shrugs and a glance up the empty beach did little to alter the situation. Assuming it was a lost cause, I walked back to retrieve my moped, casting a final look around for a face I wasn't sure I'd even recognize.

"*Okay, what are we talking here? Two thousand Riels?*" I asked myself, as I slowly manoeuvred the motorbike over a series of rough-edged stones along the sea wall. "*What is that... like 50 cents?*"

It seemed pointless to fret over such a minor amount, yet somehow the disappointment of possibly having been swindled made it linger. Several more scans down the beach proved fruitless, and I was about to head back to the lodge when another motorbike came zipping round the corner of a cement wall and stopped directly in my path. Familiar blond hair tumbled out as the rider removed her helmet and smiled. Caught unawares, for a brief moment all I could do was stare.

"Hey mate, hello again."

It took a second to recognize that the voice was not the woman before me, but that of the Englishman I'd met that morning, now walking up from the direction of the road.

"So you've ended up with one as well have you?" he said, giving my vehicle a once over.

"Yeah, yeah," I answered, switching my gaze from his partner. "Wish I'd done it sooner. Completely changes the way you experience things. What happened to yours by the way? You didn't have an accident, did you?"

"No, no. Turned it in already. Had enough for the day. Bloody tiring it is."

Although curious why his partner had held on to hers, I didn't bother to inquire. Instead, as fellow mother tongues tend to do in a foreign land, the three of us quickly fell into a conversation about our respective adventures. The man, who'd introduced himself as Lee, was particularly interested in hearing about the salt fields, and when I offered to show them some photos, both of them crowded in for a better view. Having dismissed the likelihood of their being potential serial killers, I was quite enjoying the eye contact the woman seemed to be making between photos. But never having been particularly adept at flirting, it was a challenge to determine whether it was all in my head. Over the years, experience had shown that it usually took a hammer blow to the head to realize a woman was interested in me, and a similar subsequent blow to indicate she wasn't. As a result, I'd come to develop a cautious approach when it came to assessing any perceived interest. As this internal dickering was raging, I made a concerted effort to at least keep her partner included in the conversation.

"My name is Victoria," the woman said abruptly, extending her hand once we'd exhausted the photos and there was a pause in the conversation.

"Nice to meet you," I answered just as another familiar face ran up to hand me my change.

With the unexpected encounter rapidly moving towards a denouement, I suggested that the two of them join Melissa and I for dinner. Victoria seemed agreeable but suppressed her interest when Lee mumbled something about no longer having transportation.

"Thanks all the same mate, but Vic's gotta give her bike back before six. We're stayin' in town and it's too far to walk to the Crab Market."

With the sharp edges of the afternoon and evening encounters beginning to blur, I lay in bed, drowsily observing the shadows of neighbouring trees as they swept back and forth across the wall in the dim moonlight. Sleep finally arrived, borne on the notion that for a place that was supposed to be "pretty laid back," I'd managed to pack a lot of memories into a single day.

Day Sixteen: Thursday, February 17th.

I was enjoying the silence of a near-empty patio the next morning, when my bungalow neighbours entered and asked if they could join me for breakfast. After Jonathan and Sally had explained how Eric had informed them of our mutual heritage, we exchanged the obligatory "what part of Canada are you from" inquiries, before branching off to talk about our favourite sites in Cambodia. Noticeably older than her partner, Sally effused at length about what they'd seen and done in Phnom Penh and Angkor Wat, before switching to what she called the "swimming caves," using such words as "beautiful, utterly fascinating and mysterious."

"You absolutely must see them. They're not far from here," she cooed in a voice that would have made Zsa Zsa Gabor jealous.

Seeing as I'd rented the motorbike for two days and had nothing else on my agenda, I decided to take her advice and check out said "caves." Getting off an early start right after breakfast, I travelled the same road that had led to the Anguil Beach fiasco the previous day. This time however, I passed the turnoff with a shudder and kept straight on towards Vietnam. Not long after, I entered the bustling market town of Kampong Trach, where free-roaming water buffalo and shoppers seemed to be jockeying for the same street space. Not having expected any signs for the caves, I was not disappointed. All I knew is what Sally had inferred at breakfast, which was that they lay somewhere north of the town. Taking what appeared to be the sole option in that direction, I followed a rural lane in such bad shape, I was often reduced to walking speed. After almost twenty minutes on a washboard road, during which time I passed a decreasing number of small huts, I arrived at a junction near the base of one of the isolated conical mountains I'd grown accustomed to in December. The single-lane trail to the left looked more promising, as though it would take me around the mountain. The one to the right, had an actual sign, albeit in Khmer, indicating the presence of what appeared to be a temple ruin further up the road. Flipping a mental coin, I ventured left on what quickly became a twisting path infested with jagged rocks. Suppressing a secret fear that a flat could leave me stranded for weeks, I was grateful to find I was not alone when I came upon a makeshift parking lot. There, under a thatch of trees, sat a blue and white van with a company logo on the side. Its lone occupant appeared to be busy doing what any good worker in the world does from time to time between service calls. Obviously convinced he had found the perfect location to grab a few undetected winks, I momentarily debated whether to surprise him by leaving a note on his windshield stating, "I'm reporting you." But without a Khmer translation book on hand, there seemed little point. Instead I left him in peace and began climbing a precarious trail on foot, giving a wide berth to the large boulders lodged on its steep slope. Halfway up, I stopped to rest on a small plateau where a stubbed-out campfire, ringed by a decorative necklace of empty beer cans, suggested civilization had passed this way before. Sensing success was close at hand, I moved to the far end of the plateau, and was granted a clear view down into a darkened hole at the base of an adjacent cliff face. Convinced I had found the missing caves, I cautiously inched my way down the treacherous incline for a closer look. Halting at the entrance to the cave, I was immediately overcome with the feeling I'd been had. Staring down into a subterranean pool of stagnant, scum-coated water, I could not for the life of me understand why anyone would suggest visiting, much less swim in such a cesspool.

"What was she thinking?" I thought, realizing the folly of granting people credibility simply because they were fellow citizens. Obsessed with the idea of wreaking revenge, I started back up the hill, toying with the idea of asking the lady in question, how long she and her "son" had been traveling together.

With no pressing need to return to Kep, I stopped at the junction to weigh the merits of trying to locate the signposted temple. Convinced that the chances of two bad decisions in one morning were relatively slim, I set off down the sandy trail hugging the base of the mountain. I hadn't gone more than a few hundred metres before coming upon a peculiar indentation in the rock face that at first glance looked like a giant version of the paper-mâché massifs used in decorating model-train landscapes. Equally out of place was a two-meter brick wall built across where the mountain curved inwards. Entering through an unmanned gate, I headed towards a group of people congregated under a grove of trees in the courtyard. The lone customer amongst a pack of friendly, albeit eager vendors, I agreed to hire a young man to act as my guide. Delivering what sounded like a memorized text as we walked towards yet another cave entrance, he informed me that the temple I'd expected was actually an underground shrine. Having dressed for the day's sweltering temperatures, it came as a shock to feel the sudden coolness, as I followed the weak beam of my guide's torch down into the pitch -black hole. Walking several meters in front of me, he continued to expound on the highlights of the shrine at a volume that was almost detectable. Requests that he speak louder were either not heard or ignored, but I did manage to decipher that the sparse stalactites and stalagmites, practically invisible in the poor light, had taken hundreds of years to develop.

"*Maybe so,*" I thought, "*But in this light, they could just as easily be made of plasticine and who's going to know the difference?*"

Emerging into a blinding sunlight, from a tour that rendered nothing more memorable than a stubbed toe and a lingering chill, it was clear that after sixteen days of sight-seeing, including the recent visit to the infamous "swimming caves, " I was starting to feel a little jaded. Aware however, that my current guide was not to blame for the mediocrity of the tour or my diminishing interest, I thanked him and departed.

As a result of the the morning's misfire, it was just after one when the white stallion again reared into view. A brief inspection of Eric's crinkled map confirmed that Kampot lay a mere twenty kilometres up the road. Assuming the "quaint" town had to be more interesting than the caves; what wouldn't? I headed off in the belief I could easily make it there and back before dark. As it turned out, the journey proved infinitely more interesting than the destination. Thatched-roofed huts perched on the banks of a picturesque jungle river, a tangled expanse of gnarled mango groves encroaching on the highway, and children barely old enough to walk amusing themselves on a fishing wharf in a muddy-watered harbour, all quickly became photo motifs en route.

Upon entering Kampot's city limits, I shuddered at how close I had come to staying here, and very well might have, had it not been for Jerry's warning. The guidebook had been right about buildings in the centre reflecting the elegance of the by-gone French colonial era. Many however, now appeared shabby, draped in the same spotty, black mould that adorned the walls of abandoned villas in Kep. Hoping that the opposite side of the river might provide something more interesting to see than laundry fluttering from the rusting balconies of apartments that overlooked the skeletal remains of an abandoned indoor market, I rattled across a one-lane steel-plated bridge to discover nothing beyond a few industrial machine shops. When a brief inspection of several side streets and a circular tour of a walled-in residence that could have housed an aristocrat in better days, produced nothing of interest, I'd had enough of "city life."

Beyond the mere pleasure of getting out of Kampot, the return trip to Kep was highlighted by my attempts at becoming airborne whenever a slight rise in the road surface allowed. Performing such acrobatics was admittedly foolhardy, but also incredible fun. As a bonus, the increased speed helped return me to the white stallion almost ten minutes faster than it had taken to get to Kampot. Following the highway back to Kep, I watched the land gradually taper in from the right, ultimately letting the sea creep right up to the edge of the road. Somehow the sight of a small sailboat slicing through the sun's golden reflection convinced me that a pre-dinner drink at a boat club I'd spotted on a previous tour, would not be out of line. Parking near a harbour conspicuously void of marine craft, I entered the bar to find I was the only one with the same intention. Not thrilled about nursing a drink alone, I was further discouraged by news that happy hour didn't start for another forty-five minutes, thereby providing a convenient enough excuse to exit.

Still seemingly obsessed with wringing every last minute out of the motorbike rental, I chose to follow my nose, inadvertently ending up at a gated entrance at the base of Kep's main summit, Prey Thom.

"Ticket $3.00, sir," said a yawning uniformed guard as he sidled out of his gatehouse to serve me.

"Ticket for what?" I asked.

"For National Park".

"National Park?" I repeated, naively glancing around for a sign. "And just where is this National Park?"

Pointing to a rusting cross-bar blocking the entrance to a forest path, the guard informed, "you must follow road." Once having dispensed with the required fee, I was soon zig-zagging my way up a rock-strewn trail, whose rapid ascent was not only confirmed by the straining motor, but also by occasional glimpses of the forested plain and glistening sea far below. By the time the trail turned inland however, I'd begun to doubt the existence of said National Park. It was just then that the golden-spire of a temple flashed its presence from across a sunlit valley. But with no discernible ways of reaching it through the thick underbrush, and certainly no signs to direct me to a path, I decided it less of a challenge to seek out what a rare signpost advertised as "eco-oriented" tourist bungalows. Despite their stated proximity however, the self-proclaimed "natural habitats" were so well integrated, I never did manage to find them. Giving up in sweaty resignation, I completed my circling of the mountain, considered asking for my money back at the gate, but in the end simply slinked back to the lodge.

Melissa was not at her place at the bar, having left for Sihanoukville, early that morning. The previous evening at dinner, we had briefly discussed our mutual plans for the next few days.

"This is where I'll be staying," she had told me with a smile, before handing me a slip of paper. "Just in case you decide to come."

With Jerry's remarks still lurking I had yet to fully commit, worried that Sihanoukville might turn out to be even less appealing than Kampot. After giving it some forethought however, I realized there wasn't enough to keep me in Kep for another full day. As a result, on the way to dinner that evening, I stopped off at a travel kiosk to confirm a ticket for tomorrow's early bus.

What with it being my last night in the seaside resort, I couldn't resist splurging on the most expensive item on the menu. Staring out at the becalmed sea from the same table Melissa and I had shared the previous night, I felt a pang of regret that there was no one there to enjoy the view with; that is besides the boisterous couple at the next table arguing about the lack of German magazines in town.

"Crab verry good," the Cambodian waitress assured me, issuing a nod of recognition as she retrieved the menu, "Lady no come tonight?... Verry, verry fresh... Caught today."

It wasn't long before four pairs of "fresh" bulging eyes

were transfixed on each and every one of my clumsy attempts to get to the meat of the matter, as it were. In the end I had to hail the waitress for assistance, only to discover we didn't share much of a common language. It was only thanks to a series of awkward mimes, that she finally managed to grasp my dilemma. Selecting the smallest of the litter on my plate, she nimbly snapped off the legs, peeling back the torso in one smooth movement to reveal what all the fuss was about. It struck me as an awful lot of means to justify such a limited end, but the taste was indeed exceptional.

As the heap of bone and shell continued to rise on a side plate, one of several scrawny dogs that had been keeping me under surveillance since my arrival, approached the table and settled in at my feet. Remarkably, he kept his distance, never once seeking a donation with a whine or baleful look. Continuing to munch on the treasured flesh, I was curious what had induced manners that could overpower the raw hunger of what for all intents and purposes, appeared to be a stray dog.

Too stuffed to treat myself to a final midnight ride despite an enticing moon and warm sea breeze, I returned to the inn. Citing my early start for Sihanoukville as reason for declining Eric's offer to join him for a drink, I returned the helmet and key and settled the bill. Spread-eagled on the bed, with a light wind coming through the screened window, thoughts soon turned to the days remaining. Down to a precious four, two of which were destined to be spent in Sihanoukville, I fell asleep in the hope that Jerry's predictions would prove to be wrong.

Day Seventeen: Friday, February 18th.

It was a few minutes past six, when the minibus pulled away from the early morning tumult engulfing the Crab Market. Told it would take two to three hours for the eighty-seven kilometres to Sihanoukville, it wasn't long before I decided to strike up a conversation with one of the four passengers aboard. Marla was an American; from Seattle to be more precise, and had been soloing through South East Asia for the past two months, with another two months still to go.

"So either you're independently wealthy, or you know something I don't," I said half-jokingly.

"Neither, I'm afraid. It's much more mundane than that. I was laid off a few months ago and decided to use my severance pay to see a bit of the world before tying myself back down to a job that will likely grind me into the ground."

"Are you always so optimistic this early in the morning?" I asked, shaking her extended hand, pleased to be sharing the ride with someone with a sense of humour.

"Sihanoukville, I assume?" she said with a raised brow, flicking back an errant strand of long ash-blonde hair.

"That's what it says in the script. But to be honest, I'm kind of dubious about the place. A guy I met in Phnom Penh had some rather questionable things to say about it."

Turning to face me over the seat, she asked me to elaborate.

"I can't vouch for his credibility, but he claimed there are certain sections you don't want to go to at night and that there's a big drug thing happening there."

"I never wander around at night anyways, and I'm not looking for any drugs," she interrupted, reaching down to get something from her pack and providing a brief glimpse of the substantial girth of her lower back, evidence she could more than likely handle herself in an any unwanted tangle, day or night.

"You know where you're staying yet?" I asked, changing the subject.

"Not really. My guidebook lists a ton of places, so I'm not really worried. Besides, when you're in the $12- $15 bracket, you usually don't have a problem."

The conversation remained light for the remainder of the journey, but captivating enough to condemn much of the passing scenery to oblivion. One event that didn't go unnoticed however, took place ten or fifteen kilometres outside of Sihanoukville. Forced to stop at what had all the markings of an official border crossing, both of us watched in silence as our driver handed a document to the guard on duty.

"I wonder what was that all about," I said to Marla, after the guard had conducted a quick scan of the passengers, placed several stamps on the paper, and waved us through. "Fell a little short of what I would call high security, but I'm curious what it's meant to protect against." We never did find out.

First impressions of Cambodia's main port were not stunning. Larger than anticipated, it was disconcerting to be confronted with so much civilization after several days in quiet, little Kep. Thanks to heavy traffic, something I also hadn't missed, it took a good half hour to inch our way through what had to rate as one of the most touristy areas this side of Siem Reap. Instead of dropping us off at anything that resembled a station, we were unceremoniously dumped at an empty lot fronting one of the innumerable mobile phone stores that flourish throughout Cambodia. Needless to say, a flotilla of entrepreneurs was awaiting us.

"I know good place, right on beach," one Tuk-Tuk driver boasted as he confiscated Marla's backpack from the minibus and tossed it on to his vehicle with a resounding thud. Turning his attention to me, he announced, "You no can stay at hotel... You too old."

Finding the slight hilarious, Marla turned to stifle a laugh, while all I could do was muster a sardonic, "thank you."

Picking up on his inadvertent faux pas, the driver attempted an apology as he handled my knapsack with equal finesse.

"No... Too old because hotel has many young people. Much noise."

Independent of his explanation, I was still not sure where I wanted to stay. I'd been leaning towards the hotel where Melissa was staying, but I agreed to at least accompany Marla to check out the rooms at the beach. Considerably less selective than I, she quickly booked a room at the first place we stopped. Watching from the doorway as she conducted an inspection of a room that had noisy and hot written all over it, I begged off booking a second room and instead suggested we try and meet later for dinner.

"That would be awesome," she answered, coming out of the room to shake my hand. "Here at eight o'clock sound okay, seeing as I don't know where you're staying?"

One short Tuk-Tuk ride later, I was standing in front of a modern, three-storey structure, horse-shoed around a courtyard pool and outdoor bar. I was sold on the place before reaching reception, a conviction that remained intact despite hearing it would set me back twice what I'd paid in Kep. Even the painfully slow-motion pace of the clerk at check-in failed to deter me. Finally, with key in hand, I was crossing the courtyard to my second-floor room when I caught sight of Melissa in the pool.

"Hey, you made it," she called out, swimming over to greet me like an old lost friend. "Great. That's really nice."

Ten minutes later, it was me enjoying the cooling waters as Melissa relaxed on a nearby chaise lounge. The only other guest in the pool was a man Melissa had introduced as Will, a balding, American pensioner, who claimed he lived there six months a year.

"Here at the hotel?" I asked, a little too disparagingly.

Beyond a single nod, Will remained evasive, offering nothing more than bland comments on how inexpensive and comfortable the arrangement was. I was eager to ask whether such a lifestyle didn't get lonely at times, but refrained after realizing he was not likely to answer. I was debating whether to probe any further, when Will abruptly excused himself and retreated to his room.

"He's quite mysterious," Melissa said, as she slipped back into the water to join me. "All he's told me is that he spends the other six months in Hawaii. But he won't tell me what he does. All he says is that he has 'investments'," she added, using her dripping fingers as quotation marks.

"Probably former CIA... or maybe current," I mused out loud, deliberately fuelling her imagination, while wondering what impressions she had assembled about me during our brief acquaintance. Whatever they were, there'd be a chance to pad the file that evening as we agreed to meet later in the hotel bar as a prelude to dinner on the beach.

Faced once again with time on my hands before a rendezvous, I returned to reception to inquire about renting a bike. Much to my misfortune, the same glacial clerk was still on duty.

"I'd like to rent a bike for a few hours. Do you know if there's a shop around here?" I asked.

Fumbling with a map he pulled from a drawer, the young man began scouring street names with his finger as a line of other guests began to form behind me. Finally, after several snorts and grunts from impatient clients, I was told there was one within a ten-minute walk. Standing on the curb in front of the hotel, I was about to cross the busy street when a cursory glance saved me the effort. There, no more than fifty feet from the hotel entrance, was a large neon sign touting "Bikes 4 Hire." After rejecting the option of having a few words with reception, within minutes I was cruising along the beach road, past what seemed to be an endless row of bars and restaurants. As if that wasn't tedious enough, I again had the pleasure of being aboard another one-gear wonder. I was on the verge of turning back, when I noticed that the commercial district was coming to an end and the boardwalk opened up to a clear run down to a white sandy beach. For a moment I was tempted to coast right into the water to cool off, but settled for a less dramatic entry when my wheels got bogged down in the sand. Abandoning the bike on a grassy strip above the beach, I quickly doffed boots and socks and waded into the sea for the first time since arriving in Cambodia. That pleasurable experience might have continued had I not happened to note the absence of fellow bathers. Assuming there had to be a reason why I was the only activity in the water beyond a few fishing boats anchored offshore, I withdrew to higher ground in case there was a jellyfish with my name on it somewhere. Hoping to speed up the process of drying my feet, I strolled off down the beach, walking on sand so pure and packed, that it squeaked with each skidding step. Much to the bewilderment of other beach patrons, I soon got carried away, purposely shuffling and stomping my feet like some demented drum major.

Back at reception, I was forced to wait for my key while the clerk attended to what appeared to be a dissatisfied customer. Not terribly interested in the unfolding drama, my attention fell to a rack of brochures, one of which was promoting a two-island boat trip. Closer inspection revealed that a day trip to "Cambodia's first officially protected, uninhabited island," included a snorkeling adventure, a river walk as well as a jungle trek, all for a measly twenty-five dollars.

"206 please," I said when the clerk finally turned his attention to me.

"206, Moment please."

Tapping my fingers on the countertop, I watched in mild dismay as he proceeded to slowly shuffle through a stack of papers. Tempted to tell him he was looking in the wrong spot, I remained silent so as not to slow matters down even more.

"Is it possible to book a boat trip and have it put on my bill?" I asked, briefly interrupting his search. Pausing to look up, the expression on his face told me I might as well have asked him to recite Einstein's theory of relativity in Portuguese.

"206?" he proffered, after a moment of awkward silence.

"Yes, 206."

"Must change," he announced, proudly withdrawing a sheet of paper from the pile he'd been rummaging through.

"How's that?"

"Sorry sir. Must change room. Your room booked for other person."

"There must be a mistake. When I checked in this morning, I told you I would be staying for at least two nights. You never said anything about changing rooms. I wouldn't have taken it if I thought I would have to switch. I've already unpacked my stuff, used the towels, and besides... if there's a room you can switch me to, why not just put the new guest there and leave me in mine?"

The introduction of this new option was clearly too much to absorb and I could almost see "Tilt" flashing behind his dark eyeballs.

"Hang on. I'll be right back," I told him, darting out the open doorway.

Luckily for me, earlier at poolside, Melissa had mentioned that the hotel owner was a Danish woman with a crop of short blond hair. I'd seen someone fitting that description sitting at the courtyard bar when I returned from my ride and fortunately she was still there when I emerged from reception. One short explanation later, I was back in Room 206, loaded down with an apology and the vow I wouldn't be bothered by her "new employee" again.

Despite a lengthy shower and a change of clothes, I was

still ten minutes early for our pre-dinner drink. Nodding my gratitude to the owner as I mounted a stool, I couldn't help noticing the man now seated at her table.

"*Mark something*," I said, when Melissa joined me a few minutes later."

"Mark something?" she echoed with a look of bewilderment.   "What was the name of the lead singer of Grand Funk Railroad? The guy with the four-foot hair," I asked. "And more importantly, what the heck is he doing here in Sihanoukville?"

"I have no idea what you are talking about," Melissa replied, more or less ignoring me to order a drink. Between the man's remarkable resemblance to the singer,

"Mark Farner" I blurted out to Melissa. "Between that guy over there and Jerry's depiction of hippie life in Sihanoukville, I'm beginning to think we've stumbled into a time warp where the 70's were still going strong."

"Who the hell is Jerry? Are you feeling okay?" Melissa growled.

Strands of tiny, overhead lights were starting to gain the upper hand on the last rays of sunlight as Melissa and I were shown to our seats. We'd chosen the restaurant primarily because its staff had been the only one amongst dozens along the crowded boardwalk, that had not accosted us the second we stepped into their ill-defined territory. That, and the fact there were no syrupy ballads wafting out of their in-house stereo system.

"You know," I began, after we'd settled into a pair of overstuffed chairs directly on the beach. "At the risk of sounding like a snob... Being able to sit here, enjoying all of this... the view, the weather, the company and most of all, how far away we are from a real winter, one could almost believe we must be doing something right... or? "

With her smiling eyes just visible over the top of her menu, Melissa was about to share her thoughts when she was interrupted by a young girl toting a tray of colourful string wrist bands. But rather than politely declining interest and sending the girl on her way, I was surprised to see her alternative way of responding.

"I don't want or need any of the stuff they're usually selling," Melissa said to me, as she handed the young girl an unexpected bounty from her purse. "But I know that they're doing it because they need the money. I thought this would be a good compromise because it's something they can always make use of, or even sell."

Beaming with delight, the young girl thanked Melissa before running off with her cache of hotel cosmetics.

A short while later when our drinks arrived, I noticed our waiter lingering nearby, observing that everything was to our satisfaction, while vigilantly shooing away several other prospective hawkers. Eventually, conversation turned to the boat excursion planned for the next day.

"You're welcome to join me, you know," I offered, between sips of a decent mojito.

"Thanks, but one day on Rabbit Island was really enough adventure. Besides, I think I might have a date tomorrow."

"A date as in a 'date'?" I pried.

"Yeah, believe it or not, a real date," she chuckled. "It's with a guy I met on the beach the day I arrived."

When no other details were forthcoming, I was about to broach another subject, when distracted by a voice beneath our table. Struggling to push back my chair in the sand, I looked down to see the outstretched hand of a man. As absurd as it sounds, in the dim light, my first thought was that he'd somehow been buried up to his waist in the sand. A closer look however, revealed the smooth pattern his legless torso had left in the sand as he dragged himself to our table. Even though his request for a donation had been directed to me, it was Melissa who responded, quickly retrieving another packet from her purse. Any misgivings I might have had as to the appropriateness of offering hotel articles disappeared when the man broke into a broad smile. Seemingly pleased by her gift, he turned to shake Melissa's hand, before accepting the Riels I pressed into his palm. As he started to pull himself away through the sand, he stopped just long enough to say "land mines," before moving off down the darkened beach.

Having agreed to an after-dinner drink at another bar, Melissa and I were slowly making our way along the boardwalk when I spotted Marla sitting alone in a corner of a half-empty locale. Although the weak ambient lighting on the promenade lessened the likelihood of her seeing me, there was still a chance she could glance up just as we walked beneath one of the swaying lamps. For a moment, I debated whether to go over and apologize and ask her to join us for a drink, but that plan was ditched when I realized I had no valid excuse for having reneged on our dinner date. To my fortune, Marla was too involved with her meal, allowing me to slip past, scathed by nothing more than a twinge of remorse and a new appreciation of the word "cad."

It was just shy of ten-thirty when we arrived back at the hotel. Will was sitting at the bar nursing a beer but declined the invitation to join us, mumbling his way through an apology before taking his leave. Left to our own devices, the ensuing conversation went everywhere and nowhere over the next half-hour, a sign that the evening was over but hadn't quite reached a suitable end. Aware I had an early start, and tiring of the awkward pauses, it was me who begged off a third drink, suggesting we finally call it a night; a suggestion that was met with quick approval.

Day Eighteen: Saturday, February 19th.

One of the by-products from working as a cameraman is that you become accustomed to operating in what is called the "hurry up and wait," mode. It was precisely that experience that was helping to keep me from getting rattled over the fact we had been patiently waiting for our final passenger for over fifteen minutes. Well... more or less patiently. When purchasing my ticket for the boat excursion the previous afternoon, I had been instructed to be out front of the hotel at 6:45 a.m. sharp, in order to make an eight o'clock departure from the harbour. As the minutes continued to tick by, it was becoming more and more obvious that someone had a different perception of the word "sharp." Hopes were fanned briefly when a foursome emerged from the courtyard, only to fade when they climbed into an adjacent Tuk-Tuk and disappeared into early morning traffic. A full ten minutes later, a frail white-haired gentleman was finally escorted out of the reception area by two young Cambodian women, and guided towards our vehicle. Seemingly well into his late seventies, he didn't look to be the ideal candidate for an all-day boat adventure, especially one miles from an iron lung. En route to the docks, polite chatter revealed him to be a retired Irishman, who called southern France home when he wasn't galavanting, (and I use the term loosely) around Cambodia. Reasons for his presence in Sihanoukville weren't volunteered, and I didn't bother to inquire. With their patron temporarily engaged in conversation, his two female companions had withdrawn into their own private talks, occasionally interrupted by squeals of laughter hidden behind cupped hands. When the banter with "Thomas" had run its course, I found myself wanting to believe the giggling pair were simply nurses' aides, but kept getting side-swiped by their young age and the power of innuendo.

"*That... is our boat?*" I thought, staring at the triple-decked vessel moored at the end of the pier. Sheathed in a coat of glossy, black paint, highlighted by chrome railings and an assortment of adornments, the vessel bore all the hallmarks of a sinister, futuristic pirate ship that wouldn't have looked out of place in a Star Wars re-make.

The first of the latest arrivals to reach the boat, I bounded up a springy gangway to discover I was in fact not the first of the hundred or so expected on board. That honour had been usurped by a group languishing on plush sofas at the rear of the middle deck. Lethargic glances were tossed in my direction as I entered their domain, making me feel as though I'd intruded on a private party. Nevertheless, I staked my claim to an empty chair near the back railing, which provided an unrestricted view of the groups' antics without appearing too obvious. Christening them Ivan, Boris and Olaf, I pegged the three pasty-faced men in the group to be in their late thirties, early forties tops. Judging from their attire, none appeared to be severe victims of fashion. Sprawled out across from them, oozing boredom, were three deeply-tanned knockouts in bikinis so small, they had likely come equipped with nitroglycerine tablets. Just as my gaze was moving to the other passengers streaming onboard, the recollection that, "*They were kicked out of Thailand and...*"

drifted back on to the radar.

With seats around the ship's curved bar the first to fill up, latecomers were being forced on to the upper deck. Meanwhile, back at the private party in front of me, peals of laughter kept interrupting a language I was close enough to hear but not understand. Repeatedly stealing covert glances at the group as the boat prepared to sail, I realized a strange dynamic was at play. None of the affection being shown between the men and the women seemed authentic. One minute the men were guffawing amongst themselves over a privately shared joke. The next minute, one of them reached out and pulled a woman close for a grope and a wet, sloppy kiss. It didn't take a wild stretch of the imagination to think the whole atmosphere was some sort of professional arrangement. As I continued my subtle scanning, I was startled to see one woman intently staring back. With hauntingly blue, almost translucent eyes, framed by a short crop of dirty-blonde hair, she looked to be East European. Returning her gaze for a few seconds, I looked away only to fall on what was clearly a disapproving glare from the man I'd labeled Olaf. For what I suspected might be in my own best interests, I promptly turned my chair around to the more mundane but safer view of the sea.

Once we had cleared the outer reaches of the harbour, a voice crackled to life over the intercom. Introducing himself as the captain, Thorsten issued an apology for the late start before announcing that the first stop of the day would be at an island, an hour's sailing time off the coast.

"Anyone wishing to snorkel," he continued, in what I recognized to be a heavy German accent, "can do so at no extra cost as equipment will be available at the bar."

By the time we dropped anchor off a heavily forested coastline that appeared to be uninhabited, I had made use of the ship's single washroom, cum storage closet, cum garbage bin, to change into my swim trunks. One of twenty to spring from the top deck into the warm turquoise waters, I was determined not to let my enthusiasm be marred by the murkiness of the water. Plying the waves in search of something more interesting than a reef of greyish coral, I was disappointed to find nothing more than an inexplicable pile of concrete slabs littering the sea bed. As it appeared to be the most excitement I could hope for, it wasn't long before I'd "flippered" back to the rear-staging platform and reclaimed my seat under the enduring, listless gaze of the three beauties. For a moment I was tempted to break the ice by congratulating them on their decision to pass on the snorkelling, but a quick survey of the scowling lads led me decide otherwise, lest I be granted a second, somewhat lengthier visit to the site of the mysterious concrete slabs. Leaning back to enjoy the sun's warm rays, I was in the process of losing myself somewhere between fantasy and oblivion when a familiar odour wafted into range.

"No wonder they all stayed on board," I thought, blinking one eye open to catch sight of a curling flue of smoke rising up from the enormous joint making the rounds.

Once underway again, the captain's voice broke the airwaves, his words barely discernible amidst the giggles from the group.

"Cambodia's first and only protected island," Thorsten informed us, was to be our next stop. With nothing beyond a calm and empty horizon to hold my interest for the next hour, all there was to do was doze while the drying salt caked

276 |

and cracked over my burning pores. I had been doing so for at least half an hour when I was awakened by the sound of the ladies returning from a stroll around the decks, loaded down with a supply of requisite snacks. A short while later, in a scene right off the pages of a Caribbean travel brochure, we passed through a narrow channel that opened up on a bay one or two kilometres across. Attention was immediately focused on a thin white strip of beach stretching the entire width of the bay's curved horizon. Thorsten dropped anchor approximately two hundred meters from shore in waters so clear they almost weren't there. The once boisterous crowd was awed into silence by the beauty of this tropical spectacle, as Thorsten welcomed us to what sounded like Koah Rung Samloen island, Cambodia's first officially protected reserve. As appreciative as I was to be witnessing such a panorama, I couldn't help wondering how schlepping a boatload of tourists to a remote pristine island five times a week qualified it as "protected." But now that we were here, I was willing to overlook the poetic license that had been taken in the description.

"You have two choices," Thorsten alerted passengers. "You can either swim to the beach, or wait for the dinghies to ferry you in."

A good number of people voted their choice with splashes before the static-filled microphone was even turned off. As much as I would have liked to join them, my desire to capture photos of this Shangri-La, meant it was the dinghy for me.

Storming the beach as part of the first invasion, I was surprised to hear the same squeaky sand I'd experienced in Sihanoukville. Whiter than what I had trod upon on the mainland, this sand was so fine in texture it even stuck to the dry soles of my feet. After securing my daypack and camera to the stumped branch of an overhanging tree, I wasted no time wading into the sea, slinking down up to my neck and languishing in water that must have been close to the temperature of blood. So far removed from reality I wouldn't have recognized it if it had come up and bit me on the nose, I joined with the others who'd come ashore to partake in the incomparable tranquility. With nobody expelling so much as a cough, let alone words, there was nothing to disturb the calm beyond rustling palm leaves and lapping waves at the shoreline.

"River walkers to the right, jungle walkers to the left," Thorsten's non-amplified voice suddenly rung out, as he and the last of those coming ashore reached shallow water. Irked by the disruption to my watery cocoon, it took a moment or two before curiosity triumphed over rapture. Imagining myself to be some pre-historic alligator, I slowly slithered over to the designated starting point for the river walk, remaining on the sea side of a thin white embankment that separated me from the water-way we were about to explore.

"Keep in line behind person in front you," the young Cambodian guide began his introductory speech. "River has sandy bottom but there holes in different places and I no want lose someone, heh, heh, heh."

Once all twelve in the assembled group of adventurers had immersed themselves in a small lagoon, the colour and temperature of consommé soup, it was evident that the so-called river was actually more of a creek. Nonetheless, as we headed upstream, it was surprising to see how quickly we were all in it up to our necks. The further inland we moved, the more unexplained patches of warmer water started occurring, and it was all I could do to keep from falsely accusing someone up the line. When it got to the point where the water level had reached my lower lip, and the tips of my toes were gently sinking into the mushy bottom, I found myself wondering who had originally explored this waterway and decided it safe for unsuspecting tourists. Perhaps even more importantly, how long ago had they done it? The further we got from the sea, the more the creek narrowed, enshrouded on both sides with a thick growth of overhanging bushes and trees. Highly aware of what looked to be a virtually impenetrable shoreline, I couldn't help but wonder what one could do if suddenly met by an unneighbourly snake or irked piranha. The deeper into the jungle we ventured, the darker the tint of the water became, prompting a voice from behind to ask why. Taking a break from what up till then had been a droll, rehearsed narration, the guide explained.

"The colour of water is due to tea trees falling into river and rotting."

Continuing to expand on this impromptu botany lesson, the guide halted the group alongside a grove of submerged mangrove trees and pointed to a batch of wild orchids and other exotic plants. While I listened to his account of their medicinal uses, I realized there was something missing. Here we were, inching our way up a tropical creek on a remote island, and I had yet to see or hear a single bird or animal; not even that familiar jungle-film warbler that echoes through the tree tops just as another pith-helmeted leader holds up his hand to stop his expedition and assess their lot.

"Careful please, here is big hole," the guide warned, before raising one arm above his head and quietly disappearing beneath the surface. Several seconds later, he bobbed back up, laughingly confessing to having no idea as to the hole's origin. A short while later, we rounded a sharp bend to see that a number of fallen trees had made the creek no longer navigable.

"So," the guide announced somewhat redundantly. "Here tour end. We go back now."

Judging from the chorus of moans, it was clear that many would have liked to push on despite the glaring obstacle.

"How much further does the creek actually go?" a young woman wanted to know, as the group manoeuvred to form a line for the trip back.

"No sure. Maybe two mile, maybe more."

With the image of a rogue piranha still lingering, a part of me wanted to ask the guide how he could be sure that something wasn't lurking further up the creek; something that might be upset with us invading his turf, something that might take a chomp out of my leg as revenge for not respecting invisible boundaries. Instead, I settled for making sure I was not the last person in line on the return journey.

Grateful to have made it back with all limbs attached, it was only once I'd re-submerged in the salt water, that it dawned on me I may have taken aboard any number of microscopic stowaways during the river walk. Although no new parasites had yet to make themselves known, as a pre-caution, I stepped out of the bathwater to retrieve a lukewarm cola from my knapsack. I'd just finished the last few drops of that cure-all wonder when Thorsten announced the two groups would now switch.

Having neglected to bring along any footwear for the jaunt through the jungle, it wasn't long before my feet were taking a beating from the scorching sand and sharp cones littering the forest floor. I say forest rather than jungle, as the section we were exploring looked more like an unkempt suburban park than any tropical wilderness I'd ever seen. Although several unseen birds were giving it their best to add to the ambience of a jungle setting, it was not really working. Not that I was particularly interested in encountering any wildlife in the form of a tiger or crocodile, but it would have been nice to have seen something. As it was, the only mammalian wildlife spotted in the first twenty minutes, was a lone monkey nestled up in the trees, apathetically dropping shells from whatever it was he'd been stuffing into his mouth. Then, just as things threatened to get really boring, another form of wildlife suddenly appeared on the trail in the form of two of the boat's three bikini-clad women. Realizing it represented a chance to strike up a conversation without three sets of watchful eyes, I attempted to slip into line directly behind the new arrivals, but was foiled at the last minute when a large American, clad in Bermuda shorts, a loud shirt and white socks and sandals, rudely wedged himself in between. Forced to follow his waddling frame on the narrow trail, interrupted from time to time by what I swear was the emittance of a fart or two, the rest of the walk turned out to be profoundly tedious. As a result of my thwarted plans, I'd been looking forward to sulking in the soothing seawater as compensation. But no sooner had we emerged from the forest, then Thorsten shouted it was time to return to the mother ship. Despite a strong yearning to prolong my time in the water, fears of some well-meaning but inattentive lump dropping my camera into the drink from the dingy, forced me to abandon plans to swim back. It was nearly twenty minutes before the last stragglers had panted their way back to the rear platform. By that time I'd long since changed out of my wet trunks, securing them to the arm of my chair to dry in the wind, before allowing myself the luxury of a beer. Once all guests were accounted for and the anchor hoisted, the ship began a slow arc back towards the narrows, gliding effortlessly past the outer edges of the bay and back out into the open sea, as an audible murmur of vows was made about returning one day. Settled into my chair, nursing my beer before a spectacular panorama of the sun's descent towards the churning waters of our wake, I was coasting along in all senses of the word when Thorsten made it clear other plans were afoot.

"Hey...Who out there wants to party?" he brayed into a hand-held microphone at the bar, muttering to an assistant fumbling with the stereo to "get things rolling." Only those who had been welded to the bar since departing Sihanoukville appeared up for the challenge, heartily lifting their glasses to acknowledge their approval. More bewildered than agreeable, the rest of the patrons sat in stunned silence, wondering what was about to unfold. But before any form of objection could be organized and voiced, AC/DC had broken into song at levels capable of creating a tsunami. Many older patrons quickly made for the stairwell, hoping to find shelter from the deluge on the lower deck. Egged on by Thorsten's manic banter, the more inebriated members of the crowd, of which there was no scarcity, competed to slur along to the melody. Given Thorsten's polished delivery, it was clear that this was no spontaneous shindig, but rather part of a package calculated to keep, if not all, then at least some paying customers satisfied. Exasperated at the thought of enduring "disco central" for the next two hours, but in no mood to swim home, I declined asking Thorsten to take a straw poll. Things had already become tenuous enough. During the introductory phase of the captain's nautical blow-out, two of the bikinied beauties had moved to the rear of the boat, jockeying within inches of me, for the best position to be photographed against the setting sun. With my gaze partially hidden by the peak of my tilted cap, I watched as they pouted and pranced from one artificial pose to the next. Trying my darnedest to remain outwardly motionless, I nonetheless felt a betraying grin spreading across my face as I inwardly shook my head at the absurdity of the whole scene. Hoping to draw a curtain on the current spectacle, I took a deep breath, closed my eyes and drifted back to the pristine reality just left behind.

It wasn't until I was about to step under the shower that evening, that I happened to catch the first glimpse of myself in the mirror. Even without my glasses, the redness suggested I'd seriously underestimated the protective powers of an earlier tan. Despite the apparent damage to my dermis, it was possible to wash off the day's collection of salt, grit and grime without going through the roof. It was while carefully towelling off that thoughts inexplicably fluttered back to the arm of my deck chair. True, it was just an article of clothing, but recalling all the pools, lakes, creeks and oceans my trunks had accompanied me to, it felt as if I'd lost a part of my past. Snared somewhere between mild regret and a rebuke of stupidity, I was dressing for dinner, when a scene from "Harold and Maude," helped transform the loss into a more acceptable memory. For those unfamiliar with the movie, there is a scene where the young Harold has just handed the much older Maude, a ring as a sign of his affection, only to see her immediately throw it into the lake. Much like Maude had explained her actions, I too would always know the last time I saw my trunks, and more importantly, the bevy of circumstances that played a role in my having forgotten them.

It was just after seven when Melissa and I made our way back to the same beachside restaurant we'd visited the previous evening. I was looking forward to sharing stories of our respective days, but it didn't take long to realize Melissa's sour mood risked making the evening a non-event. Sensing a dam was about to burst, I let her go first once we'd been shown to our seats.

"You're lucky I'm even here," she growled, as she absently scanned the menu. "All I've seen the whole lousy day is the inside of my hotel room. I think it's probably something I ate... hopefully not here."

As further conversation revealed, the real disappointment was not so much having been ill, as having missed the scheduled date.

"But if you're well enough to come out with me, why didn't you just arrange to meet him tonight?"

"I don't want to talk about it," she said, before proceeding to do the exact opposite. "We were supposed to meet on the beach at noon."

"So why didn't you just call and say you were sick and make other arrangements?"

"I didn't have his number and I didn't give him mine."

"So where were you supposed to meet? Back on the

beach?"

"It doesn't matter now. There's no point in dwelling on it. But enough about me. What the heck happened to you? You look as if you've been sprayed with red paint. Doesn't that hurt?"

I made an effort to expound on the day's events, but my heart wasn't in it, partly because I sensed Melissa wasn't really interested in listening about my exploits. Somewhere over dinner, I also realized that tomorrow represented the first step back towards Germany. If that alone wasn't enough to sag my spirits, her continuing exasperation sealed the deal. After reluctantly agreeing to a single drink back at the hotel bar, I made a last-ditch attempt at meaningful communication only to see it quickly fizzle. It was only when we were on the threshold of Room 206, faced with our imminent and likely permanent separation, that we were forced back into the present. Fumbling for some appropriate parting words, I suddenly felt uncertain whether she might have been seeking a replacement for today's aborted rendezvous. Whatever her intentions may have been, my hesitation was interpreted as a verdict, leaving us to part with "goodnight" and "goodbye."

Day Nineteen: Sunday, February 20th.

Despite the all too familiar benign melancholy that often creeps in as an adventure is winding down, things got off to a better than expected start the next morning. It began with something as simple as climbing aboard what appeared to be a much higher calibre of bus. Not only did this model have the added luxury of more space between rows, there was even a lunch packet and bottle of water laying on every seat booked. If there was a downside, and there always has to be a downside, it was having to share my row with a bit of an oddball. The first inclination that trouble was brewing came when I tried to take my window seat only to be greeted with a muffled grunt. It was with dismay that I watched a plump woman with inch-thick glasses defiantly juggle her position to avoid any possible physical contact as she let me through. A part of me was tempted to tell her, "not to worry, my leprosy cleared up last month," but a deep sigh sufficed.

Sihanoukville had been history for all of twenty minutes when I noticed that something was definitely askew with my new neighbour. Cocked forward in her seat so that her nose grazed the headrest in front of her, she hadn't moved an inch in over ten minutes, while chatting away to what I assumed were her two companions in the row ahead. Chatting actually, was a bit of a misnomer, as that implies having a conversation. She had taken on the role of narrator, droning on and on in what sounded like Russian. With no prospect of moving to another seat on the fully-loaded bus, the only viable option was to hope this talent wouldn't be in evidence for the entire four hours it would take to reach Phnom Penh. Observing the ceaseless barrage out of the corner of my eye, I soon became convinced that her two colleagues either had to be stone-deaf or had adopted a strategy of sitting as still as storefront mannequins in hopes of discouraging her. In a desperate attempt to distract myself from the verbal onslaught, I dug out my battered guidebook and map to track our progress. I was in the midst of learning that the rolling hills outside my window represented the tail end of the Cardamon mountains, which were destined to give way to plains and small villages before the home stretch to the capital, when the nattering soundtrack suddenly stopped. It may have been my battered imagination, but I swear the whole busload breathed a deep sigh of relief. Unfortunately, our respite turned out to be short-lived, and within minutes she was back, barrelling on and on and on. Just when complete enfeeblement seemed all but certain, a petite, young Cambodian woman dressed in a dark mauve uniform, stood up from a seat beside the driver and turned to face passengers. Enmeshed in a brief struggle to contain the screeching feedback from a microphone, she began her presentation by officially thanking us for traveling with the company, first in English and then in Khmer. She then careened off into a somewhat tedious history of said company, that was nonetheless enjoyable if for no other reason than it had silenced my grumpy neighbour. The second the hostess had finished her "Spiel" and re-taken her seat, hopes of gaining a few minutes of peace were quashed when a series of Asian music videos began their assault from a small screen behind the driver. Employing a format conducive to inciting insanity, one vignette after another portrayed sappy romances laced with intermittent doses of violence and soft porn. Defying all forms of logic, the grating music accompanying the films, gradually blended into a fog of white noise, lulling me into a stupor that put me under for a glorious half hour. That welcome hiatus might have lasted even longer had it not been for the amplified announcement that we were about to stop for a break.

Despite a mass of people milling around in the rest station's forecourt, our driver roared in, coming to a stop within inches of patrons seated on the outdoor patio. Presumably used to such theatrics, nobody batted an eye. The instant the motor died, the bus was surrounded by a frenzy of youngsters, each thrusting forward a raised tablet in hopes of a sale. As I was not in the mood for either sliced mango, syrup-coated buns or unidentifiable fried animal parts, I stayed onboard, hoping to savour the silence while other passengers, including the narrator, attended to necessities. Lazily watching the muted antics outside my window, I picked up on an English conversation coming from several rows ahead. Standing up to stretch my legs and discover the source, I was surprised to see it was a woman I'd seen on yesterday's boat tour. Casually moving forward, I listened in as she told the man across the aisle she was traveling back to the capital to meet her brother, after having spent a week down on the coast.

"Excuse me," I interrupted when there was a pause. "Weren't you on the boat to the island yesterday?"

"Yes," she answered, turning to face me. "I thought I recognized you when you boarded this morning."

"Yeah, that was quite the adventure. But we must have been in opposite groups because I didn't see you in the river or jungle walk."

"Oh, that's because I stayed on the boat. I wasn't feeling so great."

"Oh... that's too bad. You really missed out on something. At least on the beach. The water was so warm and relaxing. But speaking of not feeling so great, what did you think of the captain's disco routine on the trip back?" I asked, failing to camouflage my displeasure.

"Oh that," she replied with a snicker. "I actually didn't find it so bad. A bit loud at times I suppose, but it was those Russians that got my goat," she added, shaking her head in recalled indignation. "Strange how new money can be spotted a mile away. But what about you?... You were sitting right beside them. You must have had it full bore."

"It was tolerable," I replied, recalling the visual aspects.

"Let me tell you something. If you think they were trashy on the boat, you should have seen them the night before."

"You knew them?" I asked, somewhat incredulous.

"I didn't *know* them, just *of* them. A friend and I were in the same restaurant. He studied Russian at university so could translate what they were talking about. Believe me, they were not the kind of people you tend to miss or forget quickly. Everyone in the place noticed them. Loud, obnoxious, arrogant. You name it, they tried it."

Just as the "Russian story" was getting interesting, passengers started to straggle back on board

"You know they arrived in a Rolls?" she said, adding a final anecdote.

"To the restaurant?"

"No, no, to the boat. I was already on board, " she said, before leaning forward to avoid other potential Russian ears. "I watched them from the upper deck when they pulled up in this gold-coloured Roller. It was quite the show and they knew it."

Just then I looked up to see the narrator coming down the aisle. Rather than a simple "excuse me," a gruff clearing of her throat signalled her wish to get by. Standing aside to let her pass, I glanced over to see the woman I'd been talking to widen her eyes and silently mouth "they're everywhere."

Having fully expected the worst, it came as a godsend when the narrator fell asleep within minutes of our having stormed back out on the highway.

Although it had only taken three hours to journey from the coast to the outskirts of Phnom Penh, city traffic made it seem like it could take another three to reach the central station. With each lurch of the bus, a wincing threatened to bring the narrator snorting back to life. Amazingly enough, despite the level of street noise, she remained out of it, a remarkable but welcome feat.

In spite of the mob clogging the terminal, there was little difficulty in nabbing a Tuk-Tuk to the hotel. Normally, being back on familiar territory tended to relax me. But this time things felt different. At first I had written it off my mindset to the trying journey, but no sooner had I closed the door to my room, the phenomenon of being gone before you've left began to deepen. Hoping to avert my declining mood and reflect on the high points of the last three weeks, I decided to head for the pool. It didn't take more than a few lengths however, to realize that a more trusted refuge would be required. Just in under the wire for what would likely be my last happy hour, I ordered the usual before sitting back to observe the gathered collection of patrons. Jerry was nowhere to be seen, which all things considered, was not exactly a tragedy. While awaiting my drink, I watched a group of bewildered tourists struggle to find a table large enough to accommodate them all. At first envious at the thought they might just be starting their vacation, the arrival of my mojito brought the realization I had little to be envious of. Short of making it to Laos, I'd virtually achieved everything I'd hoped for and then some. Fuelled by a second mojito, I concluded there was little point in moping over my imminent departure and vowed to make good use of my remaining hours. After bidding the waiter adieu, I called it a night, hoping that a good night's sleep, much like it had done on my arrival, would produce a final day of inspiration.

Day Twenty: Monday, February 21st.

Those familiar with the adage, "everyone you meet in this lifetime, you will meet at least twice," can appreciate there are some people you'd prefer having never met once, let alone twice. As dawn cracked on my last day in Phnom Penh, there was nothing to suggest that such an encounter was awaiting me. As my plane was not scheduled to depart until seven that evening, I'd decided to start the day off with a long-deferred visit to the Royal Palace. It was while standing in line at the ticket counter, that my attention was snared by a familiar dyed-blonde hairdo, ten or twenty people ahead of me.

"*Ohhh, you've got to be kidding,*" I thought, straining to see the faces of the figure's two companions."*What are the odds of them showing up at the same place and time?*" In the midst of pondering the probability of running into the trio again, I was interrupted when a Chinese family directly in front of me, suddenly decided to abandon their place in line. The commotion created by others to push forward to fill the gap caused the blonde to glance back in my direction. I watched in dismay as she nudged one of her colleagues and whispered something in her ear, prompting the narrator to turn around to see for herself. Knowing there was little I could do about the chance meeting other than leave, I purposely dawdled in the inner foyer, hoping to give the threesome enough time to get lost in the crowd. By the time I did emerge into the main courtyard, I was glad to find the grounds virtually deserted. Despite my trepidation of having an encounter of the third kind, our paths didn't cross again, allowing me to stroll the immaculately ministered gardens, explore ornate temples and examine hundreds of priceless artifacts reflecting Cambodia's history, completely unmolested. As anyone who's visited large exhibits knows, unless you happen to be a historian or archaeologist, excessive exposure to displays of antiquity can eventually cause one's eyes to glaze over. Sensing that room after room of pottery fragments was turning my interest into sarcasm, I felt myself beginning to assemble an arsenal of reasons to leave. The first target was the famed Silver Pagoda, so named because of the squares of that ductile element embossed into its floor. Although cited in countless guidebooks as one of the city's highlights, I found the few sections of engraved silver not covered by faded, threadbare oriental carpets, to be dull in every sense of the word. Realizing I was just putting in time, I returned to the street to start walking back to the hotel. It wasn't until I was standing at reception to obtain my room key, that the idea of squeezing in a last-minute massage surfaced. Unfortunately, a quick phone call made by the woman on duty, brought the discouraging news that unless the masseuse was willing to treat me somewhere over Burma, I would no longer be in Cambodian airspace when the next appointment was available. Left with few options, I retreated to a place I knew could supply a reasonable facsimile of respite.

"What's with the glum, chum?" Jerry asked, shortly after I'd seated myself on the patio.

"It's no big deal. I'm flying out tonight and had been

hoping to get a massage before leaving. But the one by the hotel is all booked up."

"No worries my man. No worries. I know a place not far from here where I guarantee you can get in right away. And it'll only cost you five bucks."

"Five bucks?" I echoed, skeptically. "What kind of massage can you get for five bucks?"

"That's for the standard massage man. Extras cost extra, if you get my drift."

"But all I want is a massage," I said, vaguely recalling Franz's offhand remark about places where you wouldn't be hassled.

"Whatever, man... It's your call. I'm just sayin' you don't need an appointment because it's not your average massage parlour."

"How so?"

"Well, for one thing you get to select your own masseuse."

"How does that work?"

"It's a weird place man, really weird. They have this big, empty room with a picture window in one wall. Behind it are all these young women dressed in red and white uniforms that make them look like car hops or space cadets. You just go in and decide which one you want. You gotta see it to believe it man."

"Sounds kind of perverse if you ask me. I mean, how many of the women are there of their own volition."

"Their own what?"

"They chose to be there of their own free will."

"No idea, man. I just know if you want a cheap massage... with no waiting. That's the place to go... Hey look man. It's up to you.

Here's the address in case you change your mind," he said, jotting down the location on a piece of paper before handing it to me.

"Good to see you again. Have a good flight back, and drop in again if you ever come back this way. In the meantime, take care man." And with that he was off to pester other patrons.

An hour or so later, with my luggage safely stored with the concierge, I returned my key to reception, and decided to take one last look at the vibrant street life, hoping it might help lift my spirits. But that too turned out to be a false strategy when I discovered Sihanouk Blvd. to be practically empty.

What is it with this guy?" I muttered angrily, straining to keep my luggage from spilling out into the street. Puzzled why the driver I'd arranged to take me to the airport had been replaced at the last minute by his "brother," I watched with unease as the new driver continued to swerve in and out of traffic, cutting off vehicles left, right, and centre, and even resort to driving on the sidewalk to avoid sporadic jams.

"There's no friggin' fire, lad," I said when we were forced to slow down when a lorry pulled out of a side street. "Slow it down."

Besides the advantage of not being tossed into the street at the next sharp corner, the newly slackened pace brought the opportunity to take more notice of the passing scenery. Judging by the number of glass-fronted shops, parked SUV's and stylishly-dressed pedestrians filling the streets, it was clear we were travelling through a neighbourhood I'd not seen before. It was not a scene I was heartbroken to see left behind, when traffic thinned and we sped off into the countryside. Gazing out into the darkened fields for what I expected would now be a straight run to the airport, I was surprised when a number of gaudily painted buildings, all lit up by harsh floodlights, suddenly appeared to break the monotony. Small crowds could be seen milling behind a series of identical chain-linked fences that controlled entry to the various premises. They may have remained a mystery had it not been for a light-controlled construction site that forced us to halt directly in front of one the buildings. Suddenly presented with a clear view into one of the bright entranceways, inside I could see fifteen to twenty well-dressed women seated on opposite sides of a colourful foyer. Smoking and chatting amongst themselves, they appeared completely impervious to the loud music blaring in their midst.

"What is that all about?" I asked the driver, who was sharing my reconnaissance. "What are those women doing there? They all look bored to death. As if they're waiting for a bus that will never come."

"They wait customers come," he answered with a slight smirk.

"What kind of customers?"

"Beer customers. They beer ladies. People come drink in club. Ladies sell them their beer."

"What do you mean *their* beer? And why do they need twenty hostesses for one club? How big are these places anyway?"

Just as the light changed and further details threatened to be lost to the din of backed-up traffic, I was able to hear the driver explain that "Beer clubs" were simply popular watering holes that catered to a certain breed of tourist. The women I'd seen were hired to be representatives of various breweries, and expected to encourage thirsty patrons to select their particular brand. What the driver didn't make clear, and I didn't ask, was to what level such encouragement went.

Oddly enough there's something comforting about the anonymity of an airport lounge. Slumped in a chair, staring off into space while awaiting the boarding announcement, I felt a small sliver of eagerness poke its way through the limbo, at the prospect of being able to share stories back home. And so much of the twenty minutes still left of Cambodia, was spent recalling some of those stories.

Re-entry to the "real world" went smoother than expected. Following a short hop to Bangkok, the connecting flight to Frankfurt turned out to be one of the most relaxing and uneventful eleven hours one could ever hope to spend on a plane. It was only once we'd landed that things began to slide. Relegated to a shuttle rather than a gate, I cringed when a load of oafs insisted on shattering the early morning silence with bursts of loud-honking laughter inside the overheated bus. To make matters worse, as soon as the doors closed, a German businessman next to me, began braying details of his arrival into a cell phone and my left ear. Although one of the first from our plane to reach passport control, I was dismayed to see long line-ups at all three of the six booths open. Prepared for a glacial advance in the wrong line, it came as a pleasant surprise when a member of the airport service personnel suddenly appeared, franticly waving to passengers who's just joined the queue to follow her. Led through a maze of doors and hallways so complex I started to suspect we were part of a television game show, we finally entered at a small hall where two bored-looking immigration officers stood alone at their posts. After collecting my luggage and negotiating my way through a stalled crowd in the "arrivals" area, I paused at a bench to extract what I sensed would be much needed winter clothing, while watching more jet-lagged travellers struggle with carts of teetering luggage, as they re-united with family and friends.

Grateful for once again having declined a welcoming committee, I made my way to the underground rail station, where a scroll of the electronic schedule revealed a departure in two minutes. More crowded than I expected for this time of the morning, I nonetheless managed to find a seat amidst the crush, earning a scowl from the passenger across from me as I squeezed my knapsack between my legs.

A dull, grey icy dawn was breaking as we pulled out of the terminal tunnel to my first sight of snow in three weeks. Just settling in for what I hoped would be a smooth ride home, I was puzzled to see dozens of people waiting on the platform when the train pulled into the next station. It seemed peculiar to me that so many people would be congregated at a station I knew had been built solely to provide access to a nearby football stadium. It became even more mysterious when the doors remained closed after the train had come to a stop. Several minutes of confusion passed, as passengers on both sides of the doors started to become agitated. It was at that point that the train's intercom crackled to life. In a voice that sounded like a cross between a county-fair barker and a camp commandant, the speaker delivered a message too garbled for me to understand. Judging by the groans it elicited from fellow passengers however, it did not appear to be good news. Immediately after the announcement ended, the doors hissed open and disgruntled passengers began to shuffle out.

"Was ist los?" I asked the man sitting next to me. "Where's everybody going?"

"Die Fahrer streiken. Wir müssen hier bis acht Uhr bleiben. Scheiss Deutsche Bahn," he told me.

It took a moment to fully absorb the irony of having just come ten thousand kilometres, only to be halted less than forty from home by a train drivers' strike. Cursing the fact that the strikers had knowingly removed us from the comfort of the airport, thereby sentencing us to spend the next hour on a cold, windy platform, I swung my knapsack over my shoulder, and stepped back out into Germany. Shivering in the cold, I looked up at the same pale moon I'd just left half a world away.

Acknowledgements

To my two favourite "Deutsche Damen", Ingeborg and Ina, who have supported and inspired me in ways they aren't even aware of... my deepest gratitude. I owe you big time.

I would also like to thank Dave Gurney for his suggestions and feedback on the cover and text. Much appreciated.

Books by the same author

Episodes from a 20 Year Vacation

"Why squander your life away in your own hometown, when you can do it in London, Paris and Rome?"

Eight months after landing what many had considered to be a plum job with the Federal government, Fred Z. suddenly realizes that his safe and secure position is rapidly luring him towards an insufficient destiny. Abandoning his home and native land, Fred heads for Europe, only to be faced with the even greater challenges of a new language, new culture and a new life. After six months spent exploring the continent and a year-long respite in Cornwall, he returns to Germany and is immediately thrust into an array of lurid, sublime and downright ridiculous situations in the on-going struggle to establish himself as a freelance cameraman. Plagued by uncertainty whether he's made the right decision, it's through a chance meeting with a fellow North American that the doors to real opportunity fling wide open. From that point on, whether it's dog sledding in the Yukon, getting mugged in Naples, removing land mines in Cambodia, tracking Dracula in Romania, interviewing Hitler's telephone operator in Berlin, chasing cheetahs in Vienna, flying in a Black Hawk over Bosnia, or replacing a cancerous esophagus in Hamburg, to name just a few, all play a part in providing for eclectic glimpses of just how the world works, laying the groundwork for what would become a twenty year vacation.

Höttlland

How and why an educated man became and remained a Nazi

Why them? Why there? What caused a nation of 'Dichter und Denker' to be transformed into one of 'Richter und Henker'?

Höttlland attempts to answer those questions by examining the life and times of Wilhelm Georg Höttl, a former high-ranking member of the Austrian SS. The trail begins in Vienna in 1915, moving up through a culture of envy, past people and events that influenced a young man to make a fateful leap aboard the Nazi bandwagon at the age of 19. Tracing his rapid advance within the 'seething ranks' of the SS, which saw him emerge as a heeded advisor in the SD intelligence apparatus at 24, Höttlland documents Höttl's involvement in various wartime intrigues that included everything from a counterfeiting operation, the kidnapping of Mussolini, the rescue of Hitler's art treasure, and the occupation of Hungary, to name just a few. With priorities shifting in late 1944, the book follows Höttl as he dons the mantel of peacemaker to confer with American officials about a separate peace and the sabotaging of the much feared 'Alpenfestung'. Arrested at war's end, Höttl diligently polishes his past to salvage a future, evading post-war justice by supplying interrogators at Nuremberg with detailed information on the inner workings of the Nazi intelligence apparatus, portions of which later help incriminate such former colleagues as Ernst Kaltenbrunner and Adolf Eichmann. Part I concludes as Höttl resurfaces in Austria in late 1947, ready to resume plying his wares with various agencies clamouring for intelligence under the gathering clouds of the Cold War.

Höttlland Part II
A Life after Deaths

"He was a very dangerous person... He only looked out for his own advantage. He was very crafty and impenetrable. You couldn't pin anything on him. But he was a swindler nonetheless." Edith Frischmuth (former member of the Austrian Resistance)

Unlike many Nazi colleagues whose careers finished at the end of a rope or in exile, the former Austrian SS officer and SD operative returns to Austria in late 1947, ready to embark on a series of equally opaque activities. Taking advantage of the rivalry created by the growing Cold War, Höttl resumes plying his wares, initially with the American Counter Intelligence Agency (CIC), and German based Organization Gehlen, and later with whomever happened to show interest. Eventually outed as a dubious source and cast back into the cold, he returns to his academic roots, founding a school and assuming its directorship, while managing to publish three stylized versions of his wartime recollections. Despite suspected involvement in the 'Ratlines', a mechanism set up to aid Nazi fugitives flee to safer havens, entanglement in a Soviet-American spy scandal, a death sentence handed down by a Hungarian court, and numerous demands to testify at the trials of former colleagues, including that of Adolf Eichmann, Höttl nevertheless slithers through the jaws of justice to emerge as a 'qualified Zeitzeuge', catering to an enduring media circus willing to pay for his flawed reflections right up until his final breath.

Lightning Source UK Ltd.
Milton Keynes UK
UKHW010642050321
379837UK00002B/763